FINANCIAL SERVICES:
Insiders' Views of the Future

Mark Coler
Ellis Ratner

New York Institute of Finance

Library of Congress Cataloging-in-Publication Data

Financial services.

    Includes index.
    1. Securities—United States. 2. Financial
institutions—United States. I. Coler, Mark D.
II. Ratner, Ellis M.

HG4963.F56 1987   332.6'2   87–24839
ISBN 0–13–316837–9

©1988 by NYIF Corp.
A Division of Simon & Schuster, Inc.
70 Pine Street, New York, NY 10270-0003

New York Institute of Finance
(NYIF Corp.)
70 Pine Street
New York, NY 10270-0003

Printed in the United States of America
10 9 8 7 6 5 4 3 2 1

CONTENTS

INTRODUCTION

Forty years ago, there was no financial services industry as we know it today. There were two very good reasons for its absence: few products and even fewer customers.

Those few potential customers did not require much assistance in their investment decisions. If his forebears had failed to establish a trust to relieve their descendents of the bother of money management, then a gentleman of means entrusted his assets to the old line bank or brokerage firm with which his family had been dealing for three generations. There, an old school chum kept an eye on the money while he kept an eye on his golf game.

Outside of these circles, investors were scarcer than a hole in one. So were investments. If anything was left from your paycheck at the end of the month, it went straight to the bank. Any bank. It didn't much matter. They all paid the same rate of interest, although some gave away better toasters.

If by any chance you woke up one day feeling like a sport, and announced out loud at a family dinner that you were thinking about buying stocks, you could count on some member of the older generation pouncing on you with the tale of Uncle Louie, who also thought stocks were a good idea, and lost the family nest egg in the crash of '29.

All this has changed. America has grown and prospered. Several million Americans could now be considered wealthy, and tens of millions have sufficient disposable assets to make them candidates for some type of investment. Around family dinner tables today, you don't have to fight to justify investments.

Quite the opposite. The inflation of the last decade ended the public's love affair with the bank account. It taught the average American that you could put your money in an absolutely safe bank account and still find out at the end of the year that—in inflation adjusted real terms—you had lost money. Furthermore, the family tales of money lost in 1929 have now long been replaced by stories of money made in the stock market, in real estate, in oil, in gold, in art, and even in bubble gum trading cards.

The financial services industry is both the child and the parent of the new demographics of American investors. If a core group of several million Americans did not have substantial funds to invest, there might be no financial services industry. But if the industry had not created products such as mutual funds, which made diversified, professionally managed investments available to Americans of more modest means, many millions of other Americans would never have become investors.

To our knowledge, no one to date has marketed a mutual fund to invest in bubble gum trading cards, although one may be in formation as we write. But funds, limited partnerships, general partnerships, stocks, trusts, and accounts have been devised in seemingly endless variations for an endless number of purposes. The list is so extensive, and changing so constantly, that it is difficult for even an expert in the field to stay current. Even the experts need experts. In large measure, that is the reason for this book.

We sought out the leading companies or experts in a dozen of the most important fields that fall under the rubric of financial services. Each was asked to write about a subject within his expertise for others within the industry. Since the authors are among the nation's leading experts, we felt it inappropriate to limit or direct their scope. This was left to each author's discretion.

The dozen chapters cover three general topics—products, services, and marketing. All the chapters provide an introduction to the subject. Some speak from the more personalized perspective of a particular company; others are more general in scope. Most will be of primary interest to those concerned with identifying, developing, or marketing new products. Some are more weighted toward those advising investors.

This book primarily addresses the asset side—the investment side—of the financial services balance sheet. The liability side—credit cards and so forth—often involve quite different issues which are best left to another volume. The chapters in the marketing section, however, should prove quite useful to those marketing any financial services products.

We think the best approach to this book is to peruse the Table of Contents and turn directly to those chapters of greatest interest. But for those who prefer a very brief (and necessarily incomplete) introduction to each chapter, it is provided below.

The first chapter, *The 1980s: Decade of Tax-Free Investing,* is written by James Gratehouse, Vice President of John Nuveen and Company, the nation's oldest and largest sole sponsor/underwriter of unit investment trusts. No subject better illustrates the increase in both the number of investors and the number of products. Once a municipal was a municipal. Today there are bonds, bond funds, unit investment trusts, and money market municipal funds. Also, guaranteed bonds, zero coupon bonds, discount trusts, put trusts, and a host of others. Under the new tax law, there are even taxable municipal bonds.

This extensive article traces the development of the industry, identifies the growth rate of different products, and elucidates the variations and latest developments. It describes how to identify the product best suited for each individual, and how to market them by presenting the advantages of municipals using concepts that investors can readily understand. The article is supported by numerous statistical tables.

No name is more identified with the development and success of the mutual fund industry than Boston's Fidelity Group. In Chapter Two, Roger T. Servison, Vice President of Fidelity, addresses *New Direction for the Mutual Fund Industry: Wholesaling to Banks.* A recent study indicates that millions of smaller investors would invest in mutual funds, but only if offered by the one institution they really trust—their local bank. Drawing on Fidelity's incomparable experience, Servison analyzes this market, and offers concrete examples of how banks can work in partnership with mutual fund managers to tap its huge potential.

In Chapter Three, *Precious Metals*, nationally known expert Fred Bogart and his associate Frederick Jennings discuss the timeless allure of gold, silver, and the precious metals from the perspective of

Republic, the nation's leading gold trading bank. The article offers the reader an overview of the basic types of available precious metal services as well as some of the more esoteric ones. Among others, these include bullion coins, numismatic coins, and investment certificate programs.

In Chapter Four, the editors, Mark Coler and Ellis Ratner, principals in Mercer Financial Services and authors of books on the subject of discount brokerage, discuss *The Bank Brokerage Boom*. This chapter discusses the extraordinary growth of discount brokerage over the past few years, focusing on the fastest growing form—bank discount brokerage. It asks how are banks marketing, to whom are they marketing, how successful have they been, and what is the future of bank brokerage?

In Chapter Five, *INVEST: The Full-Service Brokerage Approach*, Burton Binner, Vice President of ISFA Corporation, a consortium of savings and loans institutions, presents the history of the development of INVEST—a brokerage service with a difference. It offers brokerage with advice and commissions that typically lie between the full service and discount brokers'. Binner's article describes the history, feasibility studies, rationale, and comparative advantages of this unique form of brokerage.

Microcomputers and the Independent Investor: Transforming Discount Brokerage in the '80s is the subject of Chapter Six, by Bruce Feiner, Lotus Development Corporation, the pioneering software firm. Noting that discounters can provide computerized information that is comparable to the traditional brokers, Feiner asks what type of computerized information investors want, surveys what is available, and suggests how banks can market these services to their clients.

If there is anything which has changed faster than technology in the financial services field, it is the law. In Chapter Seven, *Banks in the Securities Business: A Regulatory Primer*, Carl N. Duncan and Bruce O. Jolly—Partners in the Washington, D.C. office of the law firm of Barnett and Alagia—present a comprehensive but comprehensible account of the current status and developments in the law over the past few years. Among the legal and regulatory issues discussed are discount brokerage, investment advice, mutual funds, and securities underwriting and liability.

Just as the market for financial products has dramatically broadened in recent years, so too has the market for services. In Chapter Eight, *The Coming of Portfolio Management for Everyone*, Neil R. Michelsen, a partner in the national accounting firm Coopers and Lybrand, lays out a blueprint for the future of portfolio management. Analyzing the key segments of portfolio planning, he offers a compelling argument that the explosion in financial products combined with rapid advances in technology have brought sophisticated portfolio management planning to the threshold of universal availability.

In Chapter Nine, we return from the future to the present. Dr. Frederick B. Putney, a prominent consultant and member of the faculty of Columbia Business School, offers a detailed, practical analysis of current day *Financial Planning*. The chapter provides a framework for financial planning through an overview of the process, recommended steps, suggested goals, and selected examples. Using a personal financial statement as the basic source document, Dr. Putney shows how comprehensive planning can help an individual develop a financial plan addressing five major concerns: maintaining a desired lifestyle, tax planning, insurance, investment and financing, and estate planning.

The final chapters explicitly address the subject of marketing. In Chapter Ten, J. Bud Feuchtwanger, President of The Feuchtwanger Group and a frequent industry speaker, analyzes *Delivering Financial Products and Services to the Consumer*. His focus is that part of the marketing process which aims to efficiently deliver the product or service to the consumer. Using both a theoretical construct and numerous concrete examples, he analyzes many types of delivery systems—including face-to-face contact, telephone, electronics, direct response, and general advertising—and relates their use to different types of financial services and products.

In Chapter Eleven, Robert Wilcox and Diane Rosen of Wilcox and Associates, a nationally known strategic marketing and communications firm with a specialty in financial services, address *Marketing Financial Services: Competition Heats Up as Restrictions Cool Down.* In the new financial services environment, "advertising alone is not enough." Their article focuses on key communications issues. It covers the major methods, identifying and targeting specific market segments, and positioning products and services to maximize profit opportunities.

In Chapter Twelve, Irving L. Straus, Chairman of the Straus Marketing Communications Group, a division of the Financial Relations Board, Inc., the nation's largest financial communications consulting firm, discusses *Public Relations—The Magic Wand of Marketing.* Straus argues that a well-conceived public relations program can be a firm's best marketing investment. Drawing on his twenty-five years experience in the industry, he offers fifteen detailed, concrete steps that a firm can take to mount a successful public relations effort.

This is a book by insiders, for insiders. No one within the industry can fail to benefit from at least some of the chapters. But we hope and believe it will prove useful to the sophisticated investor as well. The twelve chapters provide an excellent, concise overview by leading experts of a dozen key fields. It is of more than passing interest to a sophisticated investor to know what insiders are saying to each other about products they are marketing to him.

Mark Coler and Ellis Ratner
August, 1987

PART ONE

New Products

CHAPTER ONE

The 1980s:
Decade of Tax-Free Investing

James W. Gratehouse, Vice President
Packaged Investment Product Marketing
John Nuveen & Co. Incorporated

James W. Gratehouse is Vice President, Packaged Investment Product Marketing, at John Nuveen & Co. Incorporated. Mr. Gratehouse has been employed with Nuveen for the past 15 years. He is a 1960 graduate of the University of Wisconsin with a B.S. in Economics.

John Nuveen & Co. Incorporated is an 89-year-old investment banking firm that specializes in the researching, underwriting, and trading of municipal bonds and tax-exempt packaged investment products. Nuveen is the nation's largest sole sponsor/underwriter of tax-exempt unit trusts and offers a full line of tax-free mutual funds and money market funds. Nuveen's packaged investment products are distributed exclusively through financial intermediaries.

The 1980s is the decade of tax-free investing. Individual investors from every walk of life—from the high-income professional to the middle-income salaried employee—are all interested in reducing their tax bills. To accomplish that objective, individual investors have poured *billions* of dollars into tax-free investments—tax-free municipal bonds as well as municipal bond products such as unit investment trusts and municipal bond mutual funds. The individual investor is the vanguard of a financial revolution in the distribution of tax-free investments.

It wasn't always this way. Until recently, the municipal bond markets were dominated by institutional investors, such as banks and insurance companies. But that's changed. In 1976, individuals owned 29%

of the outstanding municipal bonds issued by state and local governments, while institutions owned the remaining 71%. By 1985-1986, the
market had shifted dramatically. At the end of 1986, individuals owned
55% of outstanding municipal bonds, while the institutional slice of the
pie had shrunk to 45% (see Figures 1-1 and 1-2).

In fact, both 1985 and 1986 were in many respects highwater
marks for the municipal bond industry—years that were characterized
by enormous new issue volume, falling interest rates and increasing
prices, and the tumult of the tax reform process.

1985: INVESTOR DEMAND AND TAX REFORM DEADLINES PROPEL NEW ISSUE VOLUME

In 1985, municipalities issued a record volume of new tax-exempt
bonds, a level we are unlikely to see for some years to come. That year,
the market saw some $204 billion of new, long-term, tax-free bonds—
100% more than 1984's volume of $102 billion and more than two and
one half times as much as the $83 billion issued in 1982.

The primary reason for 1985's skyrocketing volume was the prospect of tax reform restrictions, as enumerated in a bill (H.R. 3838)
passed by the House of Representatives in mid-December. State and local governments and other qualified issuers came to market with an unprecedented volume of bonds to beat the January 1, 1986, deadline
established by the House bill.

Despite the avalanche of new issues, demand for municipal bonds
far outstripped the volume, so yields actually declined at the end of
1985. While commercial banks and casualty insurance companies re-
turned to the market more heavily than in the past, individual investors
remained a dominant force in the tax-free market.

According to the Federal Reserve, individual investors were responsible for more than 82% of net new municipal bond purchases
through the third quarter of 1985. Tax-free packaged portfolios—unit
investment trusts and tax-free mutual funds—also enjoyed record sales
in 1985, with some $35 billion of new money flowing into these prod-
ucts. To meet increasing investor demand, sponsors and underwriters
offered a cornucopia of new products, including intermediate maturity
unit investment trusts that had average portfolio lives of 5, 10, and 15
years.

FIGURE 1-1. The Municipal Market Pie—1976. % of Outstanding Municipals Held by Sector.

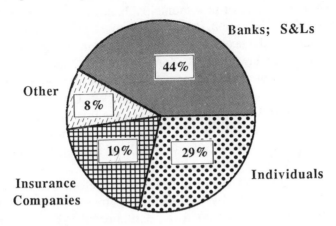

Source: Federal Reserve Board

FIGURE 1-2. The Municipal Market Pie—1986. % of Outstanding Municipals Held by Sector.

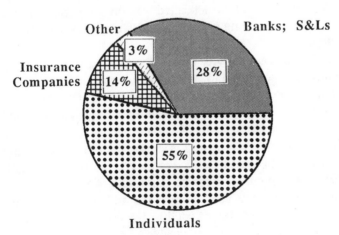

Source: Federal Reserve Board

The universe of municipal bond investors has shifted dramatically in 10 years. In 1976, institutional investors predominated. Today, individual investors own more than half of the outstanding municipal bonds in the form of individual issues, tax-free unit trusts, and tax-free mutual funds.

5

1986: A YEAR OF UNCERTAINTY AND CHANGE

In 1986, the volume of new municipal bonds brought to market declined to around $136 billion, due primarily to the confusion and uncertainty surrounding the tax reform process. Although the House bill—H.R. 3838—was not a law, it had the force of law because it contained effective dates that would have imposed deadlines for the elimination and restriction of certain kinds of municipal bonds. Until the Senate placed its stamp on the tax reform process and the final tax reform bill worked its way through the House and Senate Joint Conference Committee, both municipal issuers and investors lived in a world of uncertainty about the possible restrictions on municipal bonds.

In November of 1986, the long awaited Tax Reform Act of 1986 finally was signed into law by President Reagan, and for municipal bond investors the news was good but complicated. All municipal bonds issued before August 16, 1986 (and certain bonds issued on or before that date, but before September 1, 1986), retained their tax-exempt status. Municipals issued on or after August 16 (or September 1 for certain kinds of bonds) were placed into two broad categories: (1) public purpose or (2) private activity bonds. Public purpose bonds issued for development of what the act called "essential government functions," such as school financing or highway construction, remained federally tax exempt.

For so-called private activity bonds, the law became extremely complex. Bonds that were used to finance activities of some nonprofit institutions, such as hospitals, stayed federally tax free. Other kinds of bonds, such as those used to finance multifamily housing and port facilities, retained their tax-exempt status—but their interest income became a so-called "preference item" for investors subject to the alternative minimum tax. (This provision became effective for bonds issued on or after August 7, 1987, or September 1 for certain kinds of bonds.) Finally, Congress determined that various private activity bonds were "nonessential" (for example, bonds used to finance sports stadiums); these nonessential bonds became fully taxable.

Despite the limitations imposed upon some municipals, investor demand today remains strong due to the fact that municipals are one of the few tax-favored investments that remain. Tax reform should bode well for the future of municipal bonds, and for packaged investment products especially. Packaged products assembled by experts should have particular appeal because full-time market professionals are in a much better position than individual investors to analyze municipal securities in the complex environment fostered by the new tax law.

Let's look at a number of other forces that stimulated the municipal bond market in the early to mid-80s.

INDIVIDUAL INVESTORS STILL PREDOMINATE

Both 1985 and 1986 were tumultuous years for municipal bond investments. But the key fundamental change in tax-exempt investing—the shift from institutional investors to individual investors—began in the mid-70s. Since then, individual investors have stepped up their interest in tax-free investments spectacularly. This occurred for a number of key, interlocking reasons.

* The surge of inflation in the late 70s and early 80s pushed middle-income wage earners into higher and higher tax brackets, thus making tax-free investments an effective means of earning more after-tax income for an increasing number of individual investors.
* The surge in interest rates in 1981 and 1982 (tax-free yields peaked in January 1982 at 13.44%, according to *The Bond Buyer* 20-Bond Index) made tax-exempt investing irresistible. Many factors contributed to skyrocketing yields—most notably a 1979 change in Federal Reserve policy from controlling interest rates to controlling the money supply in order to rein in inflationary pressures. But the upshot was that investors captured some of the highest interest rates in investment history.
* The short-lived, tax-free All Savers certificates (September 1981 to December 1983), and the attendant promotion by banks, S&Ls, and brokers, educated the public about the advantages of tax-free income—specifically, the greater after-tax return from tax-free securities. That awareness has been reinforced by the media's discovery of the trend toward tax-free investing.
* Significant growth in personal income, spawned by the economic recovery that began in 1982, has prompted investors to invest in tax-free securities in order to shield their investment earnings from taxes.

- Due to a sharp decline in interest rates that began in 1982, many bondholders were afforded generous returns based partially on capital appreciation.

- Finally, owners of municipal bonds have been blessed by a historically unprecedented interest-rate spread. Traditionally, the yield on municipal bonds has been between 60% and 80% of the yield on long-term government bonds. Yet in late June 1986, the average yield on 30-year municipal bonds actually *exceeded* the yield on 30-year Treasury bonds—municipals yielded an all-time high of 117% of Treasury bonds. By the beginning of the fourth quarter of 1986, the yield ratio had fallen back, but as of early February 1987, it was still around 85%. As long as the rate spread continues to exceed 72%, "munis" will be extremely attractive to any investor whose combined federal and state tax is 28% or higher.

ANOTHER KEY REASON: HIGH AFTER-TAX REAL RATES OF RETURN

One phenomenon responsible for the enormous growth in tax-free investing has been the high *real rate of return* available from tax-exempt investments. While the inflationary surge of the late 70s made investors more sensitive to tax-bracket creep, the welcome slowdown in inflation occurring the past five years has created exceptional real rate-of-return opportunities.

The real rate of return is calculated by subtracting the 12-month pace of inflation (say, from December 1985 to December 1986) from the rate of return available on long-term, tax-free municipal bonds. For example, at the end of December 1986, the 12-month change in the Consumer Price Index was just 1.10%. During the same month, long-term, tax-free yields averaged 6.87%, according to an index compiled by *The Bond Buyer*, a trade publication of the municipal bond industry. Here's the real rate of return for that month:

> 6.87% (Tax-Free Yield)
> − 1.10% (CPI 12-month change)
> 5.77% Real Rate of Return

Thus, for December 1986, the real rate of return on long-term municipal investments was 5.77%.

Throughout the 80s, real rates of return from municipals have been at historical highs—with a record 7.18% reached in mid-1983. While real rates have trended generally downward since then—as have yields on all fixed-income investments—inflation-adjusted returns from municipal bonds are still exceptional. This is especially true when you compare these tax-free real rates with the *after-tax* real rates from a comparable taxable investment.

For example, during December 1986, 30-year Treasury bonds yielded an average of 7.68%. Compare the after-tax return from Treasury bonds versus tax-free municipals for a taxpayer in the 33% tax bracket (the top bracket, according to the Tax Reform Act of 1986).

	Bond Buyer Index	*30-Year Treasuries*
Nominal Yield	6.87%	7.68%
Less Federal Taxes at 33%	0	− 2.53%
After-Tax Return	6.87%	5.15%

Now let's take into account the effect of inflation by subtracting the Consumer Price Index:

	Bond Buyer Index	*30-Year Treasuries*
After-Tax Return	6.87%	5.15%
Less Inflation	− 1.10%	− 1.10%
After-Tax, Inflation Adjusted Real Return	5.77%	4.05%

As you can see, municipals provided 42% more after-tax inflation-adjusted real return as 30-year Treasuries.*

Despite the prospect of lowered tax rates in 1988, municipals will still remain attractive to most investors. With the loss of favorable capital gains treatment combined with the discontinuation of several popular methods for shifting income to lower-bracket family members, many moderate- and higher-income wage earners will have fewer places to turn for tax-advantaged investment income and will be looking for ways

---

*Treasury bonds are backed by the full faith and credit of the U.S. government. Treasury bonds are free from state and local taxes; municipals may be subject to state and local taxes.

to increase their real rate of return. Furthermore, many bonds and packaged products are exempt from *both* federal and state taxes, making municipals all the more attractive.

ANOTHER PERSPECTIVE: THE CONCEPT OF EXTRA DOLLARS

Another way to look at the superior earning power of tax-free investments versus comparable taxable investments is to focus on the concept of *extra dollars*. The term *extra dollars*, as we'll define it here, is just simple arithmetic: it's the additional after-tax cash flow earned on tax-free investment, compared to the income earned from a 30-year Treasury bond. We can use the interest rates in our previous example to show how it works.

Suppose that a 33% bracket investor has $100,000 to invest and that his choices are a tax-free investment yielding 6.87% and a 30-year Treasury bond yielding a 7.68%.

	Tax-Free 6.87%	*Taxable 7.68%*
Annual Income on $100,000	$6,870	$7,680
Less Federal Taxes at 33%	0	− $2,534
After-Tax Dollars	$6,870	$5,146

Take the difference between after-tax dollars, and that will be extra dollars.

After-Tax $ from Tax-Free Investment	$6,870
After-Tax $ from Treasuries	− $5,146
Extra Dollars	$1,724

What's especially powerful about this idea is this: *The extra-dollar advantage from tax-free municipals has historically always been there* in varying interest-rate markets and changing tax climates. It's the concept of relative return, *no matter where yields and tax brackets are.*

Figure 1-3 illustrates that principle dramatically; it plots the extra dollars for 28% and 33% bracket taxpayers for the period from February 1986 to February 1987. (The graph uses the weekly return on the

FIGURE 1-3. *Nuveen Extra Dollars. The Additional After-Tax Dollars Earned from a Nuveen National Trust Compared to 30-Year Treasuries ($100,000 Investment).*

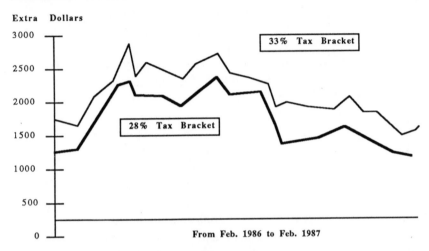

Despite falling interest rates during the period from February 1986 to February 1987, Nuveen extra dollars remained consistently high. Although it's impossible to predict the future, the municipal bond market has historically been extremely efficient, offering many investors extra dollars, no matter what the yield environment. There's every reason to think such efficiency will continue.

Nuveen National Trust as the tax-free investment and the weekly average of 30-year Treasury bonds as the taxable investment.) At the beginning of 1986, tax-free yields were nearly 8.00%; a year later, they had fallen to below 7.00%. But as the graph shows, the amount of extra dollars from tax-free investments remained relatively consistent throughout, even though nominal yields fell.

WHO SHOULD INVEST FOR TAX-FREE INCOME?

When is an investor a candidate for tax-free income? Simply when the return from a tax-free investment delivers more net *spendable* dollars than a comparable quality taxable investment. At what level of income does that start? Around the 28% marginal tax bracket for a couple filing a joint return—starting at about $30,000.

To compare tax-free securities with other taxable fixed-income investments, it's necessary to determine the *taxable equivalent yield*. This taxable equivalent yield shows the yield an investor would have to earn on a taxable investment to equal what could be earned from a tax-free investment. The higher the tax bracket, the more attractive the tax-free return.

For example, if an investor's taxable joint income is $45,000, the marginal federal tax rate for 1988 is 28%. Any taxable investment income is taxed "at the margin" for this investor—that is, 28% of investment income is taxed. Thus, if the investor earns $6,000 from a taxable investment of $75,000 (for an 8.00% return), he will get to keep only $4,320, because 28% of his original earnings go to the IRS. Thus, after tax, the investor actually earns around 5.8%.

Now suppose that the investor takes the $75,000 and invests in a tax-free security that offers approximately a 5.75% return. The investor will earn $4,312 tax free on his initial investment. As you can see, the two investments—$75,000 at a taxable return of 8.00% or $75,000 at a tax-free return of 5.75%—are nearly equivalent investments for this 28% marginal bracket taxpayer. The investor earns the same amount of money, after tax, on either investment.

Once we move up to the 33% bracket, the advantage of tax-free income becomes dramatic indeed. If an investor has a joint taxable income of $72,000-$193,000 (1988 bracket for married couples filing joint returns), the marginal federal tax rate is 33%. A 6% tax-free yield for this investor is equivalent to a 9% yield on a taxable investment. (For a complete summary of taxable equivalent yields, see Table 1-1.)

Thus, it's easy to see why tax-exempt securities have such broad appeal. It's difficult, if not impossible, to find taxable investments with comparable safety and marketability paying an after-tax yield that equals the return on a tax-free investment.

RISK AND THE MUNICIPAL MARKET

Municipal bonds are considered second only to U.S. government securities in safety. But even though municipal bonds are among the safest investments, they are not risk free—only federally guaranteed deposits and U.S. government Treasury securities can make that claim.

TABLE 1-1. 1988 Taxable Equivalent Table.

To use the Taxable Equivalent Yield Table, first determine the investor's taxable income and federal income tax bracket. Locate the current tax-exempt yield at the top of the table. Read down and across to find the taxable yield *needed to match the current tax-exempt yield.*

Taxable Income (1,000s)		Federal	Tax-Free Yields						
Single Return	Joint Return	Tax Bracket	5.00%	5.50%	6.00%	6.50%	7.00%	7.50%	8.00%	8.50%
$ 0– 17.9	$ 0– 29.8	15.0%	5.88	6.47	7.06	7.65	8.24	8.82	9.41	10.00
17.9– 43.2	29.8– 71.9	28.0	6.94	7.64	8.33	9.03	9.72	10.42	11.11	11.81
43.2–100.4	71.9–192.9	33.0*	7.46	8.21	8.96	9.70	10.45	11.19	11.94	12.69
Over 100.4	Over 192.9	28.0*	6.94	7.64	8.33	9.03	9.72	10.42	11.11	11.81

*The table reflects the effect of two surcharges, or rate adjustments, designed to phase out the effects of the 15% federal tax bracket and the personal exemptions for higher income taxpayers. The rate adjustments, in effect, raise the marginal federal tax rate to 33% for taxpayers whose taxable income exceeds $71,900 (joint return) or $43,150 (single return). The rate adjustments are subject to certain maximums, which depend on the number of personal exemptions claimed. As a result of these maximums, joint taxpayers with taxable incomes in excess of approximately $192,930 (assuming four personal exemptions) and single taxpayers with taxable incomes in excess of approximately $100,480 (assuming one personal exemption) will be taxed at a marginal federal tax rate of 28%.

The most obvious risk is that of default—circumstances where the is-suer of the bond cannot make interest and principal payments.

Despite some highly publicized municipal bond defaults (the most notable example being the Washington Public Power Supply System, or WPPSS, in 1983), it's important to note that only a small fraction of municipal bonds issued ever reach such dire straits. Even in the 1930s, when banks closed and the Depression had taken hold, no more than 2% of the outstanding par value of municipal bonds were in default—and most defaults were eventually corrected as adjustments occurred or refinancings took place. Recently, the level of default has been a fraction of 1% of outstanding par value.

While the risk of default with municipal bonds is remote, interest-rate risk is always present. Like all debt instruments—be they corporate bonds or government-issued securities—municipal bonds are affected by the movement of interest rates. Picture the relationship as a seesaw: When interest rates move up, the price of bonds moves down. This is the basic definition of interest-rate risk. But by the same token, there is interest-rate *reward*: when interest rates decline, the prices of bonds *increase*.

Many investors, though, invest in municipal bonds for stable in-come: they are not necessarily looking to realize any sizable appreciation in the price of their municipal bond investments due to the movement of interest rates. Besides, it is difficult, if not impossible, to forecast the peaks and valleys of interest rates—even the highly visible and "expert" economists at major investment firms have had an erratic track record at predicting the course of future interest rates.

WAYS TO INVEST FOR TAX-FREE INCOME

An individual investor can choose among four kinds of invest-ments that provide tax-free income:

- Individual municipal bond and note issues that have maturities rang-ing from a few months to 30 or more years.
- Unit investment trusts (UITs)—closed-end packaged portfolios of municipal bonds to which no new bonds can be added.
- Open-end bond mutual funds—"managed" portfolios of municipal bonds, with shares redeemable at net asset value.

- Closed-end bond mutual funds—"managed" portfolios with fixed capitalization; fund shares are common stock traded on an exchange at a market price.

- Tax-free money market funds—open-end portfolios of short-term, tax-exempt securities.

Each of these investment products has its particular characteristics. First, let's look at individual municipal bonds.

INDIVIDUAL MUNICIPAL BONDS

Ever since a Supreme Court ruling established the doctrine of mutual reciprocity, which prevented states from levying taxes on interest from federal obligations, and in return prevented the federal government from levying taxes on interest from state obligations, municipal bonds have played a crucial role in funding projects vital to the economic growth of our state and local governments, as well as the quality of life of our citizens.

At the end of 1986, there were $724 billion of municipal bonds outstanding—or nearly a trillion dollars. Municipal bonds are issued to raise capital for projects such as schools, hospitals, water and electric systems, highway construction, bridges, and a host of other projects needed by our communities.

Two categories of municipal bond issues are available in the marketplace. The first—general obligation bonds (known as G.O.s) are secured by the issuer's pledge of full faith and credit, or, in other words, its taxing power. These bonds are usually issued for non-revenue-producing projects such as streets, schools, and other public buildings. Communities pay the principal and interest from the taxes levied on local residents. Under the Tax Reform Act of 1986, general obligation bonds will remain exempt from federal income tax.

The second category—and the majority of bonds currently brought to market—are revenue bonds. Revenue bonds are secured by user fees generated by a specific project such as a local water and sewer system, an electric utility, an airport, a community hospital, or perhaps a toll bridge or a toll road. While tax exemptions for many revenue bonds will be retained under the Tax Reform Act of 1986, interest on certain private activity bonds may be subject to the alternative minimum tax (AMT). Because the AMT will only apply to a small percentage of tax filers, interest on many private activity bonds will continue to be completely federally tax free for many investors.

Before the 1986 tax act, private activity revenue bonds for industrial development and pollution control were always categorized as tax exempt. These bonds are issued by local and state authorities, but the issuing municipalities do not pay the bondholders. The principal and interest are paid by corporations using the facilities financed by the bonds and may be guaranteed by a parent corporation of the user. Therefore, when investors bought industrial development bonds, they were (and are) really buying the equivalent of tax-exempt corporate bonds. However, under the new tax law passed in 1986, Congress labeled these issues "nonessential" to government activities, and interest on industrial development bonds issued on or after August 16, 1986 (or September 1 for certain bonds), will, in most cases, be taxable. Specifically, the tax will apply to interest on bonds issued for sports stadiums and the upgrading of pollution-control facilities.

Tax-exempt corporate bonds may be a perfectly fine investment if the issue is backed by a major corporation, but obviously some corporations will pose a greater risk than others. An investor must judge the creditworthiness of the corporation or the guarantor, not the municipality, when evaluating the risk of these bonds.

What implications does this hold for an investor? Tax reform restrictions on the amount and types of tax-free debt should decrease the supply of municipals, and, as with any other commodity, if you decrease the supply, you increase the demand, thus raising the price. So investors astute enough to have purchased tax-free investments before January, 1986, saw their holdings appreciate in value. Moreover, due to the severe curtailment of other kinds of tax-favored investments—notably real-estate and equipment-leasing partnerships and income-shifting trusts—tax-exempt securities will be one of the few advantageous outlets remaining for upper- and middle-income investors.

EVALUATING THE RISKS OF TAX-FREE INVESTING

Most individual investors do not have the analytical experience or the time required to properly evaluate the creditworthiness of individual municipal bond issues. However, two independent rating organizations—Moody's Investors Service Inc. and Standard & Poor's Corporation—evaluate the ability of the issuer to pay interest and principal for many tax-exempt bond issues. Industry experts and individuals alike use their evaluations and guidelines.

Perhaps the most significant recent change in the municipal bond market has been the advent of insured municipal bond issues. Insured municipal bonds are rated triple A by Standard & Poor's and/or Moody's, and therefore are sold at a lower rate of interest than if they carried a lesser rating. Major insurers in the market include the Municipal Bond Investors Assurance Corporation (MBIA Corporation), AMBAC Indemnity Corporation, the Financial Guaranty Insurance Corporation (FGIC), and the Bond Investors Guaranty Insurance (BIGI). All are monoline firms that devote their entire business resources to the insurance of municipal bonds.

Municipal bond insurance provides for the timely payment of interest and principal when due. One thing must be emphasized—insurance does *not* insulate an investor from interest-rate risk if a bond is sold before maturity. Just because an issue is insured, that does *not* mean that an investor can get all his principal back at any time before maturity without loss of principal—though the insurance does guarantee the payment of principal on maturity.

As a result of the insurer's "third-party guarantee," many industry experts believe insured bonds will exhibit a greater price stability than lesser-rated, uninsured bonds during volatile markets.

In recent years, several innovative securities have come on the scene—the zero coupon municipal bond and the stripped municipal bond. Zero coupon municipal bonds follow the same principle as the taxable zero coupon bond—they are purchased at a substantial discount from maturity or par value and pay all interest and principal at maturity. For those who can forego current income, the zero coupon bond can be an attractive investment; because interest compounds automatically, it isn't necessary to reinvest the income. They have another advantage: Because zeros are purchased at substantial discounts, they're an ideal vehicle to help fund a future need—such as a college education for children or grandchildren or an investor's own retirement needs.

However, there is one caution when considering zero coupon bonds, and it's an important one. Because an investor receives no current income, the entire investment return depends upon the issuer's ability to meet its obligation at maturity. Therefore, investments in zero coupon bonds should be restricted to the highest quality issuers.

Stripped municipal bonds are also attractive investments for people who need to fund a future need and are in the higher tax bracket. Unlike zero coupon municipals, most of which have maturities far greater than 10 years, stripped municipals offer maturities of usually around 5 to 10 years, making them ideal for investors who have short-term goals.

UNIT INVESTMENT TRUSTS

Many investors have neither the time nor the expertise to select individual issues of municipal bonds or to monitor their portfolios on a continuing basis. However, there are tax-free investment vehicles that eliminate these problems for the individual investor.

One of the most popular is the unit investment trust (UIT)—a closed-end portfolio of municipal bonds selected by a sponsor/ underwriter to provide the highest possible tax-free return commensurate with safety. These sponsor/underwriters are investment banking firms that have considerable expertise in municipal securities.

During the 1980s thus far, tax-free unit investment trusts have enjoyed spectacular growth. In 1980, industry sponsors of tax-free UITs packaged for and sold to investors $4.4 billion of par value. By 1985, that annual figure had jumped to $15.34 billion—an all-time record. In 1986, deposits declined to about $9.6 million, but that was due in part to the rapidly growing popularity of mutual funds. Total mutual fund assets at the end of 1986 climbed to more than $130 billion. Figures 1-4 and 1-5 show the dramatic growth of both unit investment trusts and mutual funds over the past decade.

A UIT portfolio is selected by the sponsor/underwriter and then deposited with a trustee bank. The trustee safekeeps the bonds, collects and distributes the income, and provides an annual accounting to unitholders. Unit investment trusts are sold in minimum investments ranging from $1,000 to $5,000. Many UIT sponsors offer the investor the option of receiving interest distributions monthly, quarterly, or semiannually. An investor pays a one-time sales charge, which can range from 1.35% to 4.90%, depending on the sponsor, the amount invested, and the maturity range of the portfolio.

The sales charge is included in the price and yield quoted to the investor—that is, the yield is "net" to the investor. Many sponsor/ underwriters offer "breakpoint" pricing; when purchases reach certain

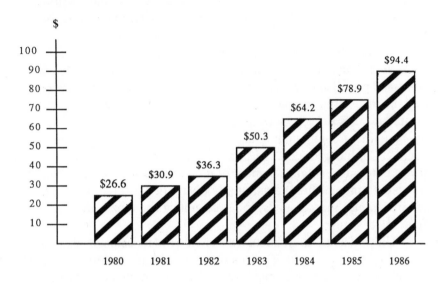

FIGURE 1-4. *Cumulative UIT Volume—Year End (Billions of Dollars)*
(Source: Nuveen Market Research.)

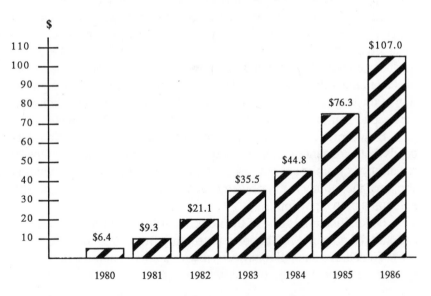

FIGURE 1-5. *Total Assets in Tax-Free Municipal Funds—Year End*
(Billions of Dollars). (Source: Investment Company Institute.)

levels, the sales charge declines, and the net yield to the investor increases. Some sponsors conduct credit surveillance of the portfolio as long as the trust is outstanding, thus providing additional value for the investor.

When an investor owns a portion of a unit investment trust, he owns *units* in that trust—a fractional undivided interest in the interest income and principal of the underlying portfolio bonds. These units represent the investor's pro rata share of the value of that trust. Some unit investment trusts offer reinvestment options so that investors can enjoy the benefits of compounding tax-free interest. For example, John Nuveen & Co. Incorporated, the largest sole sponsor/underwriter of unit investment trusts, offers a number of reinvestment options: a nationally diversified mutual fund, a nationally diversified insured mutual fund, tax-free money market funds, and state mutual and money market funds from select states.

Units in a unit investment trust are always redeemable at net asset value based on the market prices of the portfolio's underlying bonds. The trustee of a unit investment trust is legally required to redeem units any business day at their current net asset value. But of course the net asset value at redemption may be higher or lower than the original purchase price, depending upon the level of interest rates at the time the purchase was made versus the time the units are liquidated.

Sponsor/underwriters of unit investment trusts generally maintain a secondary market so that units tendered for redemption may be sold to other investors. By reselling these units in the secondary market, the trustee need not liquidate bonds from the portfolio in order to make monies available to redeem units. This helps maintain the full diversification of the original portfolio for the longest period of time and eliminates the need to liquidate bonds during unfavorable or volatile markets.

However, the trustee at the sponsor's discretion may liquidate bonds that experience credit or market deterioration or to meet unitholder redemptions if units are not resold in the secondary market. When this happens, the money is distributed proportionately to the investors who hold units in that portfolio.

Diversification is one of the key advantages unit trusts provide. A typical UIT portfolio has bonds representing from 10 to 30 separate issues. To achieve such diversification with a comparable yield on their own, an individual would probably have to invest $250,000 or more in individual bonds. That's because a purchase of less than $25,000 of a single issue would be difficult to market if an investor wanted to sell before maturity. (A "round lot," the most easily marketable quantity, is $100,000.)

Besides providing diversification, unit trusts are convenient. The bank or trust company that serves as trustee safekeeps the bonds, collects interest payments from issuers, and distributes monthly, quarterly, or semiannual checks to unitholders or to reinvestment accounts chosen by the investor. The trustee also sends principal distributions when bonds are called, sold, or mature. (An investor who owns an individual bond may miss a call on the bond or forget to submit a coupon.)

Many unit trust portfolios are national in scope—they are well diversified with bonds issued by municipalities from around the nation. These national trusts provide income free from all federal income taxes; however, a portion of the income may be subject to state and local taxes. Some sponsors also offer single-state trust portfolios, containing different issues from only one state. The income from these trusts is 100% tax-free for residents of that state: all the interest income from the trust is free from federal, state, and local income taxes—and, in a number of cases, from personal property taxes and intangible taxes as well.

The Growth of Insured Unit Investment Trusts

As insured municipal bonds have increased their market presence, so too have insured unit investment trusts. Through 1983, there were 3 sponsors of tax-free insured unit trusts; by the end of 1985, the number of sponsors offering insured trusts had more than quintupled to 16. Insured unit trust sales now account for more than 40% of unit trust sales in the marketplace.

Investors currently have the choice of two types of insured tax-free unit investment trusts. The first type is sometimes called the insured *while in trust* (WIT), because the underlying bonds are insured *only* while they are in the trust portfolio. The other kind, the *insured-to-maturity* (ITM) trust, contains bonds that are individually insured as long as they are outstanding, whether they are in or out of the trust portfolio. Thus the term *insured to maturity*.

Because the insurance on a WIT trust covers the bonds *only* while they remain in the portfolio, the bonds in these portfolios can have a variety of different ratings, ranging from BBB to AAA. In effect, the insurance on a WIT trust guarantees that unitholders will receive their pro rata share of interest and principal from their trust holdings—as long as the bonds remain in the portfolio. The insurance does not guarantee that individual bonds themselves will pay interest and principal. Thus, WIT trust units are priced daily to market value of the bonds without attributing any value to insurance obtained by the fund. If any portfolio bonds should default, the lower market price of those bonds is likely to be reflected in the trust's net asset value.

In contrast, the insured-to-maturity (ITM) trust contains bonds that are insured as long as they are outstanding, that is, until they mature or are called. The insurance is permanent. Whether these permanently insured bonds remain in the portfolio or move outside the trust, the timely payment of interest and principal from each individual bond is guaranteed. Consequently, each individual bond receives a triple A rating from Standard & Poor's and/or Moody's. The net asset value of an ITM trust reflects the market value of the triple A insured rating of the bonds.*

Many bond professionals anticipate that ITM trusts, with their permanently insured triple-A rated bonds, will have a more stable net asset value than WIT trusts, whose portfolio bonds can have a variety of ratings. For the investor, this means that the permanent insurance can enhance the net asset value when the investor wants to redeem units before maturity. The units of both trust types receive a triple A rating from Standard & Poor's, but only ITM portfolio bonds retain their triple A rating when outside the trust.

Understanding the distinctions between the two kinds of insured trusts is important for investors in determining their investment strategies. There's a cost/benefit trade-off involved in choosing between a while-in-trust only (WIT) and an insured-to-maturity trust (ITM).

While the ITM trusts have the extra protection of permanent insurance, they will also tend to have a lower yield than the WIT. And while the WIT trusts lack permanent insurance on each individual bond, their yield will tend to be higher than ITM trusts. Also investors should be aware that insurance, whether it covers one type of trust or the other, does not guarantee the market value of bonds or trust units because all securities are subject to market price fluctuation.

---

*The bond rating reflects the rating of the insurance company; if the rating of the insurance company changes, the bond rating changes as well.

Range of Maturities Available—Short, Intermediate, and Longer Term

Besides the choice of insured and traditional tax-free trusts, investors also have a spectrum of maturity choices. Longer-term trusts—state and national portfolios that have an average life of 25-30 years—have remained the most popular. The reason, of course, is that long-term trusts offer the highest current tax-free yields for the longest time and have historically outperformed taxable investments of comparable quality and maturity. In 1986, longer-term trusts accounted for nearly 78% of the tax-free UIT market.

But the intermediates—trusts that have average lives ranging from 5 to 15 years—have had a growing share of market in the UIT industry. In fact, the intermediates accounted for 14% of UIT sales in 1986, up from 11% in 1985.

The intermediates fall into three categories:

- *Short Intermediates*—trusts that have a 5-year average life, containing bonds that have maturities ranging from 3 to 7 years
- *Intermediates*—trusts that have a 10-year average life, containing bonds that have maturities ranging from 5 to 15 years
- *Long Intermediates*—trusts that have 15-year average life, containing bonds that have maturities ranging from 11 to 19 years

The intermediates have all the key advantages of long-term UITs—diversification, convenience, liquidity, and a choice of payment options—while offering higher tax-free yields than tax-free money market funds and a shorter investment period than long-term securities. Intermediates should also provide greater price stability than longer-term bond investments—a consideration should the investor wish to cash in before the entire portfolio matures.

Investors have been particularly attracted to the intermediates because they provide flexible choices to help meet financial planning goals. By purchasing one or more of the 5-, 10-, and 15-year portfolios, investors can time their tax-free investments for the years they need to shelter investment earnings from federal income taxes. The intermediate portfolios have staggered maturities of tax-free municipals, designed to return principal over a span of years as bonds mature. Both interest income and principal returns can be reinvested to create a growing pool of assets, or funds can be redeployed for other purposes such as college tuition, family gifting, paying off a home mortgage, etc.

Many investors want tax-free investments with maturities even shorter than five years. Individuals who have a short investment horizon have two choices in packaged portfolio tax-free investments: a tax-free money market fund (discussed later) and a short-term unit investment trust. A short-term trust has an average life of three years and is an attractive tax-free alternative to CDs, taxable money market funds, T-bills, and other highly liquid taxable investments.*

Several other types of specialty unit investment trust products are worth mentioning: the discount trust, the put trust, and the compound interest trust. In a *discount trust*, a sponsor buys previously issued bonds that are valued at a discount from their maturity (par) value. When investors buy units in a discount trust, not only will they receive the tax-free income generated from a trust, but there is also a built-in capital gain when the bonds in the fund mature. This same investment strategy can also be accomplished by purchasing originally issued unit investment trust units, trading at a discount from par (due to a change of interest rates), in the secondary market.

A *put trust* can be seen as a discount trust with an added feature. Put investors have the opportunity to put, or sell, their units to the sponsor/underwriter at a prescribed price after a certain period of time. To assemble put trusts, sponsor/underwriters usually buy market-depreciated bonds held in the portfolios of banks, trust companies, or insurance companies and package them into a portfolio. In turn, the selling institution agrees to repurchase these put bonds when the put period elapses at the original price for which they were sold to the trust sponsor. So if an investor wishes to put his units, the seller, who has agreed to repurchase the bonds, will provide the monies necessary to meet those redemptions.

This put option is, de facto, a kind of insurance: It guarantees that the investor will receive the original amount of principal invested at a specified future date. However, there's a trade-off: The investor must accept some reduced yield. If the investor were to invest in a comparable

---

*CDs pay fixed principal and interest and are backed by the FDIC or FSLIC; T-bills are not subject to state and local tax, pay fixed principal and interest, and are backed by the full faith and credit of the U.S. government.

discount trust without the put feature, he would generally earn more interest. However, these put trusts generally yield more than individual bonds that mature at the same time as the put date.

A *compound interest trust* is made up of a portfolio of zero coupon bonds and stripped municipal bonds. Like zero coupon and stripped municipals, the trust provides no current income. The investment is designed so that an investor makes an initial one-time payment and receives all interest and principal—free of federal taxes on income and capital gains—the year the trust matures. However, there's one key difference between an individual zero and the CIT. An investor who buys an individual zero gets one lump sum payment when the bond matures, but with a CIT, the investor receives a series of monthly payments in the final year of the trust. That's because the portfolio will contain a number of different zeros and strip bonds that mature at various times throughout the final year.

MUNICIPAL BOND MUTUAL FUNDS AND TAX-FREE MONEY MARKET FUNDS

Another popular tax-free investment is the open-end mutual fund that consists of municipal bonds. With a unit investment trust, an investor owns units in a closed-end portfolio—no new bonds can be added to the portfolio once it's assembled (although bonds may be sold out of portfolio for credit reasons or to meet unit-holder redemptions). On the other hand, with an open-end municipal bond mutual fund, an investor owns bonds that are bought and sold continually by the portfolio manager.

The managers of a municipal bond mutual fund seek a total return—a mix of appreciation and interest income—by actively trading the bonds in the portfolio. About half the assets of open-end funds are held by "no load" funds; the other half are held by funds that have a sales charge ranging from 1.75% to 8.50%, depending on the sponsor. In either case, all open-end funds have additional costs—usually an annual management fee plus a charge to cover their expenses—which in the aggregate can amount to 0.4% to 0.75% of mutual fund assets annually. For tax-free money market funds, such management fees can range from 0.5% to 0.75% of funds assets annually. (For unit investment trusts, the trustee's annual fee ranges between 0.05% and 0.1% of the face value of the bonds in the portfolio.)

The most significant development in tax-free packaged portfolios has been the emergence of tax-free, *closed-end* mutual funds that are portfolios of tax-free securities. Unlike open-end funds, which can continually issue new shares as investor funds are received, closed-end funds have a fixed capitalization. And unlike open-end mutual funds, closed-end fund shares are underwritten by a syndicate of investment banking firms, sold to the public in an initial public offering (IPO), and then traded on a stock exchange, such as the New York Stock Exchange, after the offering is complete. These tax-free closed-end funds pay a monthly tax-free dividend. The largest such closed-end fund, the Nuveen Municipal Value Fund, came to market in mid-June 1987, raising $1.58 billion—the largest initial public offering in the history of the U.S. capital markets.

Both open-end mutual funds and unit investment trusts must redeem shares or units at that day's net asset value. In contrast, the price of closed-end bond fund shares is determined by market forces on the exchange—primarily supply of and demand for shares, and expectations of future interest rates. Thus closed-end fund shares may trade at net asset value, at a premium to net asset value, or at a discount to net asset value.

Clearly, investors are attracted to some key advantages closed-end funds provide. First, closed-end municipal funds, as a tax-free dividend producing stock, offer the liquidity of a stock exchange listing. Second, since shareholders of a closed-end fund buy and sell shares on the exchange, rather than redeem shares from the sponsor, the portfolio manager of a closed-end fund does not need to keep cash reserves to meet redemptions. All funds are fully invested. Finally, given the fund's fixed capitalization and exchange trading, a closed-end fund manager can focus all his attention on the long-term objectives of the fund.

For municipal bond mutual funds, the initial investment is usually $1,000 with the option of adding to one's holdings in amounts of $100 or more. Thus mutual funds are a good vehicle to accumulate small sums and gradually build a large tax-exempt investment. Interest distributions from a municipal bond mutual fund can be paid in cash monthly or reinvested in additional shares. Shares in an open-end fund can be liquidated at any time at the then prevailing net asset value—the same as with a unit investment trust.

Because an open-end portfolio is actively managed and therefore constantly changing, the income an investor receives is *not a fixed return*, but a *variable return*. This return will increase or decrease over the course of time depending upon the general level of interest rates and the skills of the portfolio manager in adjusting the fund's holdings to take maximum advantage of the current interest-rate environment. When interest rates are declining, a municipal mutual fund can be a rewarding strategy for an investor's money, providing a reasonable tax-free return, plus an opportunity for capital appreciation.

In 1986, investors committed a record $30.7 billion of net new assets into municipal bond mutual funds. With the dramatic rise in popularity of these funds, it's critical that investors recognize the implications of an investment strategy that employs a unit investment trust, compared to a municipal bond mutual fund.

With a unit investment trust, an investor has the assurance that he has captured a stable return. As long as the UIT portfolio remains constant, the investor will earn the same tax-free yield and the same amount of annual tax-free income that he was quoted on the day he purchased. Even if the portfolio does change, the investor in most cases should earn a return close to that original yield. In contrast, an investor in a municipal bond mutual fund can anticipate that his yield will change over a period of time, providing a higher or lower return than prevailed at the time of the investment. Many investors own both a unit trust and a mutual fund—the first provides steady tax-free income, while the second offers the opportunity for an increase in total return.

For those investors who wish to invest a portion of their portfolio in readily available assets with virtually no market risk, a tax-exempt money market fund is an attractive alternative. These funds are comprised of short-term tax-exempt securities. The portfolios, by law, must have an average maturity of 120 days or less. As with the vast majority of taxable money market funds, the shares in most tax-free money market funds are bought and sold at a fixed price of $1.00. The yield fluctuates on a daily basis, reflecting the changes in short-term market rates.

Some of these funds offer check-writing privileges and the option to transfer money in and out by wire to and from an investor's bank. In addition, many investors direct their unit investment trust income into a tax-free money market fund, using it as a vehicle to "park" their money temporarily. Once sufficient funds have accumulated in their accounts, these investors have the opportunity to buy additional units in a unit investment trust or other financial service products.

THE NATURE OF THE UNDERWRITING PROCESS

Whenever an individual bond issue or a tax-free unit investment trust is marketed to the public, one of the key actors in the drama is the underwriter. Underwriting is a highly complex affair, but no matter how the underwriting is accomplished, the significant principle remains the same: the underwriter risks its capital in the purchase of securities for re-sale to the investor. The underwriter makes its profit or loss in the spread between the price at which it purchases the bonds from the issuer and the price at which the bonds are sold to investors.

But this process, simple as it sounds, entails a good deal of risk for the sponsor/underwriter. Should interest rates move up—and bond prices down—while the underwriter holds securities or units it has pur-chased, then it may find its profit "spread" narrowed considerably and sometimes even eliminated entirely. In fact, sponsor/underwriters can incur losses. Thus, during the period when the sponsor/underwriter as-sembles the trust and until it is sold to investors, the sponsor/ underwriter's capital is "at risk."

For sponsors of municipal bond mutual funds, this market-movement risk does not exist. When the fund receives money from in-vestors, shares are issued and bonds purchased with those investor funds; the shareholders then bear the market risk. Investors in a unit in-vestment trust also bear market risk once they own units. But while a sponsor/underwriter of a UIT risks its own capital to buy bonds for the trust before the trust itself is sold to investors, the sponsor of an open-end fund purchases bonds on a continual basis using monies received from individual shareholders. The open-end municipal bond mutual fund makes most of its profit from ongoing management fees, charged as a percent of the assets, and some mutual funds are sold with a sales charge (or "load"). In contrast, all unit trusts are sold with a sales charge but have no on-going management fees.

FOUR TYPES OF UNIT TRUST UNDERWRITERS

In the underwriting of tax-free unit investment trusts, there are basically four kinds of underwriters:

• Underwriters syndicating for in-house distribution.

- Underwriters syndicating for other firms.
- Sole sponsor/underwriters for in-house distribution.
- Sole sponsor/underwriters for other firms.

The distinctions among these four types of underwriting procedures are more than just technicalities. The underwriting method that brings the product to market goes hand-in-hand with a distributing firm's overall marketing strategy.

A number of the large, nationally known brokerage firms band together to issue tax-free unit investment trusts; they syndicate for in-house distribution. There are also a number of firms that do not have their own retail sales force but instead syndicate their product primarily for regionally based brokerage houses. (For a list of sponsors from all four categories, see Table 1-2 on pages 30 and 31.)

The first two types of underwriters have an entirely different marketing strategy than sole sponsor/underwriters who market in house or produce products for other firms to sell. Their strategy is based upon syndication, whereby the rewards and/or risks of underwriting are shared among a group of firms; some underwriters share profits only, while others share both profits and losses. Syndicate members may be able to make more profit per unit sold in periods of declining interest rates, but they can also be at risk if interest rates rise and bond prices fall.

Those sponsors who assemble unit trusts for syndication offer syndicate members sales support and marketing aids of various kinds and in varying degrees. But underwriter/syndicates rely heavily on the initiative and motivation of individual salespeople within member firms to move the product. Even though syndicates advertise jointly, often listing in such ads every participating firm, each member usually does its own in-house sales support. Thus, the shared underwriting approach often dilutes the identification of the specific investment product—in this case, the unit investment trust—with a specific firm.

Obviously, sponsors who sell solely through their in-house sales forces—the third type of unit trust underwriter—can overcome this disadvantage, but because such firms offer a full range of investments, they seldom devote a national marketing campaign to a single product.

John Nuveen & Co. Incorporated is unique in the tax-exempt unit trust industry: It is the only investment firm that acts as sole sponsor and

TABLE 1-2. *Major Unit Investment Trust Sponsors/Underwriters.*

Firm	Product Name	Profits/Losses on Underwriting	Syndicate Members
Sole Sponsor/Underwriters for Financial Intermediaries			
John Nuveen & Co. Incorporated	Nuveen Tax-Exempt Unit Trusts: National, State, Insured National, and Insured State series; Short Term; Short Intermediate, Short Intermediate Insured; Intermediate, Intermediate Insured; Long Intermediate, Long Intermediate Insured. Compound Interest Trust	Sponsor retains profits/losses	None
Sole Sponsor/Underwriter for In-House Distribution			
Sears/Dean Witter	Sears Tax-Exempt Trust & Sears Insured Tax-Exempt Trust	Sponsor retains profits/losses	None
E. F. Hutton	E. F. Hutton Tax-Exempt Trust	Sponsor retains profits/losses	None
Paine Webber	The Municipal Bond Trust & The Municipal Bond Trust FGIC Insured Series	Sponsor retains profits/losses	None
Underwriter/Syndicates for In-House Distribution			
Smith Barney; Kidder Peabody Drexel Burnham L. F. Rothschild *et al.*	Tax-Exempt Securities Trust (TEST)	Sponsor retains profits/losses	As Listed
Merrill Lynch	Municipal Investment Trust Fund (MITF)	Profits/losses shared by underwriters	Merrill Lynch Prudential Bache Shearson/ American Express Sears/Dean Witter

TABLE 1-2. *(Cont.)*

Firm	Product Name	Profits/Losses on Underwriting	Syndicate Members
Moseley, Hallgarten Estabrook & Weeden	Municipal Insured National Trust (MINT)	Profits/losses shared by underwriters	Glickenhaus & Co. J. C. Bradford & Co. Raymond James Lebenthal & Co.
Underwriters Syndicating for Others			
Clayton Brown	The First Trust	Underwriting profits shared, losses absorbed by sponsor	Variable: 24 participating brokerage firms
Kemper Financial Services, Inc.	Kemper Tax-Exempt Income Trust	50% profits/ losses to firms accumulating bonds, 50% profits to all underwriters	Subsidiary brokerage firms of Kemper & other regional firms
Van Kampen Merritt	"Investors' Quality:" Insured Municipals Income Trust (IMIT)	50% profits shared, losses absorbed by sponsor	Variable: 30 to 60 firms per trust

sole underwriter that produces a product solely for sale by others. While there are other firms that assemble UIT portfolios for distribution through syndicates or the general dealer community, Nuveen remains as the only sole sponsor/underwriter that makes its product available to all dealers for distribution on an agency basis only. Therefore, Nuveen has developed a total advertising, dealer marketing, and sales support program that both "pushes" and "pulls" the product through distribution channels. Witness to the success of its highly developed marketing program is the fact that Nuveen packaged portfolios are regularly sold by well over 2,500 firms and about 70,000 registered representatives nationwide. Nuveen packaged investments are sold in most of these firms in addition to in-house unit trusts, mutual funds, and/or syndicated products.

Nuveen is the nation's oldest and largest sole sponsor/underwriter of unit investment trusts, having originated the tax-free unit trust concept in 1961. By July 1987, Nuveen had deposited more than 2,000 separate trust series and sold more than $22 billion worth of unit investment trusts. Nuveen sales in 1986 alone, in both the primary and secondary market, exceeded $2.3 billion.

THE DESIGN OF NUVEEN'S MARKETING STRATEGY

Nuveen acts as a "dealer's dealer" of unit trust products and municipal bond mutual funds. Nuveen distributes its tax-free trusts and funds through a network of dealers and agents—brokerage houses, insurance companies, discount brokers, financial planners, commercial banks, and thrift institutions. Commercial banks can act as distributing agents for Nuveen products through their municipal bond departments, trust departments, and discount brokerage operations. As a matter of policy, Nuveen does not sell unit trusts or mutual funds directly to the investing consumer.

With this distribution strategy, Nuveen's marketing efforts are directed towards two separate publics: first, the dealers who distribute the product; second, the ultimate purchaser, the investing consumer.

To reach the second public—the individual investor—Nuveen has established a national brand name through multimillion dollar national advertising campaigns in major publications such as the *Wall Street Journal,* the *New York Times,* the *New Yorker, Time,* and *Newsweek.* In addition, Nuveen uses television, radio, and direct-mail advertising campaigns in its marketing efforts. This consumer-oriented strategy is designed to presell the product, creating an asked-for product. In the process of promoting its own brand name, Nuveen concurrently educates the public on the advantages of tax-free investing, ultimately benefiting the distributing dealer.

But the cornerstone of Nuveen's marketing strategy is that first public—the dealer network. While Nuveen markets the concept of a quality investment *product* to the individual purchaser, Nuveen markets both a *product and a service*—or more specifically, a *range of marketing services*—to its dealer network. This strategy differs in important respects from virtually every other sponsor.

The first and most important service Nuveen provides is a continuously offered product line. Even when the municipal bond market is declining and the risk of underwriting losses is heightened, Nuveen continually strives to have tax-exempt products available for sale through the dealer network. This constant presence in the market—a principle not always adhered to by the three other kinds of underwriters—has kept Nuveen in the forefront of dealer and investor consciousness.

To support this constant presence in the marketplace, Nuveen has established throughout the country a network of 14 sales offices whose function is to provide sales and service support to the dealer network. This support ranges from answering simple technical questions to helping a registered representative (an individual licensed by the National Association of Securities Dealers, Inc., to sell securities) use the Nuveen product line of unit investment trusts and mutual funds to help meet a client's complex financial planning needs. (For details of the Nuveen tax-free product line, see Table 1-3 on pages 34 and 35.)

Besides continuously offered tax-free products and ever-present sales support, Nuveen also provides its dealer network with a full line of merchandising aids, such as direct response mailers, access to Nuveen's municipal bond research, advertising slicks for local publications, and a comprehensive package of other marketing materials. (Other sponsors also provide a variety of sales aids.) Often, Nuveen mails to its dealer network a succinct sales and marketing idea—either in the format of a sales builder or a selling strategy—that registered representatives can put to immediate use when dealing with their clientele.

Nuveen also provides long-term, consultative, fully integrated marketing programs to select firms. Because the intensity and length of these programs demand a thorough commitment on both the part of the participating firm and Nuveen, only a limited number of qualified institutions can participate each year. These marketing programs are not promotional campaigns, though they have a promotional dimension. Rather, the programs use the building-block approach, creating a foundation of product knowledge to support the implementation of cost-effective marketing strategies. In the initial stages, Nuveen and the participating organization undertake research to pinpoint the target markets within a geographical area. Then all the integrated marketing techniques that Nuveen has developed and refined in its 20-plus years as a tax-exempt product sponsor are employed to "push" the product through the dealer's distribution base and to "pull" through orders from existing and prospective investors.

All these components of Nuveen's marketing strategy— continuous product offerings, sales support, and consultative marketing—have

TABLE 1-3. *Nuveen Tax-Free Packaged Investment Products.*

Type	Product Features
	Nuveen Unit Investment Trusts
National Trusts	Pays federally tax-exempt income from high-quality, long-term municipal bonds rated in categories A to AAA; average portfolio life: 30 years.
State Trusts	Pays in-state residents double or triple tax-exempt interest income from high-quality, long-term municipal bonds from their state. Currently available in 17 states:

Arizona	Maryland	New York
California	Massachusetts	North Carolina
Colorado	Michigan	Ohio
Connecticut	Minnesota	Pennsylvania
Florida	Missouri	Virginia
Georgia	New Jersey	

Type	Product Features
Insured National Trusts	A series of nationally diversified portfolios. Contain triple-A rated, permanently insured bonds, with timely payment of interest and principal guaranteed by the Municipal Bond Investors Assurance Corporation (MBIA Corp.)
Insured State Trusts	Currently available in California, Florida, New York, Massachusetts, Ohio, and Pennsylvania.
Intermediate Trusts	Available in three portfolios: 5-year, 10-year, and 15-year average life portfolios, 10-year average life California and 10-year average life New York portfolios also available.
Short-Term Trust	3-year average life portfolios containing nationally diversified bonds.
Compound Interest Trust	Diversified portfolio of tax-free zero coupon bonds and municipal strips, designed to return principal and interest during final year of maturity.
Secondary Trusts	A range of previously issued trust series with varying maturities and prices. Include previously issued long-term national and single-state series, and intermediate trusts.

TABLE 1-3. (Cont.)

Type	Product Features
	Nuveen Mutual Funds
Nuveen Municipal Bond Fund	Nationally diversified tax-free, long-term fund. Direct investment ($1,000 initial) or automatic reinvestment of unit trust income (no minimim).
Nuveen Insured Tax-Free Bond Fund	Nationally diversified tax-free, long-term fund, with bonds insured while in portfolio.
Nuveen Municipal Value Fund	Diversified closed-end mutual fund. A minimum of 80% of fund assets in investment grade municipals. Optional automatic dividend reinvestment.
Nuveen Tax-Free Reserves	Tax-free money market fund. Management fees shared with participating institutions. Direct investment ($1,000 minimum) or automatic reinvestment of unit trust income (no minimum). Check-writing privileges.
Nuveen Tax-Free Bond Fund—States	Diversified portfolios of bonds from a single state. Available in California, Massachusetts, New York, and Ohio.
Nuveen Insured Tax-Free Bond Fund—States	Diversified portfolio of bonds from a single state insured while in portfolio. Available in New York and Massachusetts.
Nuveen Tax-Free Money Market Fund—States	Tax-free money fund containing investment-grade securities from a single state. Available in California, New York, and Massachusetts.
Nuveen Tax-Exempt Money Market Fund	Institutional or individual tax-free money market fund. $25,000 initial investment; $500 subsequent.
Tax-Free Accounts	Institutional tax-free, revenue-sharing money market fund. $250,000 initial minimum investment; no minimum on subsequent investments.

one overriding purpose: to develop and maintain a franchise with the distribution network. The strategy is designed to establish a symbiotically profitable relationship. The dealer gets the benefit of constant sales support, while Nuveen has distribution channels without incurring the fixed costs of maintaining them. Nuveen offers dealers the riskless opportunity to participate in the marketing of this product.

Among the features of Nuveen's marketing strategy are:

• Sales training/education-oriented programs for registered representatives which are designed to familiarize them with the Nuveen product

line, as well as cross-selling opportunities with other products from
their own firm.

• Coordinated direct marketing efforts to the firm's customer base, using Nuveen-designed and market-proven direct-mail pieces.

• Local advertising using Nuveen time-tested advertising strategies—a
  particularly cost-effective effort, especially in those states where Nuveen offers single-state unit investment trusts.

Twenty-five consultative marketing programs have already been
conducted with various regional brokerage houses. In addition, Nuveen
has created a marketing program for major national discount brokerage
firms and a program especially designed for banks.

FINANCIAL PLANNING IDEAS USING
TAX-FREE INVESTMENTS

Here are some specific situations in which tax-exempt securities
and unit investment trusts and mutual funds might be good investment
vehicles to help accomplish an investor's financial planning objectives.

By now, every investor is familiar with the advantages of an individual retirement account—an IRA. Though tax reform will eliminate
the tax deduction for many wage earners, interest will still compound
tax-deferred for all IRA investors. Obviously, an investor would not include tax-free securities in his IRA account because the earnings generated in an IRA account are already tax-sheltered. However, an individual could make a one-time purchase of a tax-free unit investment trust that
would generate enough tax-free income per year to *fund the annual contributions* to an IRA account.

For example, if an individual invests in a long-term, tax-free unit
trust returning 7.00%, a one-time purchase of about $28,000 will fund a
$2,000 IRA contribution for 15 to 20 years—assuming that the unit in-
vestment trust retains its original size and composition for that length of
time. A Keogh Plan or a Simplified Employee Pension (SEP)—both of
which are tax-deferred retirement accounts for self-employed individuals
and small business owners—can be funded in the same manner, and
Keoghs and SEPs have been left relatively intact by the new tax law.

A qualified investor can shelter up to 25% or $30,000 in annual
earnings in a Keogh plan and up to 15% or $30,000 of annual earnings
in a Simplified Employee Pension Plan. Working couples where both

husbands and wives qualify as self-employed can have two Keoghs or SEPs. Keoghs SEPs and IRAs are smart investments, and they are made even better by using a tax-exempt security as the source of income for the annual contributions.

Another popular use of unit investment trusts is to fund annual life-insurance premiums. Most investors are probably paying these premiums from after-tax dollars. Instead of doing this year in and year out, an investor could make a one-time investment in a unit investment trust, where the tax-exempt income is sufficient to cover annual life-insurance premiums. Many who have used this strategy have found that they actually increase their insurance coverage.

With a bit of planning, an investor can switch from taxable investments to tax-exempt securities in order to reduce the federal income-tax bit, as well as cover fixed annual payouts such as Keogh and IRA plans or insurance premiums. The investor need not even handle these funds: he can instruct the trustee to pay the monthly, quarterly, or semiannual payments directly to the appropriate institution.

Here are some real life situations when tax-free investments are appropriate. Let's assume a newly married professional couple in their late 20s have a joint income of $55,000. They are in a life period where they need to begin to build emergency funds as well as net worth, are active consumers making major household purchases, and need some tax protection. This couple can make an initial investment in many municipal bond mutual funds with as little as $1,000 and make regular subsequent purchases of $100. The mutual fund will enable them to build assets slowly but gradually without being taxed on interest, and because many of the funds offer check-writing privileges, they'll remain fairly liquid.

Let's also look at a couple in their 30s to 40s who earn a good income, have made many of their major purchases, and are concerned about building net worth. They might consider buying a municipal bond or a unit investment trust selling at a substantial discount in the secondary market. This would not only provide them with a tax-free return, but more importantly with a capital gains opportunity. To start to fund future college expenses, a zero coupon municipal bond or a deeply discounted unit trust series is especially appropriate. A 10-year or 15-year average life intermediate trust that has staggered maturity bonds designed to return capital over a span of years is another appropriate investment vehicle to create assets for college tuition. Both income and principal could be reinvested, compounding income.

People in their 40s and 50s may be funding current college expenses, making plans to travel, perhaps buying a vacation residence, and also starting to build assets for retirement. Here they might consider a combination of tax-exempt mutual funds or unit investment trusts to provide maximum current spendable income, combined. Again, intermediate trusts can help these investors meet future needs for capital return for buying a vacation home, for retirement, or for paying off a mortgage. Another alternative for investors in their 40s and 50s is a compound interest trust that contains zero coupon and municipal strip securities. There an investor makes a one-time, up-front payment and receives interest and principal 8 to 10 years down the road. The compound interest trust is an ideal investment to help fund a future intermediate term liability.

In the 50s to early 60s, most investors have reached their peak earning years and are going to concentrate entirely on reducing or eliminating as much of the tax bite on their investment income as possible. The prudent strategy at this stage is to capture high yielding tax-free income for as long a period as possible. As they reach retirement years, their primary investment objectives should be a steady and reliable income, maximum convenience in the handling of investments, and most of all, peace of mind. High yielding tax-exempt mutual funds and unit investment trusts should represent a higher percent of an investor's portfolio at this point than in earlier years. Tax-free Nuveen products can meet these needs by providing a reliable source of income, reducing annual income tax liability, and offering the peace of mind provided through an investment sponsored by the leading municipal bond specialist with one of the most extensive market research and surveillance staffs in the industry.

But no matter what the age and stage of life, tax-free securities can be a strong foundation for any investor's portfolio. They truly are the investment of the 80s.

CHAPTER TWO

New Direction for the Mutual Fund Industry: Wholesaling to Banks

Roger T. Servison

> *Roger Servison, a graduate of Harvard Business School, is a Director of National Financial Services Corporation, our brokerage clearing company. Since he joined Fidelity in 1976, Senior Vice President Servison has been intimately involved in almost every aspect of the financial services industry. As Vice President of Marketing for Fidelity's family of mutual funds, Mr. Servison engineered one of the largest direct-mail response programs in the history of the financial services industry. In 1980 he became Vice President of Fidelity Brokerage Services, Inc., which is now the second largest discount broker. He is a former Vice President of Fidelity Corporate Bond Fund and Fidelity International, Ltd.*
>
> *Mr. Servison is a member of the Board of Governors of the No Load Mutual Fund Association and serves as Director of First Night, Inc., The Lena Park Community Development Corporation, and Digital Techniques, Inc. Prior to joining Fidelity, he was a founder of Tax Man, Inc., an income tax service, and Vice President of Continental Investment Corp. and John P. Chase, Inc.*
>
> *Fidelity Investments is America's largest privately held money management and discount brokerage firm. Based in Boston, but with offices throughout the United States and in London, Fidelity manages $85 billion in over 100 different mutual funds. It provides 24-hour-a-day, 7-day-a-week service to over 4 million customers and is widely recognized as a leader in customer service and investment innovation.*

History has come full circle. Mutual funds companies, many of which abandoned the brokerage community as a distribution channel for their products in the 70s, are returning to "wholesaling," with an even older set of partners, the nation's banking institutions. Research and forecasts point to mutual funds as one of the most desirable new products for banks in the years ahead and to wholesaling as one of the most efficient distribution channels for mutual funds.

Today, mutual funds are an $800 billion industry. Assets in equity and fixed income funds have doubled in the last three years, and the number of funds has increased by 43% over the same period of time. But that kind of growth may be just the beginning. If banks link into the distribution chain, future growth could quickly outpace the dazzling record of the early 80s.

MUTUAL FUNDS AND BANKS: STRANGE BEDFELLOWS, STRONG PARTNERS

Banks were among the first sponsors of mutual funds, both in this country and in Western Europe, when the concept of pooled equity investments gained popularity in the 20s. In 1933, the relationship between banks and mutual funds was severed with the passage of the Glass-Steagall Act. From that time, and up through the early 70s, mutual funds and banks viewed each other as participants in separate industries. Banks appealed to savers and mutual funds to investors, and the lines that separated them were clearly drawn.

All that changed with the advent of the money market mutual fund in the 70s. The exodus of depositors from banks to money market funds placed the two institutions face-to-face in competition with each other. They were competitors, but it was hardly a fair fight. At a time when money market funds were paying 17%, banks were restricted to $5^{1/4}\%$ on savings accounts. Because most money market funds offered check-writing features—and they were invested in relatively safe instruments—they threatened checking as well as savings accounts offered by banks.

The banks struck back. They lobbied successfully for the passage of Garn-St. Germain, and in December of 1982 banks offered the first money market deposit account with competitive interest rates. Now it was the mutual fund companies that watched the exodus in dollars. Deposits in money market funds fell 30%, from a high of $235 billion to $160 billion, a point from which they have now fully recovered. Deregulation of the money market business left mutual fund companies exposed. They were faced with competition from an institution that not only enjoyed an enviable trust factor among their customers, but had a local distribution network that was impossible to match.

Banks had problems of their own. Garn-St. Germain put them in the money market business, but they were forced to sit on the sidelines while other financial institutions—insurance companies, brokerage companies, mutual fund companies—offered financial products that, for them, were still off-limits. They were effectively excluded by regulation from offering some products; for others, they found themselves lacking the marketing savvy, the product expertise, the financial and human resources that were required to catapult themselves into a consumer-driven business.

Here was a clear cut opportunity for the manufacturers of financial services, with a pocketful of products, and the retailers—especially the local or regional banks—with a strong presence in their communities, to consider the possibility of attacking the market, instead of each other, to the benefit of both.

Fidelity Investments, a leading mutual fund company and discount broker, was intrigued with the possibilities. And it had a bank that was willing to explore an alliance.

WHOLESALING DISCOUNT BROKERAGE: A FIRST STEP

In 1982, the same year that Congress passed Garn-St. Germain, Security Pacific Bank of California surveyed its existing bank customers. The results of the survey revealed that the financial product they would most like to see the bank offer was discount brokerage.

Security Pacific examined the options. The bank could either "make" or "buy" the product. After calculating the costs and factoring in the time it would take to deliver a discount brokerage operation on their own, they decided to link up with Fidelity. Fidelity provided the computer software, the trade executions, securities custody, and system administration.

In a matter of months, Security Pacific was on stream with a fully operating discount brokerage business. In less than a year, they were adding 1,000 new accounts per month, more than double their original forecast. For Security Pacific, it was the first in a list of innovative products to be made available through a bank. And for Fidelity, it was an opportunity to increase its volume by tapping a market it could never reach on its own: the customer segment that wants to keep its financial business with a bank.

At the end of the first quarter of 1986, there were more than 3,000 banks offering discount brokerage to their customers. A few very large banks decided to go it alone, but for most the answer was to buy it from a wholesaler.

Today, Fidelity, the first discounter to enter the business with banks, commands a 50% market share, with Pershing claiming about 25%. Another dozen smaller discounters, some exclusively wholesalers, account for the remaining 25%.

Where did the market come from? Just as with the money fund phenomenon, there may have been some fractional exit from the manufacturers and their own retail business. But more than compensating for that was the absolute growth in discount brokerage itself. During 1983, the first year that banks entered the business, the rate of market growth accelerated by 25%! And the growth rate over the balance of the decade could be nearly double that of the early 80s, if current trends prevail. Although it is difficult to determine exactly how much of that new growth is due to bank brokerage, Fidelity reports that its wholesale bank customers are opening accounts at a rate higher than its retail operation.

WHAT'S NEXT? BANK MUTUAL FUNDS

For an entire year preceding Fidelity's announcement that it would make its mutual funds available through banks, the company researched the product and the market with its existing institutional client base. Fifty separate banking organizations of various sizes and market orientations were interviewed. Conversations with nonclient banks and vendors and market research studies of the potential customers provided additional data.

The results were resoundingly positive. Banking organizations saw the need to make mutual funds available to their customers for a range of reasons. Many had recently formed upscale or specialized retail marketing operations that require a wide range of investment products to attract their target customer; others, mindful of the enormous potential in the IRA and Keogh markets, believed that they could best compete by making mutual funds available to their IRA and Keogh account holders. Still others expected that deregulation would open the door for banks to participate fully in the mutual fund business, that they would be empowered to sponsor funds and sell them directly to their clients. Entering the business in partnership with a mutual fund company, they reasoned, could enhance the bank's position at some future date.

In 1984, a study by Market Facts, Inc. validated Fidelity's initial research and went far beyond it to describe the market potential for bank-available mutual funds in statistical detail.

THE MARKET: COLOR IT ENORMOUS

According to Market Facts, there is an untapped market for mutual funds that would equal or exceed current annual mutual fund investments. Opening investments alone would nearly *double* the annual net sales of the mutual fund industry, which was about $125 billion in 1986, to over $250 billion.

Who is the source of these new investment dollars? People who would not buy funds from mutual fund management companies or stockbrokers. People who prefer banks because they trust banks and because they find banks personal, accessible, and convenient.

The study estimates that up to 16.8 million U.S. households are prospects for bank/thrift mutual funds. The median age of a prospect is 45 years, with an annual household income of nearly $30,000. Not only do 80% of these prospects want to buy mutual funds from banks, but the Market Facts study reveals that 60% of the sample are willing to switch banks to gain access to the product.

Bank/thrift mutual fund prospects fall into two basic segments: those who value **access** to their investments above all other features and those who value **performance**. The access group also cites the importance of having a well-known fund manager. The performance group values portfolio quality and the track record of the fund.

The **access** group is evenly split between those who prefer the bank and those who prefer the mutual fund company to manage or sell the fund. (Existing legislation will prohibit banks from distributing mutual funds, but the study is predicated on expectations that the laws will soon change.)

The **performance** group, on the other hand, clearly prefers the mutual fund company as both manager and distributor of the fund. Also, the higher the income, the more likely the customer is to fall into the **performance** group, which favors a mutual-fund-managed product. The more affluent customer has little interest in a bank-managed fund; the less affluent customer is split down the middle.

The key findings of this study bear repeating:

- One out of every five U.S. households wants to buy a mutual fund, though less than one in ten currently own one.

- 80% of the prospective buyers of mutual funds, or 13.4 million households, will *only* buy a fund through a bank or thrift institution.

- The most affluent segment of prospective buyers wants to buy a fund that is managed by a mutual fund company, not a bank. Prospects are evenly split, however, on the question of who will sell the fund, the bank, or the mutual fund *through* a space in the bank.

MARKET SEGMENTATION: YOURS, MINE, AND OURS

The findings of the Market Facts study which have subsequently been confirmed by several other independent studies, have broad implications for mutual fund companies and banks alike. For one, it confirms a huge sales potential that fund companies have projected would evolve with the spread in IRA popularity, the growth in IRA account size, and a maturing, increasingly sophisticated adult population.

Most importantly, it raises the issue of distribution. These 13.4 million households want the mutual fund company's product, but they want it available through their local banks.

The wholesale distribution channel is clearly attractive to mutual fund companies. Any fear that wholesaling will cannibalize their retail business should be assuaged by the prospect of reaching a customer segment that is otherwise inaccessible and potentially very large.

And for the banks? A bank has at least three compelling reasons to enter the mutual fund business. First, expansion of the current product line with mutual funds is the cement to the all-important client relationship sought by the current bank customer. It opens up a host of possibilities for personal financial management and for bank-offered central asset-management accounts.

Mutual funds, especially when offered in conjunction with discount brokerage, facilitate personal financial management, the IRA account options multiply, and switching gives the customer an extraordinary degree of freedom. The usefulness of a money market deposit account expands as it serves as a parking lot for money in and out of an equity fund or for the purchase of stock through a discount brokerage account. The customer is looking for convenience, and the mutual fund enables the local bank to provide just that, with the widest range of products and services.

Some of Fidelity's initial Focus Group research revealed that bank customers feel compelled to consider options with greater earnings potential for the future, as, for instance, their IRA investments reach the $10,000 range, and will change financial service companies to get the products they want.

A second reason for banks to make mutual funds available to their customers is the long-term profit potential. Today's $2,000 new account owner is tomorrow's $10,000 investor and a potential millionaire by retirement.

Third, there is a market looking for a product from the bank, and all the bank has to do is make it available. The market exists, and no institution is better positioned to penetrate it than the local bank or thrift institution. This is not a market they have to win, but it is a market that the banks could lose through inaction.

There are attractive arguments for banks and mutual fund companies to hammer out a strategy that serves the interests of both. The mutual fund companies have an impressive, successful history of product development and investment management. (It is interesting to note that, during the financial disarray of the 30s, there was not a single failure in the mutual fund industry.) On the bank side, the local reputation and the bricks-and-mortar presence gives them a natural distribution channel. The news, for both to hear, is that the bulk of this potential market belongs to neither if it does not belong to both!

THE "MAKE OR BUY" DECISION UP CLOSE

The decisions a bank must make on the mutual fund issue will shift somewhat as new legislation supersedes old. However, the fundamental questions will still be pertinent: Should a bank make or buy its mutual fund products? What links in the manufacturing-distribution-marketing chain should it claim alone, now and when restrictions relax? And, to whom should it look for a partner?

For all but the largest 15 or 20 banks, cost alone will resolve the make/buy dilemma. Most banks cannot afford the salaries of a team of top-flight portfolio managers, to say nothing of the enormous overheads incurred in building the research, administrative, and record-keeping resources that are necessary to run a family of mutual funds. Marketing mutual fund products, on the other hand, carries negligible start-up costs. It also provides the bank with a high degree of flexibility and diversity in its product offering.

Time is another factor for consideration. A bank can make mutual funds available to its customers in the time that it takes to select a fund organization and negotiate a contract. Most funds available on a wholesale basis today have packaged turnkey programs, similar to bank discount brokerage programs, that could immediately be part of a product line with a green light from the bank.

Perhaps the strongest evidence that making products is not the direction the banks should take is in the results of the Market Facts survey. The majority of prospective buyers prefer a fund that is managed by the mutual fund company. A portfolio manager with a reputation is also important to many first-time investors as is the fund's track record.

According the Market Facts, the younger, less affluent prospects are willing to buy either a bank-managed and distributed fund or one managed and distributed by the fund itself. They are mainly interested in simplicity and convenience. The slightly older, more affluent prospects overwhelmingly prefer funds sold by banks or thrifts but managed by mutual fund companies. They are slightly more knowledgeable than the convenience-oriented group and more concerned about fund performance.

The bank that decides to buy today may want to rethink that position at some point in the future. More likely the bank that uses a fund company to distribute and sell funds today will rethink those issues at each juncture, and with each change in regulation and legislation.

A BIG GAME, A FEW PLAYERS . . .
WHAT'S THE SCORE?

Fidelity Investments announced its "Partners in Profit" program in mid-January of 1984. The program allows banks to make Fidelity mutual funds available to its customers in three ways: 1) as part of an IRA or

Keogh program; 2) as part of an upscale client program containing multiple services; or 3) as part of a traditional bank-client relationship.

Under the program, Fidelity allows institutions to make available any of its more-than-50 mutual funds to its customers. If they wish, the institutions may also opt to offer discount brokerage services, but it is not a requirement to participate in the program.

Here's how it works: the bank designs a program based on the choices outlined above, or a variation of its own. It selects the Fidelity funds and bank products it wishes to make available and announces its new program to prospective clients. Then, when a prospect requests information, a fulfillment kit including application form, literature on the bank products, and prospectuses for appropriate Fidelity funds is sent to the prospect by a third-party mailhouse.

Fidelity offers extensive, personalized marketing support to participating banks through two different programs. A turnkey marketing program provides advertising copy, press releases, radio scripts, promotional brochures, and other promotional material. A second option provides extensive marketing consultation for the bank, which chooses to design its own promotional materials.

"Partners in Profit" allows the bank to generate fee income in several different ways: It can establish setup, maintenance, and transaction fees, or some combination of the three; or, it can be compensated by Fidelity for providing marketing access to—but *not* the names of—bank clients.

Dreyfus Corp., another large mutual fund organization, is offering five no-load funds created specifically for marketing to banks and thrifts. The Dreyfus funds are available through the participating bank's central asset account, which requires a minimum balance of $10,000.

Unlike Fidelity, Dreyfus encourages banks to put their own labels on the funds they sell.

Dreyfus has also entered into an arrangement with Security Pacific Bank of California, the first banking company to create its own family of no-load mutual funds. In April 1984, Dreyfus announced that it would distribute six portfolios, called the Pacific Horizon Funds, on a nationwide basis. Pacific Century Group, the bank holding company's investment management subsidiary, serves as investment adviser and manager for the funds.

Security Pacific has publicized the funds to its two million customers, advising them that they should contact Dreyfus for further information. Investors can buy shares in the funds only through Dreyfus, because Glass-Steagall restrains Security Pacific from acting as the funds distributor.

A smaller, regional firm, Massachusetts Financial Service Company, has made its state and federal tax-exempt Massachusetts Tax-Exempt Money Market Trust available through Boston's Provident Institution for Savings. The fund is available through the bank's NOW account, which requires a minimum balance of $1000.

Kemper Financial Services of Chicago and Federated Investors, Inc. of Pittsburgh have also reported that they are getting into the act. Many funds, however, are moving more cautiously. Some funds are looking for more certain legal precedent, and many are still lobbying vigorously to keep the banks out of the mutual fund business entirely. The Investment Company Institute, the mutual fund industry association, is the most vocal opponent of proposed legislation that would allow banks to sponsor and sell mutual funds to their customers.

SOUTHEAST BANK: SCORING HIGH
WITH MUTUAL FUNDS

Southeast Bank N.A., located in downtown Miami, Florida, looked for several years for ways to broaden the spectrum of investment products available to customers who did not fit the profile of their traditional trust client. In 1984, Southeast conducted a series of focus groups and learned that many of the clients who had been identified as "upscale" would be interested in mutual funds if they were available through the bank. Robert Hunter, Senior Vice President for Consumer Product Management, contacted the bank's Trust Department and asked them to rate and rank American mutual funds. "Fidelity came out on top," according to Hunter. "Then we learned that Fidelity had the most comprehensive program to make its funds available to banks that was not, so to speak, experimental. And Fidelity's funds outperformed the others we looked at. There wasn't any sales potential in a poorly performing fund, so performance was important. In some instances the funds have sold the upscale program; we thought it would be the other way around."

In January 1984, Southeast opened two upscale client centers and in March 1985 added three more. Mutual funds and discount brokerage are part of the package, which also includes several bank products. The first unit turned a profit in less than six months, several months ahead of anyone's expectations.

Now, Southeast is preparing to test a combined asset account program with Fidelity. The combined asset account would further expand the product line and attract a larger share of a broader market, younger and slightly less affluent than the upscale segment.

ADD IT UP

It's a simple equation: the bank's distribution network, the mutual fund company's product and investment expertise, multiplied by the market potential. It adds up to a very attractive proposition. An alliance with the manufacturers of financial products allows a bank to capitalize on its own undeniable strengths: its strong customer base, its ability to nurture a client relationship, its standing in the community. Then, the bank benefits from the strengths of the partner organization. The product development, investment management, performance record, computer systems, and administration of the mutual fund company enhances the clout of the smallest banking institution.

It also represents the best line of defense for most banks. Citicorp may take on the First National Bank of Everytown, but look out Citicorp if Everytown has some very strong partners. The money-center bank that moves in on the coattails of deregulation may find it has nothing to offer that customers don't already have available from their local bank.

CHAPTER THREE

Precious Metals

Fred Bogart and Frederick Jennings

Fred Bogart was born in New York City on March 28, 1936. He attended Tulane University and graduated from Pace College in 1958. He went into the real-estate business until joining Republic National Bank of New York in March 1967.

In April 1968 the bank was licensed to sell gold to industry and appointed Mr. Bogart dealer. Also in the same year the bank started a wholesale gold-coin department. By the time gold became legal at the end of 1974, the bank was firmly established in U.S. markets as the largest seller of gold to industry and a major wholesaler of coins. Since complete legalization, the bank has also become a large international gold-trading house, dealing extensively with major international banks and customers.

Mr. Bogart is at present an Executive Vice President, Manager, and Chief Trader of the Precious Metals Department.

Frederick J. Jennings is a First Vice President and Chief Lending Officer for the Precious Metals Department at Republic National Bank of New York, where he has worked for the past five years. Prior to this, he was a National Bank Examiner with the Comptroller of the Currency.

The allure of precious metals dates back thousands of years to the time of the ancient Egyptians. Since then people have had an almost limitless fascination with precious metals, principally gold. By definition though, gold makes up only one part of the precious metals group. The others are silver, platinum, and palladium.

Unfortunately, most modern-era Americans were not allowed to hold precious metals in any form other than jewelry during the period from the prohibition of gold ownership in the 1930s until the end of 1974. The period since has seen the most intense scramble to invest in precious metals in the twentieth century.

The end of government restriction on public ownership of gold in 1974 removed the last major barrier to U.S. government control of the metals market.

In 1968, the government closed the U.S. Assay Office's sales of gold to manufacturing industry. At the same time, licenses were issued to approved applicants that allowed sales of gold to industrial end users. Republic National Bank of New York holds one of the first available licenses issued by the federal government. The end users who found in the bank a source of bullion are manufacturing jewelers, electronics manufacturers, and dental gold fabricators. Under current U.S. banking statutes, a national bank may deal in only two of the precious metals: gold and silver bullion. While platinum and palladium cannot be bought or sold through national banks, the New York Mercantile Exchange has been lobbying for a change in current laws to allow such sales.

In addition to the approval of public ownership of gold at the end of 1975, the other major development for precious metals was the advent of commodity futures trading on organized exchanges, beginning with the Commodity Exchange (COMEX) in 1975. Now for the first time there was an organized, well-regulated forum in which hedgers and speculators could buy and sell gold and silver futures contracts on margin.

The Republic National Bank of New York is one of a select few financial institutions to be a major domestic and international market maker in the world bullion markets. The bank's close ties with its owner, Edmund Safra, and his parents date back to nineteenth-century Beirut. These close historical links became an important part of Republic business lines when the bank opened in the United States in 1965.

The following outline sets out the many and varied lines of business in which Republic is now engaged. The purpose is to offer the reader an overview of the basic types of precious metals services as well as the current growth in more complicated and somewhat more esoteric types of services. At the conclusion of this background material, we will offer our ideas on where precious metals are going, what market mechanisms most affect these metals, and how changes in the regulatory climate, such as IRA and Keogh allowances to purchase gold and silver, could help foster a new, more robust interest in precious metals.

REPUBLIC NATIONAL BANK OF N.Y. PRECIOUS METALS BUSINESS

1. *International Arbitrage (a "paper" market) .*
   a. Simultaneous buying and selling for profit opportunities.
   b. Counterparties worldwide financial institutions, government central banks, producing nations.
   c. Close ties with European, Middle Eastern, Far Eastern countries.
   d. Augmented by bullion offices in London, Hong Kong, and Singapore.
2. *International Customer Service.*
   a. Due to historical ties with Middle East.
   b. Clients are European, Middle Eastern, Far Eastern private investors and financial institutions.
3. *Wholesale and Retail Coins and Ingots.*
   a. Based on bullion prices, not on numismatic values.
   b. Purchased directly from the government's mints (i.e., United States, Canada, Mexico, Austria).
   c. Sell at small varying premiums; premiums subject to supply and demand (i.e., over unminted bullion prices).
4. *Industrial Bullion (physical metals).*
   a. Supplier to manufacturing jewelers, electronics industry, dental gold fabricators.
   b. Purchase from major worldwide refineries, store the metal in our vault, and deliver by private armored carriers.
   c. New foreign office in Milan, Italy, expected to augment our supplies to manufacturing jewelers.
   d. Consignment lending business.
5. *Gold and Silver Investment Certificate Program.*
   a. For financial institutions, high net-worth individuals.
   b. Can be allocated Bank of Delaware per firm or per firm unallocated loco London.
   c. For brokerage houses and investment banking firms.

    d. Can be either certificates (Bank of Delaware) or unallocated loco London.

    e. For the retail investor.

    f. For retail nominal buying and selling premiums plus storage charges loco Bank of Delaware.

    g. Explain Bank-of-Delaware-type programs plus New York State sales tax on all bullion sales.

6. *Edge Act Offices in Los Angeles, Miami, and Montreal.*

    a. Serve wholesale coin dealers.

    b. Serve high-net-worth individuals.

    c. Service retail coin sales.

    d. Service other financial institutions.

    e. Service local jewelry-manufacturing clients.

    f. Supply bullion, coins, investment certificates.

7. *Republic Clearing Corporation.*

    a. Clearing membership on major organized commodity futures exchanges.

    b. Member COMEX, New York Mercantile, Chicago Board of Trade.

    c. Authorized to clear Republic's own future trades on commodity exchange as well as customer business for hedge transactions for precious-metals professionals.

    d. Customer business subject to original-margin and variation-margin requirements established by organized exchanges.

    e. Minimum net-capital requirement.

8. *New expanded Federal Reserve Bank approval for Republic Clearing Corporation.*

    a. Approval for all customer-type businesses, both hedge and speculative positions.

    b. Can deal in precious metals futures, foreign exchange, and financial futures.

    c. Augments prior approvals and establishes RCC as a brokerage firm with full service capabilities.

    d. Fees will be discount oriented with an account requirement.

9. *Options on gold and, soon to be allowed, silver.*

    a. New for precious metals.

    b. Complex and limited at present to sophisticated precious-metals professionals.

10. *Vault location.*
   a. Completion of one of the most modern storage facilities in the world, including the Federal Reserve Bank of New York.
   b. Highest security level available under United States standards.
   c. Provide gold and silver storage for COMEX.
   d. Provide silver coin storage for N.Y. Mercantile Exchange.
   e. Provide platinum and palladium storage for New York Mercantile Exchange.
   f. Provide large customer safekeeping for nominal fees.

SELECTED PROGRAM FOR FINANCIAL INSTITUTIONS

We will attempt to review a few of our bullion programs that are of greatest use to the financial institution network. These examples were mentioned briefly in paragraphs three and five of the outline above.

Wholesale and Retail Coins and Ingots

This is our basic physical gold and silver bullion sales program. Available directly to financial institutions, wholesale coin dealers, and retail investment public, its purpose is to make available to the public the whole range of gold and silver coins and ingots.

Basically, there are two types of coins: numismatic coins and bullion coins. Numismatic coins generally interest collectors who purchase them for their physical beauty, rarity, and historical value. Bullion coins, on the other hand, are far more marketable. Their value is based solely on their gold content and, therefore, they are sold at a modest premium above market price. Republic offers a wide range of high circulations coins, including the American Eagle, Mexican Pesos, Canadian Maple Leafs, and Austrian Coronas.

Republic also offers a wide selection of gold ingots in various weights and sizes ranging from the 1/2-ounce ingot to the kilobar. Each ingot has stamped on it for authenticity a serial number, a recognized refiner's name, and the fineness of the bar.

For those investors who are interested in silver, Republic offers a handsome array of ingots ranging from 1-ounce to 100-ounce bars. These are also stamped and numbered for authenticity. As a leader, Republic offers its customers up-to-the-minute market information. Although gold and silver are subject to market fluctuations, Republic continually provides a competitive buy-sell market for its coin and bullion.

Gold and Silver Investment Certificate Program

One of the best ways to purchase gold and silver is through a gold and/or a silver certificate. There is no sales tax, no assaying, and no concern for physical storage, and certificates are easy to redeem. The metal backing these certificates can be in an allocated Bank of Delaware program (retail or wholesale) or unallocated London (mostly for financial institutions and large high-net-worth individuals).

The certificate program is ideally suited to other financial institutions. These firms can either use Republic's form of certificate or use Republic's certificates as an example and offer the program directly under the financial institution's name. In either case, Republic offers a sophisticated back-office accounting program that can be adapted to the individual firm's needs.

In addition, Republic can offer a book-entry type program (either loco Delaware or loco London). This program is tailored for the trust department-type (high-net-worth) customer, investment banking firms, individuals, or the regional brokerage houses. With this program, Republic offers a monthly statement of activity for each firm's transactions, similar to the accounting provided for correspondent demand deposit accounts. This program is as easy as opening a bullion account, setting up an account for payments, and then phoning to place orders with Republic's investment trading desk.

PROSPECTS FOR PRECIOUS METALS

The last five years have witnessed an extraordinary interest in all aspects of precious metals. Price levels have been influenced by a combination of factors: principally inflation, real interest rates, and perceived levels of world tension. We have shifted from deregulation to the hyper-intense activity of January 1980 to recent relatively low levels of both price and investment interest.

At the time of this writing, both price and interest in precious metals are at very low levels. Inflation is apparently under control, and very high real U.S. interest rates have been the responsible factors. Precious metals investors are currently putting their money into better-yielding investment vehicles. Both money market funds and U.S. Treasury bills are earning positive real rates of return and siphoning off any excess monies that might be used for gold or silver purchases.

The strength of the dollar, high interest rates, reduction of inflation, and the perception that these trends will continue have reduced demand. Additionally, perceived levels of world tension have had little or no impact on world bullion prices.

Some reawakening in demand for precious metals could occur if changes are made in current IRA and Keogh plans. If precious metals are once again allowed to be maintained in these programs, more private investor interest will occur and could be the catalyst to renewed investments in precious metals. However, it is the appearance of bull markets (no matter what the price levels) that stimulates the private investor. Should interest rates go down and a decline in the current high dollar level (vis-a-vis major currencies) occur, then a gradual shift into precious metals will take place.

In this context, no matter what delivery vehicles or sophisticated mechanisms are in place, a precious-metals financial institution cannot force the public to invest. We must have programs in place so that when the "right" time comes and the investor reappears, business will flow in and both the supplier and the investor of precious metals will profit.

PART TWO

Stocks

CHAPTER FOUR

The Bank Brokerage Boom

Mark D. Coler
Ellis M. Ratner

Mark D. Coler is a Principal of the Mercer Group Companies, whose activities include investor note financing, asset-based financing, and management of oil and gas and equity investments. Mercer's Discount Brokerage Advisory Services Division is the leading independent information source for the discount brokerage industry.

From 1972 to 1977, Mr. Coler served with the federal government in various capacities, including Deputy to the Assistant Secretary and Director of the Office of Municipal Finance. In 1980 he served as a member of the Presidential Transition Team for Domestic Finance at the U.S. Treasury. He graduated with honors in economics from Harvard College in 1966 and the University of Pennsylvania Law School in 1969. He is the co-author with Ellis M. Ratner of several books and articles on financial subjects.

Ellis M. Ratner, a Principal of the Mercer Group Companies, was graduated with honors from Trinity College in 1966 and from the University of Pennsylvania Law School in 1969. With Mark D. Coler, he is the co-author of 70% Off! The Investors Guide to Discount Brokerage (Facts on File 1984).

Since 1978, he has practiced law in New York City and has served as Adjunct Professor of Political Science at York College, City University of New York. Mr. Ratner was previously a Program Director of the Federal Trade Commission in Washington, D.C.; he was given its Award for Meritorious Service and its Award and Official Commendation for Superior Service in 1976 and 1978, respectively. Mr. Ratner has taught Regulated Industries in both college and law school.

It's only human nature to be optimistic about your future. So when we conducted the first Mercer Bank Brokerage Survey in 1983, and asked the managers of nearly 100 bank brokerage operations to project their future growth, we took their answers with a grain of salt.

But we duly punched them into our computers. It therefore came as no great surprise, when we conducted in 1987 Survey, to learn that the projections of a few years earlier were far off the mark. It came as a very great surprise, however, to learn that they were too low.

Not only had the critics grossly underestimated the potential for bank brokerage, so too had the brokerage managers themselves. To cite a few examples of what the preliminary 1987 Mercer Bank Brokerage Survey disclosed:

- From 1983, the year when banks first offered discount brokerage business, to 1987, the growth in the number of bank brokerage clients approximated 200%.
- Revenue growth has generally equaled or exceeded client growth.
- Bank brokers grew faster than traditional brokers and independent discounters during this period.
- New products introduced during this period are beginning to make significant contributions to revenues.
- This growth has been achieved with minimal advertising or marketing expense.
- Whereas in 1983 critics had questioned whether most bank brokerage operations would ever be profitable, in 1987 virtually every operation had achieved profitability.

In the balance of this article, we will look at the growth and potential of the bank brokerage industry, how far it has come, and where it is going. The first section reviews the overall stock brokerage industry and the discount brokerage industry in particular, with special attention to the bank broker. The second section focuses entirely on the bank broker.

I. THE BROKERAGE INDUSTRY: TRADITIONAL BROKERS, DISCOUNTERS, AND BANK BROKERS

A. Equities—a Cyclical Growth Market

The last five years have seen enormous growth in stock trading and values. With the end of serious inflation, financial assets have boomed. "Paper" is again king, having regained the throne from the "real" assets that usurped it in the inflationary '70s. While oil and gold had fallen to half their peak values in early 1987, the stock markets, as measured by the Dow Jones Industrial Average, had nearly tripled since August of 1982.

The booming stock market attracted new investors and spurred existing investors to trade more frequently. It caught the eye of a new generation and reawakened the interest of an older one in stock trading.

While many new investors have been attracted to this market, some analysts believe there is still room for further growth. They point to evidence that the percentage of assets that the public has invested in stocks is substantially below the levels in the fifties. Therefore, they believe public participation in the market is at sustainable levels, and could increase further.

Other trends also point to a favorable environment for equities over the next decade. First, the persistence of low inflation rates favors equities. Second, the graying of America is conducive to stock trading: the older investor has more money and trades more actively than the younger one. And finally, the rise in stock values in the last few years has restored equities' tarnished record in the 1970s, which, together with the liquidity which can be found in few other places, will assure continued strong participation by institutions with longer run objectives.

In short, the future of the stock market is looking brighter than ever. And if the market's future is looking bright, so too is the future of the purveyors of stocks, the brokers. Servicing the public are three types of brokers: independent discounters, bank discounters (whom we sometimes call "bank brokers"), and the traditional brokers.

We use the term "traditional" instead of the frequently used term "full service" because discount brokers today provide a range of services that is very wide, the execution is at least as good, and, apart from investment advice, the personal service level is comparable to traditional brokers for most investors. Therefore, we think that the term "full service" is too misleading. Since "full commission," another term sometimes used, sounds pejorative, "traditional brokers" offers the most neutral and accurate description.

B. Discounters Market Share Growing Rapidly

While all brokers have prospered, the Mercer Bank Brokerage Survey reveals that bank discount brokers have experienced significantly higher rates of growth than traditional brokers over the past four years.

The limited amount of publicly available information tends to confirm these conclusions, and indicates that independent discounters are growing faster than traditional brokers as well.

For example, using the Value Line Investment Survey we analyzed the growth in overall commission revenues over the 1983-87 period of 3 major national brokerage houses (Merrill Lynch, EF Hutton and Paine Webber) and 2 regional firms. Their commission revenue growth during this period is estimated to average approximately 64%. By contrast Charles Schwab, the largest discount broker in the country and an affiliate of Bank of America during this period, showed an astonishing 190% increase—nearly 3 times the growth rate of the traditional brokers. And most bank brokers have grown at rates much closer to Schwab's than to traditional brokers.

The publicly available data concerning independent discounters is limited. Apart from Schwab, the only two publicly traded firms of which we are aware are Quick and Reilly, one of the country's largest, and Waterhouse securities, a smaller but substantial independent that recently went public. Quick and Reilly showed a growth rate approximately 25% higher than the traditional brokers, while Waterhouse's growth rate was substantially higher than Q&R's.

One might be tempted to dismiss the bank brokers' high growth rates because they started recently and their growth is therefore measured against a low base. But in 1983, Schwab's base was already a hefty 645,000 accounts, yet it grew at 3 times the rate of traditional brokers. Then one must conclude that the whole discount brokerage industry is likely to continue growing significantly faster than the traditional brokers in the foreseeable future.

It could be argued that we can't really assess the bank brokers' future growth because, since they entered the picture in 1983, we have only seen a bull market. But while the entire brokerage industry would suffer in a downturn, there is no reason to believe the bank brokers would lose market share. Quite the contrary. After all, a higher commission can look like a very small price to pay for advice when the stocks you have bought are soaring. But when prices are dropping, that additional commission is like adding insult to injury; the investor feels that he not only lost money on the advice, but paid a lot to get it.

C. Discounters Potential Market Share

A few years ago, we were asked "How large is the potential market share for discount brokerage?" At that time, discounters were estimated to have 15% of the retail market. Our estimate of the discounters' potential market share: "Perhaps one third." That estimate looked very high at the time. It doesn't look high any more. It may prove low.

Most estimates currently suggest that discounters have 20–25% of the retail trade. (Mutual funds are excluded from the equation.) Due to the limitations of the available data, it is hard to tell precisely where they lie in that range. But it doesn't really matter. If discounters continue to grow at the current rate, they will soon break out of that range altogether.

A number of factors favor discounters' growth continuing to outpace traditional brokers:

A Society of Shoppers. As one Arkansas bank broker told us: "A few years ago, the little old ladies just put their money in the bank. Now they shop around. They want to know the rates on deposits and CDs. They've become sophisticated shoppers."

It's not just in Arkansas that the public is shopping. The staple of financial magazines and newsletters are stories ranking investments, mutual funds and other investments. Once esoteric magazines like *Consumer Reports* are now mainstream. Everywhere, discount stores flourish. Whether they're out shopping or out investing, Americans, like the little old ladies in Arkansas, are becoming a nation of selective shoppers.

Perhaps that is why the "Financial Supermarket," the hot marketing concept of the '70s, has cooled down. If investors really wanted to buy everything at one place for convenience, it would have spelled trouble for discounters. Legal as well as capital limitations prevent them from offering as large a range of products as traditional brokers.

But that wasn't what investors wanted. They wanted to buy stocks and bonds through Merrill, and they loved Merrill's CMA (Cash Management Account), but had no desire to buy a house or insurance policy from the same folks. So the Merrill insurance and real estate units, acquired in the 1970s, are up for sale in the '80s.

It is well for discounters that the investor is shopping selectively, because the discounter appeals to the savvy, selective investor. He can make an offer that the sophisticated investor can't refuse: "You tell me what stocks to buy, and I'll buy them for you at half the usual commission—or less." In increasing numbers, the American investor is accepting that offer.

The Mutual Fund Factor. A notable distinction between the bull market of the 1980s and the bull market of the 1960s, is that to a much greater degree, today's small investor invests in equities through mutual funds. How does this impact the brokerage industry?

It is generally assumed that the larger mutual fund slice of the pie has been cut out of the brokers' share. But part of the mutual funds' growth has come about through broadening the market rather than at the expense of the traditional or discount brokers. Many investors might never have purchased stock, or as much stock, if they did not have the mutual funds' comfort factor—diversification and continued professional management.

To the extent that mutual funds have cut into the brokerage business, however, it is likely the traditional brokers that have borne most of the impact. That is because, apart from diversification, the principal appeal of mutual funds is continuous professional management.

Mutual funds tell the investor: "You don't have to spend time reviewing stocks. Pay us a management fee, and our professional advisers will invest for you." That is essentially the same offer that the traditional broker makes: "You don't have to spend time researching stocks. Pay us a commission, and our professional research department will tell you what to do." Therefore, mutual funds and traditional brokers are in direct competition.

The discounter is not in competition. He does not appeal at all to the investor who wants advice; he can only help people who know what they want. So the discounter appeals to a different investor, or a different instinct in the same investors. It would appear, therefore, that the continued growth of mutual funds will far more adversely affect the traditional broker.

Favorable Demographics. Brokers are benefiting from the graying of America. The older investor is a richer investor and a better client.

These demographics favor all forms of stock brokerage, but they favor discount brokerage more.

The explanation is that the older investor not only has money; he also has more time. If an investor does not have the time to decide which stocks to buy, he will use a traditional broker or mutual fund. This is reflected in a preference of many younger investors for mutual funds. But as he begins to have more time, he becomes a better candidate for discount brokerage.

Older investors tend to have more time, either because they are retired, or their families are grown, or they are at a less demanding stage in their careers. Many are willing to invest this extra time in selecting stocks. Some enjoy stock analysis; others just see it as a necessary part of safeguarding their financial future. Whatever their motivation, we have seen the time factor at work in statistics reflecting the strength and growth of discounters in retirement areas. Consequently, the graying of America bodes well for the longer term growth of discount brokerage.

Equilibrium Market Share. As our college economics professors might have phrased the question: What is the equilibrium market share, the point at which discounters' and traditional brokers' market share will thereafter remain in balance?

Unfortunately, the real world is not so simple. If there is an eventual equilibrium point, it is too early to estimate it. But one thing is clear. They are not at equilibrium yet. The discounters are currently growing much faster than the traditional brokers, and we don't see anything that is immediately likely to slow them down.

The future for discounting looks quite bright. If the discounters' current market share is 20–25%, as groups such as the Securities Industry Association have estimated, it's hard to see how the discounter's share could stabilize much below a third of the market. And judged by past experience, ours and the managers' themselves, the growth of this industry may surprise even its proponents.

II. THE BANK BROKERS

The Fastest Growing Discounters

The discounters are the fastest growing sector of the brokerage industry and the banks appear to be the fastest growing sector in the discount brokerage industry. We cannot draw this conclusion with complete confidence, since there are very few public discount brokers, and the private ones tend to hold their data close to the vest, but the conclusion appears warranted.

To take the previously cited example, we can compare Schwab with Quick & Reilly, the two largest discounters whose stock is publicly traded. Quick & Reilly showed an approximate 80% increase in commission revenues during the 1983–1987 period, whereas Schwab, which was part of Bank of America during this period, grew more than twice as much. Most of our bank brokers show growth patterns closer to Schwab's than to Q&R's.

Costless Marketing

But as striking as the growth, and perhaps even more surprising, is that the banks have, for the most part, achieved this growth with little increase and frequent cutbacks in their marketing budgets. Many of the banks that we have seen growing 30–50% in the last year or two have essentially no advertising budgets!

The ad campaign in some banks consists of printing up discount brokerage posters to be hung in the branches; in many others, it consists of occasional mailings or a once a year "statement stuffer." These are not the types of campaigns that will put a gleam in an ad man's eye, or threaten Merrill's $250 million per year ad budget.

This minimalist approach to advertising contrasts with the bank brokers' attitude when we interviewed them in 1983. At that time, there was much emphasis on deciding which type of advertising campaign to use. Today, most bank brokers scarcely mention traditional ads at all. That is because they have found a better way.

It has become apparent that bank brokers have two great resources that were not available to the independents who pioneered discount brokerage and currently offer it:

First, banks have a name. Most of the banks offering discount brokerage already have strong name recognition in their geographic areas: they don't need advertising to create it, maintain it, or differentiate themselves from other brokers. They are The Bank; their investors know them. This is in sharp contrast to the traditional and independent discounters who must actively advertise to maintain their market identity and generate new accounts.

Second, every bank broker has a highly qualified list of potential prospects that he can reach easily and cheaply: the bank's depositors.

And a client relationship with the institutions already exists. It's the type of prospect list that independent discounters, and traditional brokers, could only dream about.

With these resources, bank brokers have discovered that it is easier to find gold by mining their own customers' ranks than by panhandling for new accounts through the newspapers. Direct mail, handouts, statement stuffers, or simply adding a reference to discount brokerage whenever the bank advertises are proving to be very effective marketing tools. They are also dirt cheap.

Branches: The Sleeping Giant Awakens

In a 1983 article in *American Banker,* we called branches "the sleeping giant of bank brokerage." That has changed. The sleeping giant is no longer asleep and snoring; he's now awake and roaring. And it is one of the major reasons that banks have been able to market brokerage to their clients with minimal costs. They have learned to effectively utilize what one banker called "the branch franchise."

Outside of unit banking states, and even in them through the bank holding company, every bank of size has branches that reach out into the community. Even if the personnel in these branches didn't know anything about securities, which was often initially true, it is an enormous resource. It gives the investor, especially the inexperienced investor, a great sense of security. He can see the branch, he can visit it, and he can talk to someone. He feels like he can "kick the tires."

The reality is that in modern computerized securities trading, personal contact has little to do with the business being transacted. The transaction generally takes place by computer in a distant market in New York, or elsewhere in the country, through the network of interlocked video screens that constitute the Over-the-counter market. In the high tech world of securities, personal contact is an illusion.

But in the low tech world of marketing, personal contact is a powerful tool. It was this type of geographic saturation through branching that built the giants of the brokerage and discount brokerage world, the Merrill Lynchs and the Charles Schwabs. And the banks already have these branches in place without paying a dime for the bricks and mortar.

As might be expected, the role of branches in the discount brokerage system has evolved along varying lines. They reflect the priority of brokerage within the bank, the management styles of their managers, and the personality of the bank. One might characterize these approaches as passive or active.

In the *passive style*, branches are primarily used to help open accounts and as a conduit for questions. Branches also accept or sometimes make delivery of securities. In many ways, they act somewhat like the traditional teller in the bank. They perform a function competently when requested.

In the *active style*, the branches play a more active marketing role. They will still funnel most questions through to the central discount brokerage operation, since many security questions are too specialized for branch personnel to answer. But branch personnel can be very effective in spotting opportunities for brokerage business, and referring the client.

Some banks have told us that half their business comes from branch referrals. If the branch manager and personnel are enthusiastic and alert, they have many opportunities to spot potential clients: when opening accounts, in personal discussions, when funds are transferred in and out.

The ability to enlist branch cooperation depends in part on the skills of the discount manager and the amount of time they elect to spend communicating and motivating the branch system. It also depends upon the personality of the bank. Where does brokerage fall within the bank's hierarchy and priorities? Does the bank have a marketing oriented branch system? Is there an organization-wide premium on cooperation, or does each manager run his branch like a personal fiefdom? How well can the broker reciprocate through referrals, cross-sales, etc.?

The most successful practitioners of active branch marketing tend to be good managers in cooperative, market oriented banking organizations. They spend a lot of time communicating with the branches, through meetings, manuals, seminars and field trips. As much as anything, they prepare the branches to spot brokerage marketing opportunities and act when the opportunity appears.

The Bank Brokerage Niche

While each bank has its own approach, the bank brokerage industry as a whole has developed a distinctive appeal to the investor, a market niche that distinguishes bank brokers from the traditional broker or the independent discounter.

If the traditional broker in effect says "I can give you good advice about which stocks to buy" and the independent says: "If you don't need the advice, why pay the price?" the bank says this: "I can give you the greater convenience and security of working through your local bank at a price that is competitive with most major discounters."

And a lot of banks are saying something else. They are saying that they can give better execution and service than a full service broker. Not merely "as good" but "better." And they are saying it with apparent conviction. Said one successful discounter whose comments were not atypical: "I can give good execution, get stock registered quickly, and straighten out any problems quickly unlike those wire houses who go through New York and can't get their problems straightened out for months."

We're hearing a new confidence in the voice of bank brokers. It's a different type of confidence than five years ago. It sounds more convincing. It's the confidence of managers who've been tested over the past five years, and delivered. If they say their service is better than the traditional brokers, their claims can't be lightly dismissed. Their growth gives credence to their claims. These days, when the Bank Brokers talk, E.F. Hutton listens.

Profitability

The consequence of the bank's ability to market to their client base, utilizing existing branches, is that the bottom line is looking very healthy. The brokerage operation of virtually every reasonable size bank with whom we spoke was profitable on a stand alone basis. And some were extremely profitable. This was in contrast to 1983 when many were startups or just turning profitable, and many critics felt that most banks could never make a go of discount brokerage.

While the clients' deposit relationship with the bank is an enormous advantage, it also has drawbacks. The bank broker must take special care to service its clients, because there is more at stake than a commission; there is a relationship. The bank can't afford to jeopardize its relationship with a good client because he is miffed about slow call answering or reports or some other minor matter. So bank brokers tend to hold themselves to higher standards in certain matters than an independent or traditional broker. They may be less willing to keep customers waiting on the telephone line; they may feel more compelled to be able to straighten out minor mix-ups quickly. For these and other reasons, bank brokerage may frequently require higher staffing levels than independent discounters. But this is a small price to pay for the many advantages of the bank affiliation.

Limited Service: The Agency Brokers

There is another sector of the bank brokerage industry that we have not addressed up to this point because it represents only a small fraction of the actual bank brokerage trading. But it is worth mentioning because it includes a large number of banks, although their aggregate impact is small. This is the limited service discount broker, or what we call the "agency broker."

These are predominantly small banks that basically offer brokerage as an agency for a third party that does all the trades and provides all the record keeping. The third party may be a larger regional bank that offers discount brokerage to its correspondents, or a large national company like Fidelity. The bank's name may be on the product, but basically, the bank is receiving a fee for introducing the client, rather like an insurance agency.

By and large, these banks have shown good growth in trading, but not as much as the larger banks with a stronger commitment and larger investment in discount brokerage. With agency brokerage, the capital investment is virtually nil, and the time commitment is minimal—usually part of the time of one or two people. The return on the small time and investment is therefore probably quite good, but the revenues are not significant.

Yet this type of brokerage fills a real need. It permits the bank to present a complete range of investment services to its clients, and therefore to better attract or retain them. And to make a modest profit in so doing. Once a bank has offered this type of service, it tends to retain it, even when it is not working out very well.

One example of this pattern is a small community bank on the West Coast with $10 million in deposits with whom we keep in touch. It is a rural community within driving distance of a major city. Our contact there, who is in charge of discount brokerage, is also the chief cashier, and wears several other hats. He reports that business has slowed: "We're down to a trade every few months," he says.

We silently noted in passing that this was not the type of trading which built Charles Schwab, and inquired about what had caused the slow down. "We used to have two active traders," he said, "but I told them I didn't want to be taking their calls at 6:30 in the morning. (When the market opens in New York.) I said if they wanted to do trading at that time, they should go somewhere else."

Since it had become apparent to us by this point that discount brokerage was not the top priority at this bank, we asked why they offered it. "We like to be able to tell people that it [discount brokerage] is available when they open an account."

That answer tells us a great deal about how far discount brokerage has come in the last few years. Even the banks that don't need brokerage, and aren't making any money at it, feel that they should offer it. This says that brokerage has moved from the periphery of banking services to the inner circle. Like traveler's checks and credit cards, it has become one of the core services that banks are expected to provide.

Variations and Casualties

As in any industry, the wealth has not been distributed equally. Some have done vastly better than others. Regional and demographic trends are starting to become manifest. Competition has cut into profits in some areas more than others.

While it has been a very good few years for most bank brokers, it has not been a bed of roses for everyone. A few of the early players have fallen by the wayside. More than once we were told, upon calling back to resurvey an old friend, "We don't offer discount brokerage here any more."

If there is pattern to these drop-outs, it is that they bit off more than they could chew. They were smaller banks that decided to bypass the agency option, which almost all banks of comparable size were using, and go straight for the full brokerage. This meant carrying a full complement of overhead with a comparatively limited client base. Even with good management, the cards are stacked against the smaller bank going all out.

Client Profile

As in most businesses, the 20/80 rule applies here: 20% of the clients produce 80% of the business. The 20% consists of a very small percentage of highly active traders, trading at least 20 times per year, and a much larger group, trading at least five times per year.

The 80% of the clients producing 20% of the trades include a large number of "liquidators." These are persons who make one time or sporadic sales (liquidations). Usually, this stock has been acquired through a company stock plan, by inheritance, through corporate stock options, etc. Tax season also generates a fair number of once a year traders buying for their IRA accounts.

In contrast to their notable success in winning the individual investor's business, most bank brokers have had a hard time securing institutional business, especially from pension funds and other money managers. Despite the fact that they can offer comparable block transactions at half the price or less, it has proven difficult to break the grip of the existing relationships and "soft" service—notably the free investment advice—traditional brokers offer.

Banks have been much more successful in making inroads into the ranks of automatic stock purchase plans. For example, some companies or employee stock plans will periodically acquire stock in their company. Since they know they are purchasing their own stock, they don't need investment advice. Therefore, commission costs become a decisive factor.

In asking bank brokers about prospective clients, we used to hear a lot about "targeting the affluent market." Since then, bank brokers have learned that affluence is a necessary but not sufficient condition for a potential prospect. If you don't have the money, you can't buy stock. But having money doesn't mean you are interested in buying stock. Unfortunately, good stock traders can't be identified just by zip codes. They may live in the affluent areas, but it is hard to tell which houses.

If a client is not interested in buying stocks, it's hard to promote an interest through traditional marketing incentives. As one frustrated manager observed after a "one time, half price trade" mailing to his clientele failed to produce even a single trade: "Maybe people who don't trade much just don't trade much."

New Products

The question we are most frequently asked about discount brokerage is whether discount brokers will soon be offering the same wide array of financial products as full service brokers.

The most pronounced trend in the securities industry over the past two decades has been a diversification away from their historic dependence on stock trading commissions. Today, even among the retail firms, stock commissions account for a minority of the revenues. Are discounters following in their tracks?

Bank brokers today do offer a vastly wider range of products than they did a few years ago. In 1983, products other than stocks were unusual. Today, banks offer mutual funds, precious metals, municipal bond Unit Investment Trusts, corporate and municipal bonds as well as other products such as money funds and IRAs. (See other articles in *Financial Services*.)

While revenues from these products have increased nicely, they are not yet as large a share of total revenue as this proliferation of products might suggest. It's rare for revenues from these products to account for as much as 20% of bank brokerage revenues. Under 10% is more typical. By contrast, non-commission revenues typically account for 70% or more of the revenues of many major brokers.

Ironically, apart from regulatory restrictions, the main reason that non-stock products have not grown so fast may well be the very success of discount brokerage itself. Trading has increased so fast that the significant gains made by non-stock products still remain small by comparison with booming stock trading. Secondly, with stock trading doing so well, there is no strong incentive to aggressively market new products. After all, the traditional brokers moved into new products because their stock commission base was approaching maturity, with no fast growth in sight. That is not the case with bank brokerage.

Over the longer run, assuming that regulations continue to loosen, revenues from new products should increase in both absolute and relative terms. Eventually, too, stock trading growth will slow down. If the paw of the bear replaces the horns of the bull as the reigning symbol of Wall Street, then the slow-down will occur quite rapidly. At that point there will be significant incentive to develop contracyclical products and a lot of free time on brokers' hands to do it.

Regulatory Environment

To a large extent, the growth of other financial services hinges on the course of future government regulation. The banks have had their hands tied in offering mutual funds and fixed income products such as municipal bonds, corporate bonds and unit investment trusts. The problem is uncertainty about both the law and the respective jurisdictions of the Securities and Exchange Commission and the Federal Reserve Board.

The current regulatory climate is described in an excellent companion article in *Financial Services* so it would be superfluous to address it here, except to note that bank brokerage is a child of deregulation. It could be a harsh winter if the cold winds of regulation were to blow again.

Organization: Brokerage within the Bank

On the whole, there seems to have been a perceptible lessening of the culture clash in many banks. Brokers have become a bit more bankerish, and bankers, a bit more brokerish. Partly, it is just the normal accommodations that accompany the passage of time. But it may also reflect the more competitive, deregulated climate.

In the good old days, or bad old days, depending upon your perspective, a banker could sit in his office, wait for supplicants to appear requesting loans, say "yes or no," and go home at 4:00. This function did not require exceptional sales skills. In fact, it did not require any. Selling skills were downright unbankerly.

With deregulation, changes have come about. That former quasi-monopoly, the bank, now competes for deposits with institutions near and far, banks and non-banks. Loans too are competitive; in many areas, loan brokers provide more home loans than banks. The sales skills that were frowned upon when banking was a quasi-monopoly are essential now that banking is competitive. So bankers have moved closer to the world in which brokers always lived, the world in which there are competitors at every corner, sales skills are essential, and the customer is always right, even when he's wrong.

The problems now are as much organizational as cultural. From the bank's perspective, brokerage is part of the overall relationship with the client, not a completely autonomous profit center. Therefore, even when the brokerage unit is an independent subsidiary, some of its most vital functions seem to remain under control of other parts of the bank—notably the operating budget, the advertising budget, and the degree of access to the banks' client base.

This is not culture clash; this is an organizational clash. The bank feels that brokerage can better contribute to the bank's overall performance by placing some of its functions under controls of other parts of the organization. The bank may well be right, but the bank broker often feels like his hands are tied.

This raises a more fundamental issue; whether discount brokerage is a logical adjunct to banking or whether its value is greater as an independent unit. It is the same issue that is being faced by many American companies today.

Richard Ferris, former Chairman of United Air Lines, thought the company was in the travel business, and that travel related acquisitions were logical adjuncts to the airline business. He acquired Hertz Rent-a-Car, a string of hotels, and changed the company's name to Allegis. But, the Board and shareholders disagreed. So did the stock market. Two months after the name change, Ferris left, and the stock shot up 50% when United agreed to sell off its assets. The parts were worth more than the whole. Rent-a-cars are apparently not a logical adjunct to flying.

On the other hand, the traditional brokers like Merrill Lynch have been very successful in launching many financial service products from their brokerage base. And Merrill is certainly not contemplating the sale of its brokerage division. Clearly financial services have proved to be a logical adjunct in the context of an organization where the parent is a brokerage company.

But what if the parent company is neither an airline nor a broker but a bank? Is it a logical adjunct? Clearly, it has worked to date. But what happens when the growth slows, and the bank's depository client base is tapped out. Will the strains then show?

In one case, they have shown already. The bank brokerage industry was born in 1983 when Bank of America decided to buy the then independent Charles Schwab and company. Other banks followed. An industry was created. But in 1987, it was decided that Schwab would do better as an independent than as part of the bank. The company was sold back to a group led by its president, Charles Schwab, and taken public as an independent.

Will banks become spawning grounds for discounters, growing them and then spinning them off at massive profits? It is intriguing to note that Schwab became Bank of America's best investment—its crown jewel in a difficult period—far more profitable than banking.

As a practical matter there are many aspects of the Schwab situation that were unique, and only a few banks are of a size that they can contemplate growing discounters to the point where their sale is a realistic alternative.

But both the synergy that aided Schwab's growth and the conflicts that ultimately led to its sale are inherent in the relationship between every bank and its broker. During a rising market, the synergy may prevail. In the next down market, the strains will show. The organizational resolution of this conflicting relationship remains one of the major challenges to bank brokerage in the years ahead.

CHAPTER FIVE

INVEST: The Full-Service Brokerage Approach

Burton C. Binner

Burton C. Binner, 48, is Vice President, Marketing Research and Planning, of ISFA Corporation. From 1978 until his employment by ISFA, Mr. Binner served as Principal Consultant with PA International Management Consultants, Inc. In that position, Mr. Binner was responsible for the operation of all client projects within the Strategic and Marketing Planning Division. For 19 months prior to joining ISFA, Mr. Binner supervised "INVEST Project" assignments conducted by PA. From 1968 to 1977, Mr. Binner was a Senior Consultant with Marcom Incorporated, a management consulting firm. Prior to joining Marcom, Mr. Binner held marketing research positions with the Glass Container Manufacturers Institute, Olin Corporation, and the Flintkote Company. Mr. Binner received B.A. and M.B.A. degrees from Dartmouth College.

The piecemeal deregulation of the banking industry that has occurred over the past several years, particularly with respect to the "thrift" segment, has resulted in the addition of a plethora of products and services by the banking industry. Whether deregulation was caused by or was the result of economic conditions is not particularly relevant here; the fact is that it has occurred and among the major results are that the structure of the business and the approach of its managers to the business have changed profoundly. Development of fee-based revenue sources has moved up the priority list, and income statements are beginning to show the wisdom of diversified, fee-based lines of products and services.

This chapter will examine one of these fee-based revenue sources: securities brokerage. We will focus on full-service brokerage and will compare and contrast it with discount brokerage. In doing this, we will journey through the legal and regulatory environment and review the historical record of INVEST. INVEST is a service of ISFA Corporation, a full-service brokerage operation developed by a consortium of savings and loan associations and now offered on a subscription basis to thrifts; national banks; FDIC-insured, nonmember commercial banks; and federally chartered credit unions across the country.

We will review the development of INVEST from its original concept through the thinking process, rationale, and research results that shaped its ultimate design. We will discuss the securities products that are offered and how they are offered, and we will discuss the many customer services that are provided with the program and why these services represent the critical difference between "full-service" brokerage and "discount" brokerage.

The Full-Service Brokerage Concept

Full-service bank brokerage programs are designed to provide a full range of brokerage products and services, including objective investment advice tailored for the individual needs of banking institution customers. The programs are offered through registered brokers located on banking floors, so the services are conveniently available to customers who wish to discuss their investments in person or by telephone.

The importance assigned to customer-oriented investment research and advice within full-service programs is a direct reflection of customer needs and desires. Most current and prospective investors do not have the background or training in finance and economics needed to make rational investment decisions without advice. Others do not want to devote the time required to conduct the research needed to make such decisions. Customers want research and advice. The full-service programs provide these.

The emphasis on the customer by full-service programs ties in closely with a comparable emphasis within the banking industry. Consumer attitudes regarding banks and savings institutions are highly positive because these institutions generally are perceived as working to help customers. Employees are trained to talk objectively with customers, but in a friendly and understanding manner. This comparability between the customer-service orientation of banking institutions and full-service brokerage programs is a principal reason why an increasing number of bank managements have concluded that a full-service program is the most appropriate alternative for their customers.

Legal and Regulatory Environment

Savings institutions have been given approval by the Federal Home Loan Bank Board to become subscribers to the INVEST program and to offer the program to their customers and others. The authority of the Bank Board to give this approval has been verified by the U.S. District Court for the District of Columbia.

The Federal Deposit Insurance Corporation (FDIC) permitted participation as subscribers for FDIC-insured, nonmember commercial banks in 1983. The Comptroller of the Currency gave similar permission for national banks in 1985. In 1986, the National Credit Union Association gave its permission for participation to federally chartered credit unions. Through a "no action" letter, the Securities and Exchange Commission (SEC) has indicated that INVEST subscribers do not need to individually become broker/dealers because ISFA Corporation is a broker/dealer and the INVEST program is provided by ISFA, not the individual subscribers.

That is the legal "bottom line" as it applies to INVEST. The evolution of this approval structure has had an important influence on the development of the INVEST program as it exists today.

The Federal Home Loan Bank Board regulates federally chartered savings and loan associations and savings banks. The legislation that created the Bank Board separated these savings institutions from commercial banks. This distinction has proven to be significant. State-chartered S&Ls and savings banks are regulated by state banking departments, the Federal Savings & Loan Insurance Corporation (FSLIC), the FDIC or the Federal Reserve, depending on the type of deposit insurance carried and whether the institution is a Federal Reserve member.

The regulatory environment for commercial banks is quite different. Prior to 1933, what we now refer to as the commercial and investment banking industries were one single industry. Then, as now, institutions could elect to participate in only portions of the range of businesses encompassed by the industry. However, there was no prohibition against an institution's involvement in both commercial and investment banking. Critics of the banking industry of that era attributed part of the responsibility for the 1929 stock market crash to abuses by the banking industry during the 1920s. As a result, the Glass-Steagall Act of 1933 produced a restructuring of the banking industry that included a separation of investment banking from commercial banking. Each group was permitted to engage in certain activities, while prohibited from engaging in others.

The various elements of New Deal legislation and subsequent additions/revisions produced a virtual segmentation of the entire financial services industry that prevailed through the mid-1970s. Each segment (e.g., commercial banks, S&Ls, brokerage firms, insurance firms) had its particular market niches from which other segments were excluded. By the late 1970s, however, the "mood" in Washington had shifted toward deregulation. The barriers against entry by one segment into another's "turf" began to fall away. Institutions in one segment were allowed to cross traditional competitive boundaries and redefine their roles in the market place.

Within this deregulatory environment, the four S&Ls that joined to sponsor the development of the INVEST concept applied to the Bank Board in August 1981 for permission to:

- Create service companies that would own the equity in a registered broker/dealer firm (now called ISFA Corporation) through a holding company.
- Allow ISFA to provide a full-service brokerage program (now called INVEST) on a subscription basis to the four founding institutions and others on a basis where the brokerage service would be kept separate and distinct from other services provided by these institutions.

In May 1982, the Bank Board approved the application of the four founding S&Ls.

In the same month, the number of savings institutions accepted as prospective owners of ISFA Holding Company, Ltd., was expanded by 24 institutions, each of which subsequently applied for and was granted approval to become an owner. Among the 24 new equity owners were three savings banks that are FDIC members.

In September 1982, the Securities Industry Association (SIA), a trade association representing conventional stock brokerage firms, filed suit against the Bank Board, claiming among other things that the Glass-Steagall Act had been violated and the Bank Board had exceeded its authority in granting approval for institutions to offer INVEST. A decision by the U.S. District Court for the District of Columbia upheld the FHLBB action.

While the Bank Board was evaluating the application of the four founding S&Ls, these institutions submitted a request to the Securities and Exchange Commission (SEC) that subscribers to the INVEST program *not* be required to individually become broker/dealers. In a "no action" letter, the SEC accepted ISFA's position that because ISFA was a registered broker/dealer and would itself provide brokerage service to customers of subscribing institutions using ISFA employees as registered brokers, it would not be necessary for the institutions to become broker/dealers. In the SEC's view, a key element of the INVEST program that must be followed for the no action position to remain in effect is that INVEST activities be conducted on a basis that is "separate and distinct" from other services of a subscribing institution.

In the fall of 1983, ISFA requested that the Federal Deposit Insurance Corporation (FDIC) permit participation in the INVEST program by state-chartered, FDIC-insured, nonmember banks. When granting this permission in December 1983, the FDIC indicated that participation in INVEST by these banks would not be in violation of the Glass-Steagall Act. The primary substantiation for this position was that:

- ISFA and not the bank is the broker/dealer in all transactions.
- This point is made clear to all customers and prospective customers in a variety of relevant ways.
- INVEST activities are conducted in a manner that is separate and distinct from other activities at the institution.

ISFA also requested that the Comptroller of the Currency permit participation in the INVEST program by national banks. This permission was received in June 1985.

The National Credit Union Association gave comparable permission in June 1986 for federally chartered credit unions.

HISTORY

Concept Development

The genesis of today's full-service bank brokerage programs can be traced to actions taken at Coast Federal Savings and Loan Association in Sarasota, Florida, in 1980. At the time, the thrift industry was experiencing rapidly declining earnings, and many individual institutions were suffering significant losses. The industry was beginning a "shake-out" that would soon result in the disappearance of many associations through mergers with their stronger brethren. The primary cause was high interest rates during a period of rate deregulation on the liability side of the balance sheet coupled with the inability to restructure the largely fixed-rate loans on the asset side. The result was referred to as "negative spreads" and an interest-rate gap. This situation created an erosion of net worth and an inability at many institutions to compete for high cost deposits, resulting in an outflow of deposits.

In an effort to stem the outflow of funds, Robert Antrim, President of Coast Federal, began assessing several plans aimed at attracting new deposits. Coast and a small number of other savings institutions joined together to take advantage of deregulation and technological innovation in financial services delivery by creating a brokerage service specifically designed for banking institutions and their customers. The service also would be offered to other institutions and their customers on a subscription basis to develop a nationwide network of institutions that offered the brokerage program. The specifics of the proposed program represented the conceptual beginning of the program now known as INVEST.

The goal was to develop a fee-based program that was service oriented, conservative, competitively priced, low risk, and integrated with other banking services. Extensive market research was conducted and, as a result, discount brokerage was rejected as an inappropriate service for savings institutions. The reasons are critically important:

- Discount brokerage has only limited appeal. The absence of investment advice is appealing to only a small portion of prospective customers: those that have the ability and inclination to do their own research prior to reaching investment decisions. More than 80% of all consumer (as opposed to institutional) brokerage transactions are executed by full-service brokers. More than 90% of brokerage customers have active accounts with full-service firms. More than 90% of brokerage commission revenues are earned by full-service firms. Very simply, the vast majority of existing and prospective bank brokerage customers need and want the advice that is an inherent feature of full-service brokerage. Thus, full-service would provide more trading volume.

- The portion of commission revenues per transaction that would accrue to subscribers would be far higher with full-service than with discount. So much higher, in fact, that INVEST could offer commission rates that would be lower than those of conventional full-service firms and still produce more revenues than discount brokerage. The combined impact of higher trade volume and higher revenue per transaction was powerfully persuasive.

- The manner in which discount brokerage is generally offered is atypical of the way banking institutions conduct business. Banking institutions have achieved a high level of consumer respect over many years because of their personal relationships with customers. An 800 telephone number is generally viewed as impersonal, distant, and cold. Most banking customers do not wish to adjust to an approach based on telephoning an individual they do not know and who may not be the same individual from one call to the next using an 800 number.

- A full-service approach would provide an institution with much greater control of the business. Employees of the subscribing institution would become registered representatives and would deal directly with INVEST customers on a face-to-face basis. Cross-selling of other services of the institution would be encouraged. The institution would control the promotional information about the brokerage program provided to its customers and would determine which investment products would be offered. The sanctity of the institution's customer list would be protected and preserved.

Discount brokerage simply did not have features that could compare with those of a full-service program.

Market Feasibility

The concepts developed at Coast Federal were reviewed with a number of knowledgeable individuals within the savings and financial services industries. Three large savings and loan associations agreed to join with Coast in sponsoring the further development of the program. Executives from financial firms that would not be directly involved in INVEST were asked for advice. All believed the proposed program offered great promise of success. Its emphasis on the customer, its concern for consistent and objective investment advice, and its efforts to remove the opportunities for conflicts of interest were viewed as features that offered consumers a meaningful alternative. Equally important, savings institution branches were viewed as especially appropriate locations for brokerage activities.

Agreement on the prospects for success among industry experts was not enough. ISFA realized that an evaluation of the feasibility of INVEST from marketing and financial/operational standpoints was necessary.

The marketing feasibility study, conducted by PA International, consisted primarily of a consumer concept test form of market research. It primarily was concerned with determining:

- Whether certain premises upon which the INVEST concepts were based were indeed valid assumptions and whether conceptual "revisions" were required. The issues investigated included the following questions:

  —Are likely customer prospects aware of and concerned about the existence of inconsistent investment advice, the opportunities for conflicts of interest, the fact that brokers are paid on a commission basis, etc., when dealing with conventional brokers?

  —Do customer prospects really need and want investment advice from their brokers?

  —Are customer prospects more interested in investing or trading, and what level of transaction activity might be expected from those interested in investing?

  —How knowledgeable are customer prospects about conventional brokers, savings institutions, and commercial banks, and how do these prospects comparatively view these institutions in terms of factors that affect business relationships?

  —Which investment and financial services would customer prospects accept from savings institutions?

—Is there a "base" of brokerage-service prospects among individuals who have never dealt with brokers or who have dealt with brokers only occasionally?

• What is the level of interest in INVEST as a service among individuals who are current customers of savings institutions, former customers, and noncustomers, and how does this interest in INVEST compare among different demographical groupings (e.g., age, annual income, sex, geographical location, educational background)?

• What marketing approaches are likely to be most effective in reaching target prospects?

The marketing study findings were extremely positive with regard to the feasibility of the INVEST concept.

Financial/Operational Feasibility

The financial/operational feasibility study, conducted by Arthur Andersen & Co., was intended to determine whether an organization of the type needed to operate the INVEST program could operate profitably both for the parent company, that is, ISFA Corporation, and subscribers to the program. The feasibility effort involved:

• Development and evaluation of a series of fully documented assumptions, based on the best available information, that were used to define the proposed structure of ISFA, the service elements of the program, and how these elements would be provided. These covered:

—The step-by-step handling of each customer order, including subsequent paperwork and reporting for each type of security.

—EDP and communications configuration requirements for four years, including mail, in-house and shared computers, and public and dedicated voice and data telephone lines.

—Approaches for providing investment advice, portfolio valuations, and portfolio analysis.

—Relationships with the clearing broker and other key vendors.

• Projection of revenues, costs and profitability for ISFA, the four originating associations, and participating subscribers for a four-year period as influenced by the various operating assumptions, and including a sensitivity analysis to measure the impact of more- and less-favorable operating results than those considered most likely.

• Projection of the "seed capital" requirements, as well as the return on investment.

Again, the findings were extremely positive.

Subscriber Profitability

A key characteristic of full-service brokerage programs is the expectation that the programs will be profitable for the subscribing institutions. Full-service is not intended to be a break-even, defensive activity. It produces profits.

INVEST has been operational at subscriber locations since November 1982. Experience gained during the interim indicates that the operation of a typical subscriber becomes profitable within two to four months. For a typical new subscriber with a single INVEST Center, the break-even point is month 2, and the internal rate of return over 5 years is almost 600%. In the first year, approximately 40% of the subscriber's share of commission revenue goes to the bottom line.

Each subscriber's actual experience varies from this average, often depending on the level of marketing expenditures and the number of registered representatives assigned at each INVEST Center. For example, INVEST Centers where there are two full-time registered representatives and two modules normally generate significantly higher trade volumes than Centers with a single full-time registered representative and a single module. The additional commission revenues accruing to the two-module Centers more than offset the additional operating costs.

RATIONALE FOR THE UTILIZATION OF A FULL-SERVICE BANK-BROKERAGE PROGRAM BY THRIFTS AND BANKS

Earlier, we briefly discussed how ISFA management concluded that a full-service bank brokerage program is the most appropriate type of brokerage program for banking institution customers. This, in itself, is an important justification for a bank management decision to introduce such a program. However, there are many other justifications.

The banking industry is in the midst of major changes, the institutions most likely to survive will be those that are most responsive to customer desires in combination with attention to the profitability of specific activities. Bank brokerage generally is accepted as a prime example of a new service that most surviving institutions will be providing by 1990, if not well before. Full-service programs represent the approach to brokerage that is most likely to be profitable.

The changes occurring within the financial services industry have allowed institutions to cross traditional competitive boundaries and redefine their roles in the market place. Banking institutions, brokerage firms, and insurance companies are all in the capital acquisition business—capturing and controlling customer financial assets.

The market also has changed. Customers are demanding more and better financial services and will move to those institutions that provide them. Customers want to deal with institutions they can trust and that offer a complete array of financial services. Commercial banks and thrifts can no longer prosper simply as deposit gatherers and money lenders. Their survival depends on being able to offer a broader range of products and services.

For banking institutions, offering brokerage services is a logical and aggressive response to competitive pressures and market opportunities.

- The competition is already offering brokerage services.

    An estimated 75% of all banking institutions will provide brokerage services by 1990 and will control at least 25% of the transaction volume. It makes sense to remain competitive.
- Banking customers are already investors and are dealing with the competition.

    The consumer research that paved the way for INVEST indicated that 79% of thrift customers with annual incomes of more than $20,000 own securities, and 62% have brokerage accounts. The proportions of comparable commercial bank customers owning securities and having brokerage accounts are only slightly lower. Not offering investment services to these customers is tantamount to a giveaway. Further, because the brokerage competition offers banking services, the opportunity for losing these customers increases daily. It makes sense to offer what customers want.

- Brokerage is big.

  More than $7 trillion in investment transactions occur each year. Some $4 billion in commissions were generated in 1983. Eighteen percent of all U.S. households, or 15 million families, currently own stocks or bonds. Six million families have more than $25,000 presently invested. The average investor conducts 6.5 buy/sell transactions each year, and the availability of IRA and Keogh accounts has raised investor interest and activities significantly. One hundred fifty million share trading days are now commonplace. In the capital acquisition business, it makes sense to go where the money is.

- Brokerage is growing.

  The growth rate for revenues from private and business investments is estimated at 15% to 20% annually. While 18% of U.S. households currently own securities, another 16%, or 13 million families, have owned stocks or bonds in the past. The right market conditions could almost double the number of investors. It makes sense to go where the money will be.

Banking institutions already offering brokerage services have listened to what the market has been telling them and now have a lead on their competition. The timeliness of their decisions is paying off. Additional banking institutions need to recognize that capital acquisition and control are major objectives and that nontraditional banking services are essential elements for achieving these objectives. Unless these new services are introduced, current banking customers will seek the services elsewhere. Once customers leave, it becomes nearly impossible to get them back, or even replace them.

Full-service bank brokerage is designed to help stop this customer loss and to beat the competition on its own turf. It is capturing the brokerage business of existing customers and attracting new business to the institution. Between 10% and 40% of INVEST business is with noncustomers of the subscriber, and these individuals often establish a deposit relationship. For its banking institution subscribers, INVEST represents a major entry into a new financial services arena, and it is working. However, it is working not because it is bank brokerage. INVEST is working because it is full-service brokerage where customers bank.

What Are the Alternatives?

In deciding to offer brokerage services, an institution must consider its available capital—time, money, and people—and its marketing strategy. The objective is to ensure that the type of brokerage service offered takes full advantage of the institution's individual opportunities to increase its share of the financial services marketplace in a cost-effective way.

Offering brokerage services is a complex undertaking, requiring special expertise. Few banking institutions are positioned to accomplish it independently.

A banking institution entering the brokerage business has a number of alternatives to choose from:

1. Purchase an established brokerage firm.

The advantage of acquiring a brokerage firm starts with the complete control and autonomy obtained through ownership. Policies and procedures can be set that are consistent with those of the institution. There is no need to share profits or lose control of customers. The firm's services can be offered to others. However, there also are disadvantages. Foremost are the major capital expenditure required and the lengthy time frame needed for approval. There are extensive regulatory and legal complications in addition to the management problems of integrating the brokerage operation into the existing system. Ongoing expenditures are also significantly greater, primarily in the marketing arena.

Acquisition is complex. While the rewards may be great, so is the risk. Acquisition is the least cost-effective way of entering the brokerage business and is suitable only for a small number of large institutions.

2. Create an in-house brokerage service.

Developing an in-house brokerage operation has advantages and disadvantages similar to those of acquisition. The capital required is enormous, and the start-up time is lengthy. You start at the bottom of the learning curve. Legal and regulatory compliance needs to be managed. Securities marketing and product expertise is needed. A large number of qualified people need to be attracted, and operations and trading facilities need to be developed. These problems are compounded in the full-service arena with the need to hire, train, and manage brokers, and develop research and investment advisory systems.

Developing an in-house brokerage operation can be a more complex undertaking than acquisition. For this reason, it is most appropriate for discount brokerage. This alternative has the highest risk and, as a result, is not particularly cost-effective. Like acquisition, it is likely to be viable only for a limited number of large institutions, particularly those with long-term marketing and product strategies already in place.

3. Affiliate with a regional or national brokerage firm.

A banking institution can refer customers to a specific broker for securities business. The rewards are limited, and the referral can be dangerous since most brokerage firms also provide near-banking services. It is also possible to permit commission brokers on the banking floor and retain a share of commissions (usually 20% to 25%). This approach has the advantage of limited capital expenditure, short start-up time, limited marketing costs, and limited personnel requirements. The major disadvantage is the loss of control over the handling of customers and the products that they are sold. The institution's customer identity can become confused when a customer's financial business is shared with a competitor.

Brokerage firm affiliation has limited financial risk and limited revenue potential because of the small share. The customer base risk is significant. This approach to entering the brokerage business is sensible only for institutions wishing to take advantage of their customer base, but not wishing to take an active role in doing so.

4. Affiliate with a banking institution brokerage service.

This has been the most widely chosen means of entering the bank brokerage business. The reason is the limited requirements for capital—time, money, and people. The brokerage industry is extremely competitive and requires special expertise. Affiliation is the least expensive way to acquire it. Reduced cost means reduced risk and cost effectiveness. However, some of the advantages of affiliating with a bank brokerage service are offset by the loss of control and the reduced revenue share. These problems are most evident with discount brokerage operations. The discount broker is remote to the customer and to the participating institution, and the participant's revenue share is low (generally less than 20% of gross commissions). This translates into a limited risk, limited return opportunity—purely a defensive strategy. INVEST is the largest full-service bank brokerage operation. INVEST offers its subscribers significant control over their individual brokerage service and a much larger revenue share (50% to 78% of gross commissions, including bonus). INVEST is primarily an aggressive strategy, but has the flexibility for defensive posturing.

Bank brokerage services offer the easiest, lowest-risk means for banking institutions to enter the brokerage business. It is suitable for most institutions.

INVEST and Full-Service Bank Brokerage

Considering the control and revenue sharing arrangements, INVEST is the most cost-effective means for a banking institution to enter the brokerage business while maximizing market share and profit potential. The program was designed specifically to ease the entry of banking institutions into the brokerage business and represents a significant departure from the way brokerage services have traditionally been offered to the public. The arrangement not only provides the necessary securities service and expertise to host subscribers, it also greatly reduces their attendant risks in entering the brokerage business. The INVEST program is designed to take advantage of banking institution strengths and minimizes their weaknesses by providing services they could not offer individually in a cost-effective manner. This is done by:

- Positioning brokers on the banking floor. This approach takes investment services *directly* to the customer and takes advantage of the branch distribution network of banking institutions across the country.
- Offering reduced commissions. This provides a complete array of services at very competitive prices.
- Providing investment advice. This appeals to the largest segment of the investing public and the traditional banking customer who seeks full, personalized service.
- Offering conservative investment strategies and eliminating conflicts of interest. This enhances the trusting relationship banking institutions have maintained with their customers over the years. Customer

trust is a primary banking institution strength in the marketplace and a significant brokerage firm weakness.

- Providing the investment research for all of its brokers. This allows the broker to concentrate more fully on customer sales and service and insures that investment recommendations are made only by knowledgeable experts.
- Not offering competing products. The intent is to supplement traditional banking products and allow each host institution to retain and enhance its customer identification.
- Providing securities and sales training to subscriber personnel. This offsets the lack of brokerage experience of its subscribers and eases their entry into the investment services arena. It opens new career opportunities for subscriber personnel and enhances their productivity.
- Offering sales management and marketing support. This helps subscribers establish the goals and direction needed to succeed in the brokerage business.
- Handling regulatory compliance and customer accounting. This minimizes the risks of offering brokerage services to the public.
- Providing a complete program of technical assistance for start-up. This reduces the time, cost, and the management burden of designing and implementing an appropriate full-service brokerage program.

INVEST is a complete, full-service bank brokerage program that represents a true partner relationship between ISFA Corporation and the subscriber. It is designed to ensure that the subscriber retains control over its customers and the way brokerage services are offered to them. However, it also ensures that the brokerage service offered is consistent and of the highest quality, and that the customer receives the best investment advice available tailored specifically to his or her needs. INVEST competes through price and product differentiation. It serves the largest potential market through convenient locations. It attracts new customers and makes existing ones more productive. It is market tested and is working across the country.

CHAPTER SIX

Microcomputers and the Independent Investor: Transforming Discount Brokerage in the 80s

Bruce W. Feiner

Bruce W. Feiner is an Account Manager in the Information Services Division of Lotus Development Corporation. During the past fifteen years he has participated in several management projects within the information industry. His experiences with microcomputers, software, and financial data have given him the opportunity to keep pace in this fast-moving industry. Mr. Feiner is a graduate of Hofstra University with a degree in economics.

The proliferation of the personal computer and the unprecedented participation in the securities markets have sired a new phenomenon: independent investors. Their consumerist attitude toward banking and investing is supported by easily available financial data and deregulation in the financial services industry. These investors, who are driving the rapid growth of the discount brokerage industry, caused a fundamental shift in the way individuals traded stocks in 1985 and continue to do so.

The potential pool of independent investors has grown with the increased availability of the personal computer. Between 10 and 12 million microcomputers are now in American households—a 10% to 13% market penetration, according to Future Computing, a market research firm. This foothold is expected to increase to nearly 40% by 1990 with 28 to 33 million units in homes.

What kinds of information and services are these independents seeking? Stock quotes, business news, financial indicators, statistics, portfolio accounting, tax reporting, and analysis are all in demand. Until a short time ago, all these data and the investment capability were available only to professionals. But, thanks to the microcomputer, independent investors now have the tools to choose stock market investments themselves.

As they begin to make their own investment decisions, many investors are questioning the need for services offered by traditional full-service brokers at high commission rates. They recognize that using discount brokers to execute buy/sell orders can more than offset the investment in microcomputer technology.

Meanwhile, seeing a scattering of their client base due to deregulation, the banking and brokerage industries are packaging comprehensive, hybrid financial investment vehicles to compete for one diffused market. Just as brokerage houses crossed the line to compete with banks by offering money market funds to their trading clients, the banks are selling discount brokerage services to depositors.

Banks have moved swiftly to meet the sudden competition within their marketing territory. More than 3,000 banks currently offer discount brokerage services, and more are planning to join the ranks. The service is an important avenue to attract new money. It can also help to stem the flight of funds to brokerage-controlled money management systems.

The creation of this brokerage/banking supermarket has occurred during a time of historically high market volume. The heaviest expansion is seen in the over-the-counter market; inexpensive OTC shares are favored by independent investors. Banks view this growing activity as evidence on which to base their expansion into discount brokerage in the 80s.

DISCOUNT BROKERAGE: A NEW BANKING DIRECTION

Over the past several years discount brokerage activity at banks has increased to approximately 25% of retail trades. Yet this move should *not* be perceived as merely a defensive tactic on the part of the banks; rather, it opens up opportunities to enhance bank profits: Discount brokerage can generate traffic and interest in retail branches. Banks can produce better revenues by capitalizing on the cross-selling benefits of a full range of financial services. Securities transactions are usually settled through various demand/deposit accounts, with dividends and interest reinvested in creative ways. The bank's public image of safety, combined with a geographical saturation of branch offices, encourages the creation of complementary services.

WHAT THE MICRO-REVOLUTION MEANS FOR BANK DISCOUNT BROKERAGE

Traditionally, the market for discount brokerage has embraced a regional, sophisticated clientele that didn't require outside research and recommendations. Now this market is changing to include the new generation of independent investors across the nation, who increasingly will own personal computers.

The three reasons why investors are turning to discount brokers haven't changed: money, inclination, and time to trade. What has changed is the gigantic increase in the availability of financial information, made possible by the microcomputer. Once-privy information can be tapped by independent investors, which broadens the market for discount brokerage considerably.

Discount brokers obviously can't make recommendations. But the gap between financial information and what constitutes a "recommendation" is narrowing. Therefore, bank discount brokers should consider providing their clients with hard financial facts. Support is necessary for them to make decisions and manage their own portfolios, without outside advice. An investor information service will become a marketing necessity in a few short years to come—for microcomputer-owning clients *and* for those independent investors who haven't yet become part of the computer generation.

Discount brokerage is a low-margin, highly competitive business. Banks will have to create a differentiating service, one that will build good client relationships and encourage frequent trading activity.

THE BRANCH AS PRODUCT CENTER: WORKSTATION SUPPORT

New computerized investment tools let bank discount brokerages offer information products similar to what full-service brokers tapped to justify their high commission rates. These investment facts, figures, and information aren't "advice." But they do provide decision-making tools to consumers.

Investment workstations are information resources within the branch network. By linking microcomputers to off-site data bases, branches have access to real-time stock quotes, SEC filing information, and business news affecting the market.

Many banks offer discount brokerage services through dedicated areas at their branches. These outlets create a good marketing strategy for encouraging new account walk-in business and drop-in trading. Branch workstations give these product centers a new twist: a full-service brokerage image. Investment facts *plus* discount commissions create a magnet for drawing depositors into the discount investor fold.

On-site staff can easily call up the requested investment facts on workstation screens. Information available on-line can include company profiles, earnings projections, balance sheet information, high/low of the year, options, and bond ratings. Graphics can illustrate long-term moving averages and other comparative data.

In addition to disclosure and market information, bank discount centers can also provide financial "tearsheets." These preformatted fact sheets are drawn from financial data bases and can include a wide variety of commonly requested facts. Also to be considered are information menus from which customers can pick and choose customized tearsheets.

Similar reports can be made for clients who conduct their brokerage business over the telephone, and they can be sent by regular or electronic mail. This capability gives off-site brokers an information edge beyond merely quoting securities prices.

Investor workstations will provide a unique degree of information support. The branch office as financial product center can easily turn banking customers into discount brokerage customers by offering them comprehensive investment facts.

MICRO-INVESTOR DECISION-MAKING TOOLS

The computerized independent investor can apply investment software for sophisticated at-home research. Financial data bases provide the basics: on-line stock quotations, either real-time or delayed; historical information on companies and securities from on-line access to SEC files; and news affecting financial markets and individual companies. Investment software uses data base information in the following ways:

1. Portfolio management and reporting, to handle year-end tax accounting; updating portfolios once buy/sell orders have been executed; providing current portfolio value and position; and accounting for a wide variety of financial instruments (bonds, options, municipals, futures, mutual funds, etc.).

2. Fundamental analysis for stock screening and reporting, the method by which investors determine if securities are good investments by checking company balance sheets, income statements, and other SEC filings.

3. Technical analysis for graphing, displaying, and manipulating stock price and volume data to look for investment buy/sell signals.

4. Spreadsheet modeling, for the more involved investor who wishes to develop his own investment criteria by working within a spreadsheet package.

SELLING INVESTMENT INFORMATION SERVICES

How should the bank discount broker tap the independent investor market, including both microcomputer owners and nonowners? There are several ways banks can attract their business through financial information services. The least-cost route obviously would be to charge discount brokerage clients for providing financial tearsheets, access to on-line market information and data bases, spreadsheet analysis, and portfolio management software. This approach creates the potential for fee-based revenue, or at least recouping the bank's cost for these services.

A second approach puts the bank at a distinct competitive advantage: providing complimentary on-line quote capability, software, or access to the financial tearsheets. The cost of this marketing approach should be weighed against the benefits of increased trading activity due to a well-informed, loyal, and growing customer base.

A third approach combines the two: offering financial information services on a flat fee or piecemeal basis to small-volume traders, and on a cost-reduced or free basis for high-volume clients. Smaller-volume customers are given an incentive to increase their trading activity: the promise of no- or low-cost investment information to ensure their trading success.

Whatever the implementation strategy, financial information services can draw investors away from full-service brokers. Offering both novice and experienced traders the necessary financial information and tools produces confidence to invest with their bank's discount brokerage.

FULL SERVICE VS. DISCOUNT BROKERAGE: STALKING THE MICROEDGE

The independent investor phenomenon is putting pressure on full-service brokerage firms to seek new ways of securing their customer base. Brokers who are primarily salespeople are increasingly forced to reevaluate their role as investment advisors in a do-it-yourself, computerized investment world. Tapping microcomputer technology helps them reposition themselves as total financial planners.

A growing number of full-service brokers are using the same data bases and software capabilities as microcomputerized independent investors. They're acquiring their own "intelligent workstations" linked via local area networks to their firms' mainframes. The goal: to offer more sophisticated financial information and improved service to existing clients and prospects, to justify their high commission.

For their micro-owning clients, they're offering on-line personal account information, including daily portfolio values and securities, cash, and margin balances. Their desktop microcomputers can print out similar reports for mailing. The firms' research reports are available for customer perusal, along with stock quotes and news affecting securities in clients' portfolios. Electronic mail lets investors leave buy/sell requests for their brokers to execute at the opening of the next trading day. Some full-service brokers are offering customized technical analysis, including tax projections and reporting, "what-if" scenarios, and other special features.

In the future, full-service firms are likely to offer trading-only accounts at reduced commissions and even pay-by-the-piece advice. They may even acquire discount brokerages themselves to accommodate independent investors who balk at top commissions. This will pressure the already crowded discount brokerage market even further.

For banks, the growing importance of investment information services and discount brokerage clients cannot be overemphasized. As more banks expand their services to attract the independent trader, full-service brokers are responding aggressively with a wider array of information/advice services. Both aim to capture the new mainstay of the discount business, the independent investor. Neither will succeed without both the highest level of information services and customer support that this new breed soon will be demanding.

CHAPTER SEVEN

Banks in the Securities Business: A Regulatory Primer*

Carl N. Duncan
Bruce O. Jolly, Jr.

Carl N. Duncan graduated from Central State University in 1967, where he was inducted into the Alpha Kappa Mu National Honor Society and was a Gold Cord Recipient for Academic Excellence. In 1970 he received the J.D. degree from New York University, and in 1977 he received the M.B.A. degree from American University. He was an Instructor at Strayer College in the fall of 1976.

Mr. Duncan has co-authored numerous articles, which have appeared in a wide range of publications. He is a member of the Illinois State Bar, The District of Columbia Bar, and the American Bar Associations.

Bruce O. Jolly, Jr. is a partner in Barnett & Alagia's Washington office, specializing in financial-institution law. Prior to entering private practice, Mr. Jolly was the Washington Counsel for the Credit Union National Association until 1984. He has also been Federal Regulatory Counsel for the Independent Bankers Association and Associate State Legislative Counsel for the American Bankers Association. His responsibilities have included representing financial institutions before all the federal agencies, including the Internal Revenue Service, Federal Trade Commission, Federal Reserve Board, FHLBB, FDIC, Comptroller of the Currency, and National Credit Union Administration.

*This article updates 1984–5 overviews of the topic styled "Banks and Thrifts in the Securities Business: A Regulatory Primer," co-authored for the Inter-Financial Association, San Rafael, California, by Mr. Duncan when he was a partner at Abramson & Fox, Chicago, Illinois, and Lawrence A. Herst, an associate at that firm. Mr. Duncan and Bruce O. Jolly, Jr. are partners in the Washington, D.C. office of Barnett & Alagia. Mr. Duncan and Mr. Jolly wish to thank Mr. Herst and Ms. Ruby Ng Lau, an associate at Barnett & Alagia, for their invaluable contribution to this article.

Mr. Jolly has written extensively in the area of financial-institution law and regulation, worked closely with state commissions in revising banking codes, and lectured frequently in the area of consumer credit and regulatory compliance.

He has also testified before Congress on tax reform and actively worked on major financial-institution legislation since the mid-1970s: Truth-in-Lending reform, the Monetary Control Act of 1980, the Equal Credit Opportunity Act, and the Withholding legislation, along with implementing regulations, are among his efforts. Mr. Jolly was also deeply involved in the efforts to amend the bankruptcy laws that culminated with the enactment of P. L. 98-353, the Bankruptcy Amendments, and Federal Judgeship Act of 1984. He has authored two bankruptcy manuals, a one-volume retail credit compliance manual covering more than 30 federal laws, a manual on dividend and interest withholding, and publications on electronic fund transfers, branch banking, director and officer liability, and state banking boards.

Mr. Jolly graduated from the University of North Carolina School of Law in 1973. His undergraduate degree in journalism was also from the University of North Carolina. He is a member of the U.S. Supreme Court Bar, North Carolina, Virginia, District of Columbia, and American Bar Associations. He is active in the Credit Union, New Investment Services, and the Consumer Financial Services Committees of the ABA.

I. GLASS-STEAGALL: AN INTRODUCTION

The Act:

The National Bank Act of 1933, commonly known as the Glass-Steagall Act ("Glass Steagall"), divided one industry into two by separating the business of receiving deposits from that of underwriting or acting as a dealer or market maker. Hence, the purpose of Glass-Steagall may be described as follows: depositors who put their savings in a bank were to be insulated from the vagaries of the stock market and the conflicts of interest that had tempted banks in the past.

New Competition and Profit Potential:

In the past decade, banks have aggressively challenged the limits of the Glass-Steagall barriers to meet growing competition from the nonbank sector and to respond to the changing financial requirements of commercial bank customers. Put most simply, the larger banks, faced with declining profits and the increased ability of corporate treasurers to manage and raise funds without using a bank, must change or perish.

The result is that although Glass-Steagall remains in effect as of August 1987, it no longer presents the barrier it once did. For example, while §16 of Glass-Steagall permits national and state member banks to act as agents for customers in purchasing and selling securities,[1] early Comptroller of the Currency ("OCC") regulations and interpretations precluded banks from acting as securities brokers. Those early decisions have long since been repudiated. The current view, including the major cases interpreting Glass-Steagall, is that such prior limitation was not supported by the express language of §16 and its legislative history.

II. RECENT DEVELOPMENTS

Events of the past 40 months can only be labelled revolutionary. From the approval of the acquisition by Bank of America of discount broker Charles Schwab & Co.[2] in 1984 to the April 1987 Federal Reserve Board ("FRB") approval of bank holding company applications to underwrite commercial paper, mortgage-backed securities, municipal revenue bonds, and consumer-related receivables through subsidiaries which underwrite U.S. government securities, the breadth and pace of change has been breathtaking. (The FRB's underwriting approval has been temporarily stayed by a May 19, 1987, 2nd Circuit order and, in addition, is encompassed within a Congressional moratorium precluding new bank securities-related activities described below.)

At each step, banks have been opposed by securities industry trade groups. The SEC, seeking to address these changes, adopted Rule 3b-9 to require SEC registration as brokers by banks engaging in securities related activities. Banks, in *ABA v. SEC*,[3] scored an impressive victory when the Court of Appeals for the District of Columbia invalidated the SEC Rule.

---

[1]"The business of dealing in securities and stock by [a national bank] shall be limited to purchasing and selling such securities and stock without recourse, solely upon the order and for the account of customers, and in no case for its own account; a [national bank] shall not underwrite any issue of securities or stock. ..." §12 U.S.C. §24.

[2]*Order Approving Acquisition of Retail Discount Brokerage Firm*, 69 Fed. Res. Bull. 105 (1983). See also *Securities Industry Association v. Board of Governors of the Federal Reserve System*, 468 U.S. 207, 104 S. Ct. 3003, 82 L.Ed. 2d 158 (1984).

[3]*American Bankers Association v. Securities and Exchange Commission*, 80 F.2d 739 (D.C. Cir. 1986).

To give itself time to grapple with the question of expanded bank powers, a moratorium on regulatory approval of new securities activities, effective until March 1, 1988, was imposed by Congress in the Competitive Equality Banking Act of 1987. Specifically, the moratorium prohibits banks from undertaking any additional securities activity not previously authorized by the pertinent bank regulators on or before March 5, 1987. While Congress has indicated that it will not extend the ban, it remains uncertain whether and when new laws will be enacted establishing a bright-line test to delineate possible bank securities activities.

Key recent bank advancements include not only the Schwab and underwriting decisions, but newly won authority to: (1) place commercial paper without recourse and solely upon order for the account of a customer; (2) transfer this commercial paper activity to a holding company subsidiary[4]; (3) issue, underwrite, and deal in collateralized mortgage obligations through finance subsidiaries[5]; (4) offer securities brokerage and investment advisory services to institutional customers through a single subsidiary[6]; (5) offer and sell units in a unit investment trust solely on the order and for the account of the bank's customer through a bank or bank holding company subsidiary[7,8]; (6) make limited investments in an investment bank[9]; and (7) create and sell interests in a publicly offered common trust fund for individual retirement account assets.[10]

---

[4]*Securities Industry Association v. Board of Governors*, 807 F.2d 1052 (D.C. Cir. 1986); Federal Reserve Board Order (December 24, 1986), Fed Banking L. Rep (CCH) ¶86,770 at 92,138.

[5]Comptroller of the Currency's No-Action Letter (May 22, 1986), Fed Banking L. Rep (CCH) ¶85,532 at 77,826.

[6]Federal Reserve Board Order (June 13, 1986), Fed Banking L. Rep (CCH) ¶86,610 at 91,689.

[7]Comptroller of the Currency's No-Action Letter (May 23, 1986), Fed Banking L. Rep (CCH) ¶85,533 at 77,828.

[8]Federal Reserve Board Letter (June 27, 1986), Fed Banking L. Rep (CCH) ¶86,620 at 91,752.

[9]Order of the Federal Reserve Board (November 19, 1986), Fed Banking L. Rep (CCH) ¶86,735 at 92,039.

[10]*Investment Company Institute v. Clarke*, 789 F.2d 175 (2d Cir. 1986); *Investment Company Institute v. Conover*, 790 F.2d 925 (D.C. Cir. 1986); *Investment Company Institute v. Clarke*, 793 F.2d 220 (9th Cir. 1986).

Absent Congressional retrenchment, the battlefront has moved from a bank's authority to own and operate a discount brokerage to the scope of investment advice permitted and the limits of bank underwriting authority. Each issue is explored below.

III. ALTERNATIVE MEANS FOR BANKS TO ENTER THE SECURITIES BUSINESS

A. Discount Brokerage

Acquisition. The January 1983 FRB approval of the agreement between BankAmerica Corp., the holding company parent of Bank of America, to acquire Charles Schwab & Co., commenced the rush for banks, bank holding companies, and thrifts to get into the brokerage business. Chase Manhattan, First Union, Union Planters, and approximately 2,000 other banks and bank holding companies now offer brokerage firm services through established firms that have been acquired, or by joint venture or *de novo* entry.

The threshold decision in considering an acquisition is whether the purchase will be made by the bank, the bank holding company, or a subsidiary. If the acquisition is made by the bank and carried on in a subsidiary or made by a bank holding company or a holding company subsidiary, *SEC registration will be required.* The Supreme Court's opinions in the Schwab and Security Pacific cases have assured protection from court challenge for those that decide to purchase, whether through the holding company or the bank.

Joint Venture. Security Pacific National Bank pioneered the joint venture route in February 1982, when it linked its Security Pacific Brokerage, Inc. unit with an existing broker, Fidelity Brokerage Services. Several banks and full service brokers are now offering to banks and S&Ls a discount brokerage package, including marketing, training, and back-office assistance on a wholesale level.

De Novo. A number of large banks have entered the securities brokerage business by either setting up the brokerage business *de novo* within the bank or by establishing a discount brokerage subsidiary. Because of the high volume needed to justify the cost of acquisition of exchange memberships and the administrative costs of clearing their own trades, these operations typically utilize a nonaffiliated clearing broker. Otherwise, the operation is basically built from scratch or by expanding the accommodation services that traditionally have been provided by bank trust departments.

De novo operation may be accomplished either by (1) operating as, or within, a division of the bank (the advantage of which is that the unit *does not have to register* with the SEC and is not subject to the SEC's "net capital" requirements); (2) creating a subsidiary of the bank; or (3) establishing a separate subsidiary of the bank holding company. See Part IV, Regulatory Requirements, for discussion of the rationale for and consequences of these alternatives.

B. Investment Advice

Routine Banking Activity. The OCC and FDIC have long taken the position that investment advice is a traditional banking function. Glass-Steagall limitations had, however, been read by federal bank regulators as limiting the investment advice that could be given to bank discount brokerage customers.

The FRB's 1986 approval of NatWest Holding Inc.'s application[11] to offer a joint service of providing securities execution *and* portfolio investment advice for a fee to sophisticated institutional investors, e.g., an insurance company or bank, through a *de novo* subsidiary opened yet another Glass-Steagall door. Although the order prohibits the subsidiary from purchasing securities for its own account or underwriting securities, it did find the activity closely related to banking and not a prohibited "public sale" within the meaning of Section 20 or 32 of Glass-Steagall.

De Novo. The June 13, 1986 *NatWest* approval goes beyond *Schwab* because *Schwab* specifically provided that the authority granted did not include authority to offer investment advice. In *NatWest* the FRB stated, "[e]ven if the joint offering of securities and investment advice is viewed as a distinct new activity," banks already provided both

---

[11]Federal Reserve Board Order (June 13, 1986), Fed Banking L. Rep (CCH) ¶86,610 at 91,689.

investment advice and securities execution service in separate departments for a fee, and "at least to some extent, banks combine their separate investment advisory and securities execution services," e.g., bank trust departments.[12]

The choice of a *de novo* entity was designed to help insulate the bank and holding company from association "in the public mind between the bank and the investment company."[13]

The NatWest approval was challenged by the SIA, but in July 1987 the D.C. Circuit ruled that combining securities trading and investment advice does not constitute underwriting or the public sale of securities.

Bank Department. Shortly after the *NatWest* decision, the OCC granted the First National Bank of Whitehouse, Texas, authority to offer brokerage and investment advisory services through its retail and trust departments, respectively. The OCC's no-objection letter approved a stand-alone, fee-only financial planning and trust department service. The bank's brokerage activity was limited to acting as introducing broker with no referral fees with commissions being shared with the executing broker. Bank personnel are licensed salesmen and the bank was registered as a corporate dealer under the Texas Securities Act.

Limitations on Investment Advice. Banks, bank holding companies, or their nonbank subsidiaries have also been allowed to serve as investment advisers to closed-end investment companies. However, in view of the potential conflicts of interest, the FRB amendment to Regulation Y imposes a series of restrictions on banks' advisory power in this regard. These limitations include a prohibition on: (1) bank or bank affiliates acquiring an ownership interest in the investment company and (2) extending credit or accepting the securities of such investment company as collateral for a loan. Also, a bank or bank holding company or its subsidiary may not sell securities of any investment company for which it acts as adviser.[14]

Currently, Chase has applied for permission for its subsidiary to act as sponsor *and* investment adviser to its "Market Index Investment,"

---

[12]Id.

[13]*Federal Reserve System v. Investment Co. Institute,* 450 U.S. 46 at 64 n. 39.

[14]*See* Fed's Letter to Sovran Bank, (June 27, 1986), Fed Banking L. Rep (CCH) ¶86,788 at 92,215, including 14 enumerated conditions.

a product that links yield to stock market performance. It has already obtained approval from FDIC to market a certificate of deposit to institutional investors and consumers that ties return to stock market performance. ICI has filed suit to block the product, arguing that the product is the impermissible sponsorship of a mutual fund.

While banks remain subject to a series of limitations on their power to provide investment advice, the ability of national banks to advise and manage investments on a fiduciary basis is well-established under 12 U.S.C. 92a. This authority extends to unit investment trust activities under Part 9 of the OCC's regulations and led to three recent U.S. Courts of Appeals rulings holding that the creation, sale, management, and advice of publicly offered common trust funds for individual retirement account assets constitute a sale of "fiduciary services" permissible under Glass-Steagall.[15]

C. Sale of Mutual Funds

Glass-Steagall prohibits banks from sponsoring or distributing mutual fund shares which by definition are securities. Traditionally, bank trust departments have served as transfer agents and custodians for mutual funds as well as service automatic purchase and dividend reinvestment plans. In the past few years, banks in conjunction with investment companies have been providing mutual fund products to their customers while remaining within the spirit, if not the letter, of Glass-Steagall.

Joint Venture. The mutual fund industry has proved a much more willing "partner" than the brokerage industry. In the typical relationship, the bank provides the customer base and the investment management company provides the product. In some cases the bank may act as the investment adviser, but generally the investment manager provides that expertise. The investment manager will also distribute and operate the fund. In terms of the breadth of such activities, at the conservative end of the spectrum, the bank will do no more than notify its customer, perhaps by an insert in its monthly statement, that the mutual fund is available from the investment manager. The customer must contact the investment manager for additional information, including a prospectus and

---

[15]*See* n. 10, supra.

subscription account forms. At the other end of the spectrum, banks are providing customers directly with the prospectus and applications and answering questions. Additionally, some banks are advertising in the public media that investors can come to them to buy mutual funds. The degree of bank activity, as discussed under regulatory requirements, will determine whether registration by the bank is required.

For a while, the permissibility of bank involvement was uncertain since the banks' activities could arguably be labelled "distribution" of securities prohibited under §16 of Glass-Steagall. But in a June 5, 1986, no-action letter, the FRB approved an arrangement whereby a bank's brokerage subsidiary could sell its customer list to a closed-end mutual fund underwriter for a fee and act as a selling agent for its customers in return for a transaction fee if, among other things, the broker did not provide investment advice to purchasers.

Bank Division or Subsidiary. The OCC, in a letter to the SEC, has opined that the acceptance of Investment Company Act Rule 12b-1 funds earned for "record keeping" services is not illegal. Other activities when performed by banks, such as prospectus delivery, are also permitted. Nor is compensation limited to Rule 12b-1 payments, although care has to be taken to avoid having payments considered compensation for "distribution" of securities.

Once a customer has established an account, permitting the customer to call in by telephone and move funds back and forth between the mutual fund and savings or checking accounts would appear to fall within the exception in §16 of Glass-Steagall allowing securities purchases "upon the order, and for the account of customers."

FDIC's rules affecting state nonmember banks permit insured banks to become affiliated with, organize, or acquire a subsidiary corporation that engages in the business of issuing, underwriting, selling, or distributing certain securities.

Regulation Y (12 CFR 225.25) permits, within limits, a bank holding company subsidiary to engage in the sale of securities, including mutual funds, as agent for the account of customers.

Other Services for Mutual Funds. A bank may also act as custodian and depository for a mutual fund. Included within the services that may be performed are: the safekeeping of mutual fund securities; purchase, sales and exchanges of securities as directed by the fund; collection of income on securities held for the fund; receipt of payment for shares and investment of payments according to the instruction of the fund; all record keeping related to custodial activities, redemption of shares and making of payments to the transfer agent; and the registration of shares held as custodian. A bank could also act as the transfer agent.

D. Securities Underwriting

Section 16 of Glass-Steagall prohibits a bank from underwriting (except for private placements, U.S. government bonds, foreign securities, and municipal general-obligation bonds). In the past, the Supreme Court has ruled that the placement of commercial paper and the management of open-end mutual funds constitute ineligible underwriting and thus are illegal under Glass-Steagall. However, the barriers prohibiting banks from underwriting municipal revenue bonds (which totalled about $140 billion in new issues in 1986), commercial paper, and corporate equities are falling rapidly. In fact, the trend of cases permitting these substantial inroads for banks into the securities business may suggest generally that, unless specifically prohibited (such as corporate equities or revenue bonds), bank underwriting activities may be possible so long as it is not a firm underwriting, i.e., there is no principal risk. That thesis may help reconcile the breadth of activities (sometimes called best efforts and/or agency and/or riskless principal and/or not the public sale of securities) that are now possible today or will be available after the current Congressional moratorium is lifted.

In March 1987, the FRB gave Chase Manhattan authority to underwrite commercial paper for its own account through a lending subsidiary. The FRB has, however, limited Chase Manhattan's activity to 5% of its total gross revenue and 5% of the total commercial paper market share. These restrictions are aimed at addressing § 20 of Glass-Steagall, which prohibits bank affiliates from engaging "principally" in underwriting securities.

More importantly, in April 1987, the FRB further broadened bank underwriting powers by permitting Citicorp, Morgan, and Bankers Trust to underwrite municipal revenue bonds, commercial paper and mortgage-backed securities subject to the same 5% limit on gross revenue and market share presently required in the Chase Manhattan order. Not surprisingly, the FRB's approval has been challenged by the SIA.

In July 1987, the FRB approved applications from seven large bank holding companies to underwrite and deal in consumer-related receivables (e.g., auto or credit-card loans). The FRB's decision will not take effect immediately because of the Congressional moratorium, as well as the issuance of a temporary stay by a May 19, 1987, Second Circuit order.

Notwithstanding these challenges, Chemical, Manufacturers Hanover, and Marine Midland have filed applications to engage in broader underwriting activities, including the underwriting of mutual funds. The OCC and the FRB have indicated that they will receive and review applications during the pendency of the moratorium, although any approvals would not go into effect until the current ban is lifted.

Finally, the OCC has issued Liberty National Bank a no-objection letter permitting it to underwrite and deal in collateralized mortgage obligations ("CMOs") through a finance subsidiary. The SIA has challenged the OCC's ruling.

IV. REGULATORY REQUIREMENTS

Brokerage Service

If a bank holding company subsidiary or a bank service subsidiary offers brokerage services, unless exempt, the entity's brokerage activities are subject, among other requirements, to the following: SEC registration, SIPC membership, new capital requirements, NASD inspections, and NASD examination and registration of its representatives and principals. With the exception of brokerage activities conducted within a bank, all brokerage activities must meet the SEC's "net capital" requirements.

Rule 3b-9

On the other hand, if a bank offers brokerage service through a division or department, typically the trust department, it does not need to be registered with the SEC as broker-dealer. In 1985, the SEC promulgated Rule 3b-9, which on its face required any bank receiving "transaction-related compensation" to register. Approximately 170 banks registered as brokers before the rule was overturned in May 1986.

In overturning the SEC proposal, the Court of Appeals for the District of Columbia found invalid the SEC's attempt to "amend by regulation the explicit statutory provisions that govern the division of responsibility and jurisdiction between the SEC and banking regulatory agencies."[16] With appeal to the Supreme Court uncertain, the SEC must now ask Congress for explicit authority to regulate the brokerage activity of commercial banks.

Ironically, the OCC proposed a rule in 1985 which, based on principles of bank safety and soundness, would have accomplished much of what the SEC's (largely unilateral) Rule 3b-9 sought to do. That proposed rule, at least as to national banks, would have required securities activities to be carried on in a subsidiary, the practical consequence of which would be to require SEC broker-dealer registration. The proposed rule was withdrawn because of "changed circumstances"—a polite way of saying the SEC and the OCC could not agree on a common approach to the issue of "functional regulation." Hence, the SEC's Rule 3b-9 has been overturned because the SEC had exceeded its authority, while the OCC's approach (based on traditional safety and soundness principles), which could more clearly be established as being within its authority, has been withdrawn.

Possible NASD Action

In December 1983, the NASD moved to amend its by-laws[17] to require its members to register persons employed by certain non-broker-dealer organizations who perform activities similar to those performed by registered representatives. Under the proposal, employees of banks and S&Ls that have an arrangement with a broker-dealer (whether it is a subsidiary, service corporation, or joint-venture) would *not* be allowed to perform certain functions relating to the securities business without NASD registration. Employees who make recommendations and give advice to customers or transmit orders to the broker would have to be registered. Employees who simply hand out brochures, assist with account application forms, or dial an "800" telephone number—i.e., perform only clerical and ministerial functions—would not have to be registered. The NASD's Board of Governors approved the proposal and

---

[16]*See* n. 3, supra.
[17]NASD Interpretative Release 85-4.

forwarded it to the SEC. Currently, the SEC has resumed consideration of this proposal after the D.C. Circuit's recent invalidation of its Rule 3b-9.

Investment Advisers Act

As to banks' investment advisory activities, the Investment Advisers Act of 1940 requires any individual or entity who "for compensation, engages in the business of advising others as to the advisability of investing, purchasing or selling securities" to be registered with the SEC as an investment adviser. However, banks are exempt from such registration, and SEC registered brokers are exempt from such registration when the advice is "solely incidental" to the entity's brokerage activity.

If such investment advisory activities are conducted through a bank holding company or a subsidiary of a bank holding company or bank, unless otherwise exempt, it must be SEC registered in such capacity. In addition, such entities which are in the business of offering investment advice must obtain approval from the FRB or OCC. For example, in the FRB's decision allowing NatWest's subsidiary to engage in the business of offering investment advice to institutional customers in addition to its brokerage activity, it noted that the subsidiary must both register with the SEC (and pertinent states) and obtain approval from the appropriate banking agencies.

Choice of Structure

The choice of structure for engaging in securities activities, pending expiration of the moratorium, is (to a large degree) driven by business judgment, not Glass-Steagall. In choosing the corporate structure to enter the brokerage business, for instance, the major factors to be considered are cost, timeliness, and potential liability. Cost and timeliness will, in large part, be determined by the means of entry but are also influenced by regulatory requirements. The legal limitation of the institution's liability for its brokerage activities is largely a function of the structure chosen. Assuming that the appropriate corporate structure has been selected and maintained, liability generally is limited to the capital committed to the affiliate or joint venture. It is possible, however, that compelling business considerations might dictate the institution to absorb any losses incurred by a corporate subsidiary or affiliate. The possibility was recognized and acknowledged by the FRB in its *NatWest* holding.

a) *If Offered by Bank Holding Company*

A bank holding company setting up a subsidiary to provide brokerage services must receive clearance from the FRB. In August 1984, the FRB issued new regulations specifically adding securities brokerage to its list of activities generally permitted to bank holding companies. Similarly, the list was "expanded" in the FRB's approval of applications to allow a subsidiary to place commercial paper, underwrite commercial paper and mortgage-backed securities, provide brokerage and investment advice to institutional customers, and "sell" mutual funds or units of a unit investment trust.

Liability for permitted securities activities is generally limited to the subsidiary since, as a matter of law, assets of the bank holding company (other than the capital committed to the subsidiary) generally are not at risk. SEC broker-dealer registration of the subsidiary must be obtained. In addition, it must set aside capital for each of the subsidiaries.

b) *If Offered by Bank Subsidiary*

A national bank must obtain clearance from the OCC to establish a subsidiary that will offer brokerage services. This has been a fairly quick and simple process. The establishment of a subsidiary by a state-chartered member bank subsidiary generally does not require FDIC approval. (See 18 CFR §337.4 dealing with impermissible securities activities of nonmember banks' subsidiaries where consent of a Regional Director is required.) Whether national or state-chartered, assets of the parent bank (other than the capital committed to the subsidiary) generally are not at risk. The FDIC has proposed allowing an insured nonmember bank and its securities subsidiary to use a common name. However, the proposal would require separate offices and an affirmative disclosure that recommendations made by the securities subsidiary are not insured by the FDIC. SEC broker-dealer registration of such a subsidiary must be obtained.

Guide. Current general banking and securities requirements are outlined in Table 7-1 (see page 114). The guide is introductory in scope and speaks only as of the date of publication; it is emphatically *not* a substitute for legal advice. The discussion contained in this guide is ne-

TABLE 7-1. *Guide to Required Securities Regulatory Registration(s) and/or Approvals.*

	SEC Registration	SIPC Membership*	NASD Membership*	OCC or FDIC Approval	FRB Approval	State Registration
Bank Division or Department	No	No	No	No	No	Possibly**
Bank Subsidiary	Yes	Yes	Yes	Yes	No	Yes
Bank Holding Company Subsidiary	Yes	Yes	Yes	No	Yes	Yes
Nonbank Participants in a Bank Joint Venture	Yes	Yes	Yes	No	No	Yes

*If broker-dealer activities are to be conducted, unless exempt, registration and membership in such capacity is required.
**Certain jurisdictions including Minnesota, Oklahoma, Texas, Washington, and Wisconsin currently require state broker-dealer registration. Some other states such as Colorado require only a notice filing if the bank is federally registered.

cessarily general and summary in nature. The factual setting is different for each institution and therefore the specific application of banking, thrift, and securities law will vary from institution to institution. *Specific advice of legal counsel should always be sought before entering the securities business.*

V. SECURITIES LIABILITY STANDARDS

General Standards of Care

Generally, brokers whose services are limited to the ministerial acts entailed in executing customer orders are liable only for fraud or negligence. Brokers who provide investment advice, manage customer money on a discretionary basis, or enter into some other relationship of trust with a customer are deemed to be fiduciaries and are held to a considerably higher standard of care.

Over-the-Counter Brokers

Registered representatives of the broker generally must know the financial condition for a particular customer before processing his order and, if he makes a recommendation, must expressly make a determination of suitability. Moreover, registered representatives must not trade or make recommendations solely for the sake of earning brokerage commissions—i.e., must not "churn" an account. Conflicts of interest between the customer, the representative, the issuer of the securities, and the institution must also be avoided. If the extent of the entity's activities is restricted—by, for example, not offering investment advisory services—and reasonable standards of care are exercised, potential liability as a practical matter may be limited.

Investment Advice

Section 206 of the Investment Advisers Act of 1940 ("Advisers Act") proscribes compensated advisers from the fraudulent practice of "scalping," in which an investment adviser publicly recommends the purchase of securities without disclosing to his clients that he is also purchasing the securities on his own account. Additionally, §215 of the Advisers Act *voids* any contract where performance thereof would violate the Advisers Act.

These federal fiduciary standards are in addition to those provided in the fraud provisions of §17(a) of the 1933 Act as well as Rule 10b-5, and §9(a)(4) and §14 of or pursuant to the 1934 Act, the latter dealing with proxy solicitation and tender offer fraud provisions. These statutory standards also apply to broker-dealers and others. Generally, the SEC enforces the Advisers Act, but an injured plaintiff is entitled to a private right of action for damages under §205 in seeking to void an investment adviser's contract.

Underwriting

In addition to all of the above statutory, regulatory, and civil liability standards, underwriters are also subject to §11 of the 1933 Act, which imposes virtually absolute liability for any material misstatement or omission in the registration statement. In today's market, underwriters have sought to protect themselves by conducting increasingly thorough "due diligence" examinations in which the underwriters become as familiar with the offering as the issuer.

Civil Actions

Banks, subsidiaries of banks, or bank holding companies may be exposed to administrative or civil actions brought by the appropriate regulatory agency (the OCC, the FDIC, or the FRB) as well as by the SEC and/or the states. Under state and federal securities laws, in appropriate circumstances, arbitration proceedings and private lawsuits may also be brought by customers alleging violations of the pertinent standard of care. Similarly, state and federal regulatory agencies may institute administrative actions to suspend, revoke or fine registered entities as well as enjoining such firms from engaging in any future violations.

Criminal Sanctions

Federal and state securities laws also provide for criminal sanctions in certain circumstances for certain classes of persons, including issuers, underwriters, and dealers. Criminal actions are basically limited to willful or grossly negligent violations of applicable standards of action, disclosure, or conduct, e.g., insider trading, intentional omission of material information, or embezzlement of entrusted funds.

VI. CONCLUSION

Looking back to the time when the Schwab decision was promulgated in 1984, commercial banks have come a long way toward overcoming the rather outdated barriers presented by Glass-Steagall. Very simply, those banks that have challenged the status quo have been richly rewarded. There are few (mostly underwriting—meaning principal risk) activities that banks cannot pursue today. The question to a large extent today is not whether, but how—truly a radical change from those "frontiersmen" who dared to venture into "discount brokerage" or "made available" mutual funds less than 4 years ago.

For example, as this overview is being published in September 1987, banks have the power to generate more fee revenue by underwriting municipal revenue bonds, commercial paper, mortgage-backed securities, CMOs, and possibly some consumer-related securities. Although these new powers are currently subject to FRB limits of 5% of a bank or a bank subsidiary's gross revenue and a 5% market share in order to comply with § 20, these ceilings may be increased in view of the Fed's statement that it would consider allowing a higher level of activity within the year.

On the other hand, banks have not been given the clear mandate to underwrite corporate bonds, equity securities, and mutual funds. Greater clarity or actual expansion of permissible investment advisory factions would also be part of the new "frontier" for banks in the securities business. Pushing for more powers remains high on banking's legislative agenda. Despite the moratorium adopted by Congress, future congressional action is uncertain, and the battlefield is likely to remain with the regulatory agencies and in the courts.

PART THREE

Services

The Coming of Portfolio Management for Everyone

Neil R. Michelsen

Neil R. Michelsen is a financial services partner in the New York office of Coopers & Lybrand, specializing in the domestic and international banking and securities industries. He is currently the partner in charge of the New York office Banking Practice for Coopers & Lybrand.

He is a Certified Public Accountant and has an undergraduate degree in Accounting as well as a graduate degree in Investment and Finance. He has extensive international experience, which includes having been partner in charge of a financial services public accounting practice in Rio de Janeiro from 1979 to 1983.

Mr. Michelsen has authored publications and articles and has spoken on banking and the securities industry topics, in addition to having actively chaired and participated in numerous industry conferences, committees, and seminars.

QUESTION

Q. What are the most important possessions of any individual?

A. His assets.

Q. And what is the most important thing one must do regarding those assets?

A. Take care of them.

Taking care of one's assets is a management function which we will call Portfolio Management. The term also includes managing one's liabilities.

The task of Portfolio Management can appear to be such an obstacle that one is often afraid to even take a stab at starting: the "Where do I begin?" syndrome.

An examination of all the facets of that undertaking may appear to be such a monumental and confusing task that one is literally stopped in one's tracks. Thinking that one does not have a large enough portfolio to be worthwhile may also be an obstacle.

THEME

What we are going to address is portfolio management as it historically has been and what it might look like in the future. It must be borne in mind that any projection of how things will be involves the risk of inaccuracy due to errors in assumptions and perceptions. The longer the period of projection, the greater the possibility of new, outside events completely changing the course of events.

Our discussion will not only pertain to the management of traditional, large portfolios; it will also pertain to the moderate-sized and even small portfolios of individuals of moderate means.

HISTORY

In preceding centuries the only people who had portfolios of assets of any kind were royalty, landowners, and businessmen. Even then, the things they could do with their assets were limited. They were limited by economies that had no breadth, limited by primitive communication and transportation systems, limited by weak competition due to the limited number of players in the market, limited by volume and turnover, and limited by the state of the art of portfolio management itself.

As time progressed and as those limiting factors began to diminish, managing investments began to take on more interesting characteristics. More opportunities arose as trade and communication developed and as economies became more organized and centralized.

Still, portfolio management was relatively unsophisticated, and no high powered techniques existed. Investments were either blessed with very high returns or, more commonly, cursed with devastating losses. There seemed to be no middle ground. Making investments was time consuming and very burdensome, and required significant amounts of capital. Shifting assets from one investment to another was an ordeal and often liquidation losses were real possibilities. Predictability and stability of investments were not common, except for those who could afford to perhaps invest in land. The ability to monitor and track one's investments was still sorely deficient. Finally, portfolio management continued to be restricted primarily to the rich; the common person with limited resources and limited opportunities was left out.

TRENDS

Things have changed. Economies and markets have further expanded; transportation, trade, and communication have improved dramatically, and competition has heightened. There exist many new opportunities—even for investors of moderate means. The number of investment products now available is mind-boggling, and there seems no end in sight to the continued development of new products. The speed at which one can execute investment activity has also greatly improved and the means to track performance has now become much easier. Shifting assets from one investment to another can be accomplished more easily without incurring disastrous liquidation losses.

ON THE BRINK OF SOMETHING NEW

These recent trends have brought us to a point where it appears that we may be on the threshold of something new and spectacular. With modern tools, techniques, and available financial products and their unique market delivery systems, we may be at a turning point in financial management. The substantial possibilities for portfolio management have applications and benefits for all of us.

No one can predict with any precision whether things will ever develop along the lines we will discuss, either on a short-term or a long-term basis, or whether they will ever reach all the people they could possibly reach. But the moment has arrived when we can make some projections about what is coming in the future.

KEY INGREDIENTS

What are the primary ingredients involved in bringing us to the brink of these new possibilities? There are of course many, but there are three that are more prominent:

- The multitude of financial products.
- Reduced investment entry level.
- Computerization and technology.

FINANCIAL PRODUCTS AND THEIR DISTRIBUTION

Markets, whether they be food markets or financial markets, bring a large number of products into one or more centralized distribution locations. In order to have an effective market, however, there must be a sufficiently large number of products. Over the years, we have seen more and more new products being developed.

The products being developed today are quite unique. Traditional investment products have undergone so many enhancements that they have become separate products in and of themselves, in many cases.

Bonds, for example, were fairly standardized products. They were long term, had fixed rates, and were issued by large public corporations.

Today investors can choose bonds issued not only by a large number of major corporations, but also from a greater than ever number of smaller corporations, both public and private, and by a large number of government agencies. With the advent of floating interest rates and the elimination of the confining restrictions of fixed rates, as well as the ability to link the interest rate of one investment vehicle to the interest rate of another investment vehicle (e.g., the treasury bill rate), financial paper has taken on a whole new aspect. It has created the environment for development of a myriad of new financial investment vehicles.

Products such as revenue bonds and tax-free municipal bonds have been expanding very rapidly.

In addition, the growth of stronger secondary markets, which have benefited from better communications and delivery systems and from active participation and help by the government, has also contributed to new product development.

Bonds are not the only products that have exploded into a variety of new investment vehicles. There is an equal number of equity stock products as well to choose from, and more are being created on an on-going basis. Asset-based investments such as leasing and other collateralized products have also multiplied rapidly. Even the simple bank deposit account has taken on new product dimension thanks to the creation and proliferation of the certificate of deposit, NOW account, money market account, daily compounding of interest, and floating interest rates and the like. There is also a vast number of retirement and tax incentive products generated from 401(K), Keogh, and IRA plans. Today we also have such products as swaps, instant home equity loans, credit card loans, options, futures, options on futures, and options on indexes, just to name some others.

The products that have been developed today seem to cover every financial and investment aspect of our daily business and private lives. Investment opportunities include a vast, growing list of international as well as domestic products. Having all these products to choose from now, with the prospect of more and more coming in the future, has created a whole new market base.

Many financial service institutions, including banks, stock brokerage firms, insurance companies, and retailers, have considered developing the concept of the financial supermarket. The financial supermarket would be a place, theoretically one financial institution, where one can obtain a substantial number of the financial products one needs. It could be analogous to the one-stop banking concept, providing the means to efficiently select and accumulate financial products.

Whether one gains access to financial products through the theoretical financial supermarket or by some other means will be discussed later, but the concept of the financial supermarket obviously has some potential benefit for all of us. From the point of view of the institution offering an array of financial products the rewards may also be great, enabling that institution to service all the financial needs of its customers, thereby increasing its earnings potential from each customer relationship.

REDUCED INVESTMENT ENTRY LEVEL

Investment in the financial and capital markets had been pretty much the province of the rich, or at least of those individuals with large capital resources at hand. The common person has progressed to the point of obtaining access to a greater selection of investment vehicles but has not really participated to a significant or sophisticated degree.

That financial institutions avoided, or at least did not cater to, the investor of moderate or limited means partly stemmed from the fact that the types of investment products that they had developed in the past were just not geared to reach such an investor. The entry level of investment was high, preventing many potential investors from choosing financial products. While banks and insurance companies had given customers a number of reasonably priced investment vehicles, too many other investment vehicles required larger sums of money that in many cases would have absorbed much of the average customer's available resources. Investment firms usually directed their efforts toward the high net worth individual, the person who had an asset base large enough to make it worthwhile to do business. The result was that the majority of potential players was excluded.

The concept of mutual funds was one of the ways in which the entry-level barrier was broken. Mutual funds created a whole new approach to unlocking the individually small but collectively large resources of the masses. Portfolios could be created by the "pooling" of funds. This, of course, is not a novel idea. Individual savings accounts at banks are pooled funds as well, providing financial benefit to both the bank and the small depositor.

Mutual funds allowed an individual to buy an interest in a stock or a bond if he could not afford the entry-level price of buying the stock or bond itself. Today we are experiencing phase two of that breakthrough. Not only have mutual funds allowed more individuals to participate in the market by reducing the amount of investment at the entry level, but also many of today's new products are individually priced in such a manner that they are within the reach of the person of moderate means. The family of mutual fund products itself has expanded to a point where the moderate investor is permitted access to an even larger number of new investment products.

The lowering of the entry level of individual investment products and the expansion of mutual funds products have enabled individuals to diversify their limited resources and create real "portfolios" by all definitions of the word.

COMPUTERIZATION AND TECHNOLOGY

The third ingredient of the change is computerization. Computer technology has made it possible to categorize large numbers of portfolio assets and liabilities and other data, to analyze the various quantity indicator statistics applicable to each, and to balance portfolio composition and monitor portfolio performance more easily than before.

Portfolio accounting can be accomplished with reasonable care and in a cost-effective manner regardless of the size of the portfolio. Changes in portfolio composition can also be made rapidly and easily without losing accounting control.

In the past, portfolio management was cost effective for the larger portfolios. With the arrival of "high-tech" portfolio management programs, the smaller portfolios of individuals can be managed just as easily. Through these highly developed programs, even small and medium-sized portfolios can be profitable for the managing institution as well as meaningful for the individual. In the same way that banks benefited from individuals' small deposits or mutual funds from small mutual fund investments, asset managers can profit from the management of small portfolios.

Therefore, portfolio management now requires only an overall investment plan and some form of a computerized management program in order to effectively manage any size portfolio with ease.

ACCESS TO FINANCIAL PRODUCTS AND THE FINANCIAL SUPERMARKET

It may not be necessary to have one institution offering all the various financial products in the market under its own roof. An alternative may develop whereby products could reach everyone not by means of the one-stop financial supermarket, but through one or many investment placement service centers acting as conduits for the placement of funds for investments in various other institutions offering them. These entities would have access to all the available financial products in the market offered by all financial institutions and could assist finding the desired investment product based on selected investment criteria. This data-based funds placement entity would specialize in organizing, cataloging, and analyzing the market products for suitability to its customers.

Acting in a broker/agency capacity rather than in a principal capacity, any member entity could place funds for its customers at another offering institution. The financial institution not only retains the customer but also earns a referral fee while retaining control over the management of that customer's portfolio.

Under this scenario, having access to the entire market is effectively the same thing as having the financial supermarket itself.

In the future, even having to go through a financial institution or a funds placement center may not be necessary. Access to the market may occur through home linkups permitting an individual to select from a menu of financial products right on a home computer terminal.

THE SHOPPING LIST

The development of varied financial products and having increased access to them has certainly expanded investment opportunities. Having access to varied products solves only one problem. The other problem is a bit more complicated—how do you know what to buy? What individuals need is guidance on what products to select.

Going down the aisle of the financial supermarket or looking at a menu of financial products and reading all the labels and descriptions is one thing, but being able to put it all together and make a logical and balanced choice is another. Does the average investor have enough skill to properly understand and interpret all the selection criteria? With so many products on the market, one is faced with information overload. What is needed now is a sort of shopping list, something prepared ahead of time based on established investment criteria.

The list would contain all the types of products one needs before one even goes to the market. While at the market, one would use the shopping list to select the right product as well as to pay the right price.

How does one go about developing a shopping list? This question hits at the very core of what is involved in portfolio management.

THE STANDARDIZED PORTFOLIO MANAGEMENT PROGRAM

With the existing and future availability of financial products by means of the financial supermarket, at investment entry levels that permit the selection of varied products, and with the availability of the computer to handle activity from the selection phase to the day-to-day maintenance phase, we still are missing a key ingredient: standardized portfolio management programs having application to just about everyone.

Portfolio management programs do exist today in varying degrees. They have always existed, in one form or another, for the high net worth individual or the institutional customer, but even then an investment manager was its focal point. Small portfolios cannot support a full-time portfolio manager. What is needed is the development of standardized programs to handle the selection and management of portfolios, with perhaps very limited involvement of an investment manager.

In subsequent sections we shall be exploring the parameters of what would be involved in such future portfolio management programs if financial trends continue.

FACETS OF PORTFOLIO MANAGEMENT

What is involved in terms of portfolio management? There are many facets involved but they can be generally compacted into the following broad categories:

- Establishing portfolio objectives.
- Selecting portfolio investments, i.e., asset allocation.
- Monitoring performance.
- Evaluating changing situations.

Within each one of these facets, there exists an interplay of input and output of information to make it work. The portfolio owner would input certain critical data, and the computer would use that data to make "suggestions" in each category, from which the owner could make his choices. Each of these facets could be aided greatly by sophisticated computer programs from which the portfolio owner could draw analysis and advice. Standardizing this input/output process through the computer eliminates the need for a full-time investment manager, reduces costs, and enables the portfolio owner to participate in the process. The beauty of computerized portfolio management is that it assists those individuals who otherwise would not have the skill to manage their portfolios. Even if one had the skill, one might not have the time.

It's like the story about the shoemaker's kids always being bare-foot. The shoemaker had all the skills to make shoes for his kids, but he didn't have time to do so because he was so busy making shoes for other people's kids.

Any individual whose personal financial affairs sound like that story should be looking forward to the time when the art of portfolio management will be so organized and developed that he or she would not need much time to manage a portfolio cost effectively as a result of state-of-the-art computer techniques. Even for those individuals who have both the time and the skill to manage their portfolios, but who do not have the inclination to do so, the ease of a computerized management portfolio program should go a long way in overcoming that problem as well.

ESTABLISHING PORTFOLIO OBJECTIVES

Where does one begin? The process should start with establishing viable portfolio objectives corresponding to one's particular financial and economic situation.

An individual may start a portfolio managing process by merely inputting a list of assets and liabilities, income stream, and a few other basic items such as age, family status, and number of children, and obtain as output a complete analysis of the portfolio in terms of its present risk, distribution, liquidity concentration, and the like. From this point, structural changes could be made to meet various objective alternatives. The alternatives could even be listed by the computer in the form of a menu: a standard "objectives list" for an individual having input the financial characteristics.

Portfolio objectives could be as simple as "maximum investment security" (no risk), "low risk," high risk" or "medium risk," "capital preservation," "high yield," "capital gains," or any number of other objectives. Portfolio objectives can be combined with others to arrive at more sophisticated objectives such as "medium risk, well diversified, highly liquid," for example.

Guidelines as to how to interpret these objectives and what objectives would normally be associated with one's particular situation would be made available. The computer program might suggest, for example, that a man of moderate and steady income of $30,000 per year, having a nonworking wife and two children of high school age, might want to consider the objective of "low risk with a reasonable degree of liquidity." Without the assistance of the computer, one often does not have an effective way in which to evaluate what objectives and objective combinations are best suited for him.

Determining what one's objectives should be is not a stand-alone process, however. The list of objectives one may choose from may be limited by the ultimate size of the portfolio. An investor of limited means might not be able to achieve her objective of maximum diversification because the amount of her resources are just too limited, or because she might not want to commit enough resources to the portfolio. She may therefore have to settle for different objectives. Such alternative suggestions could easily be developed by the computer, from which she could make her selection.

SELECTING PORTFOLIO INVESTMENTS— ASSET ALLOCATION

One of the most significant benefits of the computerization of the individual portfolio management process will be selection of the investments the portfolio should contain. Second to that will be the allocation of assets between categories and types of investments. This selection and allocation process will naturally be guided by the previously selected "portfolio" objectives criteria discussed in the preceding section. The choice of portfolio investments, including liability changes, will always be guided by the selected investment portfolio objective. At the end of the day, the chosen portfolio will be assigned various indicators to measure such important characteristics as liquidity, diversification, risk quality, expected yield, or capital growth expectation.

Given the input of the general portfolio objective and the amount of resources available, the computer could develop a number of different portfolio possibilities, each having different characteristics from which one could make the ultimate selection.

One of the chief benefits of this envisioned computer program would be the reduction of the overload of information that has resulted from the recent explosion of financial products. Having too much information creates an overload situation; one cannot effectively analyze it all, much less evaluate how each possible investment portfolio choice interacts with the others in terms of meeting overall objectives. The computer can make that portion of the decision process relatively manageable.

The process of selecting portfolio investments would begin with an analysis of one's present portfolio and a determination of its investment characteristics in terms of liquidity, risk, and diversification. It should be mentioned that some securities firms offer this service today, allowing an individual to get a "feel" for how a portfolio is structured. Combining that result with the amount of resources available for the portfolio and the portfolio objective, one could be presented with a series of recommended portfolio structures with various investment characteristics: the ultimate shopping list.

Analysis of any portfolio may, for example, show that for one's designated objectives and available resources, one is too heavily concentrated in low-yielding bonds, all of which in turn are concentrated in one industry, making the whole portfolio too sensitive to adverse change in that particular industry or to any change in interest rates. Working from this, the program could develop a list of alternative investments that might better meet one's objectives. It could also recommend various allocation percentages so that the portfolio is well balanced. Through the envisioned investment placement bureau, the computer may actually be able to recommend specific available products from offering financial institutions.

In many situations today, one's mind boggles when trying to evaluate what type of investments one should make, and how much to invest in each. Asset allocation is a major problem. With a computerized program specifically geared to asset portfolio management, this problem should be greatly diminished.

MONITORING PERFORMANCE

Monitoring the performance of existing portfolios has always been another difficulty. Having assets centralized into one portfolio and monitored under one portfolio management program would eliminate most of that problem.

Sophisticated techniques could easily calculate portfolio growth and yield and match them against general market performance indicators, such as the Dow and Standard and Poors indexes. Capital growth trends could be calculated to determine whether performance has at least kept up with inflation and general interest rates. Performance can be monitored against the performance of other similar portfolios. If performance is not up to expectation, we must consider changing portfolio composition or changing the portfolio manager/program. It must be assumed that in the future there will be a number of portfolio management programs available, each one operative under varying portfolio management techniques.

In any event, the computer had the distinct advantage of being able to handle all the calculations needed to effectively get a handle on the question of whether one's portfolio is performing up to expectations, from which decisions can be made.

EVALUATING CHANGING SITUATIONS

No situation remains the same for very long. Market conditions under which prior assumptions were based often change radically, perhaps leaving the portfolio severely off the course of its original objectives. Inflation rates change, interest rates change, and recessions occur in the real estate market. In addition, new financial products are always being developed.

How can these products be evaluated for their effect? You guessed it—the computer program would make such evaluations and suggest specific portfolio modifications. Without the aid of the computer program, organized to evaluate new products and events, monitoring the portfolio would be difficult, and one would never fully know the true impact upon vital portfolio characteristics. Once advised of the impact on the portfolio, the investor can choose either to act or not to act on such information; but the point is that the portfolio owner would be advised of the impact beforehand.

DEGREES OF PORTFOLIO MANAGEMENT

In the future there will be many varied types of portfolio management packages available to choose from, covering the four facets of portfolio management. The degree of user sophistication, the size and complexity of the portfolio, the time available to evaluate all investment alternatives, and the cost involved must all be figured in.

A person limited by time, user skill, and portfolio size probably would select a basic management package with the capacity for meeting basic portfolio objectives, very standardized in its predetermined portfolio investment alternatives and geared to suggest changes only when major market changes occur.

On the other hand, there will be programs that will cater to the sophisticated portfolio owner: portfolio characteristics will be more precisely calculated, the effect of portfolio suggestions more accurately determined, and recommendations for portfolio changes triggered by a high degree of sensitivity to changes in the market and other conditions. "What if" features will also be important.

Differences in the degree of sophistication of these programs would naturally be reflected in the cost of the program itself.

It should also be remembered that, again depending upon sophistication, the portfolio management program should always be performing liability management functions as well as asset management functions, and no real program can be productive without including that feature. The larger the portfolio and more varied the income sources of the portfolio owner, the greater will be the range of suitable products, the flexibility in risk/reward objectives, and the possibility of options for implementing strategy and diversification techniques.

Risk management, through the use of risk and risk-hedging instruments, and tax planning considerations will play much greater roles. True centralized portfolio management becomes a reality.

PORTFOLIO MANAGEMENT AT HOME

The individual who has the time and portfolio management and computer skills, of course, does not have to rely on a basic portfolio program managed by others. He may purchase various portfolio management software programs himself and load them onto his own home computer. He could also tie his home computer to a service center, which might contain a myriad of larger capacity and more advanced, high-powered portfolio management programs, if he felt that his own computer was not large enough or his own programs not sophisticated enough.

In the investor's centralized portfolio management cockpit, the methodology of this portfolio management process could be simply demonstrated in the following scenario of events:

Manager: Inputs assets and liabilities and other financial information

Computer: Catalogues and analyzes the portfolio for balance, diversification, risk, etc.

Manager: Selects from a menu of objectives.

Computer: Makes recommendations for structural portfolio changes and produces a menu of financial products that will accomplish selected objectives.

Manager: Asks the computer to calculate the portfolio characteristics under the selected assumptions—then makes the final selection.

Computer: Periodically analyzes and makes recommendations as new financial products are developed and/or market conditions change.

What we are talking about here are expert systems where a resident knowledge of investment expertise and analysis is made available in menu form to the user. The user is presented a menu of items to choose from and is prompted all along the way to arriving at portfolio composition decisions.

ADD-ON FEATURES

There could be a multitude of add-on features or enhancements to add sophistication to the process.

For example, in addition to inputting such basic financial information as one's assets and liabilities, more detailed information could be inputted that would, depending upon the program involved, enable one to achieve a very sophisticated degree of portfolio management. This could cover everything from daily personal life to long-term investment strategies.

Expert programs could be developed that would handle the risk management through insurance or other products, educational needs such as college education for a child, financing of a major personal or business acquisition, a retirement program, tax sheltering, estate planning, and the like.

In addition to accepting financial data, the computer could accept such data as birth dates, passport and social security numbers, job histories, and educational information that would enable a family to have all static pertinent information catalogued and available for reference. A major financial institution is presently offering the ability to collect such nonfinancial information as an add-on feature to its central management account in order to enhance its push for one-stop financial and accounting services. Although still in the early stages of its development, it is a step toward the future.

To demonstrate how nonfinancial information may directly relate to portfolio management, the following example may be appropriate. Depending upon the sophistication of the program, changes in the portfolio could be suggested when the birth of a child is input. Changes may be recommended in reallocating one's income stream and/or capital base toward the future funding of the new child's educational needs. The program might suggest channeling some short-term, more risky assets into more secure, predictable assets. With the new addition to the family, coupled perhaps with the acquisition of a new home, one's whole financial plan might call for a review by the computer program/manager whereby new objectives would probably be required. Furthermore, a whole new set of health, medical, educational, and insurance products may have to be chosen. A greater part of one's income stream may have to be diverted from one investment to another in order to fund the new home. All these factors can be quickly converted into a new set of investment choices and portfolio restructuring suggestions by means of sophisticated portfolio management programs.

In addition, financial assets are becoming more and more fungible and more easily converted into other assets. This opens up new possibilities for portfolio management strategies that the computer can handle.

Evidence of increased fungibility and convertibility can be seen in the case of the ease with which loans can be obtained from the equity in one's home. Obtaining a second mortgage is nothing new, but in the past, and to some degree today, this process has been a major project for both the lender and the borrower. Why? Because no one was geared up for this type of product in any standard way. Such loans were handled on a case-by-case basis. Although there were standard procedures involved, there was a myriad of paperwork and processing that had to be done beforehand. There was no way to easily evaluate the market value and borrowing potential of one's assets. In the future, the computer will probably be able to process a request for a loan by tapping into its data bank of assets under centralized management and immediately convert that market value equity into available funds. In fact, the need for funds, coupled with a request for the computer to produce an array of financing alternatives after its analyses of market conditions, will be an easy task for the computer. For example, depending upon the liquidity and strength of various markets and level of interest rates, borrowing against portfolio bonds rather than against equity stocks may be a better choice; it may avoid more adverse portfolio effects and may in fact enhance one's overall portfolio objectives. Through the great ability of the computer to track market values of all portfolio assets as well as market conditions in general, there is a greater chance that all assets can be considered fungible to some extent or at least more easily converted from one to the other.

Another example of a sophisticated portfolio capability would be a case where one is considering switching from a mutual fund to, say, a high-risk bond, but did not want to get out of a mutual fund position. Depending on market conditions, the computer might recommend that one borrow against one's equity in one's mutual fund portfolio and then invest in the speculative bond.

If tax sheltering is a major consideration, portfolio management programs could be selected that, in addition to evaluating economic and financial consequences, could also figure the tax ramification of any potential portfolio selection.

Another add-on feature possibility might be the ability to actually execute transactions automatically. Under a situation where all assets are centralized under the control of one institution, execution might be performed as easily as pushing the right button. Even if assets are not centrally controlled, execution could be accomplished through a centralized exchange system by merely pushing the button to authorize the transaction. Because the market values of centralized assets would probably be constantly updated, transaction values and collateral values would always be current. Liens and other types of collateral arrangements could be automatically executed, and one's centralized data bank could be updated for any new asset composition, asset value, and collateral borrowing power. The credit evaluation process will be much more easily and scientifically accessed, and instant financing made available. Paperwork would be reduced to a minimum as most transactions would be standardized, functioning from the centralized asset and liability account. In addition, international and domestic financial, stock, commodities, and other exchanges will probably be linked with ever-increasing interfacing mechanisms.

ACCOUNTING AND TAXATION

With the advent of centralized portfolio management, all accounting aspects of an individual's financial affairs would be greatly simplified. Just having one's portfolio organized and categorized into a logical financial order would be an immense accounting control benefit. Once that is done, income and dividend receipts and market value changes can be calculated and recorded in easy statement form. Each statement would show all capital transactions that occurred, all income receipts and expenditures for mortgage payments, telephone bills, groceries, etc., as well as any capital gains or loss transactions that occurred. Statements would be available not only once a month but at any time that one requests it. Cash transactions can be input as well to make the record keeping complete. In addition, noncash activity such as depreciation and amortization of business investments can be calculated automatically. Because all transactions would be centralized, one would have all the ingredients to enable the computer to prepare a full set of personal or business financial statements for the month, the year, or any other period.

At this point one's income tax return could easily be prepared at the end of the year, since all relevant information would be available. All the mathematics, the test limitations for deductions and capital gains treatment, and the calculations of depreciation, etc., could be performed automatically by the computer. Of course, there are service corporations now that perform this function, but think of the time saved in having them performed directly from one's portfolio data bank instead of having to collect and codify data from hard-copy records and then having to input such data on complicated input forms for end-of-the-year processing.

Another accounting feature would be the ability to make budgets and projections of future profitability on certain investments given certain assumptions, such as interest rates being 8%, 10%, or 15%, or to ask "what" would be the expected financial "if" I sold my IBM stock now and invested the proceeds in a money market account. Another simple budgetary computation might be determining how much one would have to allocate from one's income stream, and at what interest rate, to ensure that at the end of 15 years one could finance a child's education, projecting that a 4-year college education in 15 years would cost $50,000 per year.

With the computer collecting all pertinent information, a clear historical pattern of success or failure in portfolio performance can easily be measured, from which one can make clear evaluations of performance and develop new strategies for the future. Trends in asset growth and profitability can better be seen by comparing past historical information year by year. These trends can then be used to make future projections, performing sensitivity analyses by adding in various "what if" conditions, e.g., what if interest rates rise by 5%. Because one's portfolio would be comprised of both assets and liabilities, reasonably accurate projections of what would result might be produced, which would enhance planning. To emphasize it once again, effective liability management is as important a part of what we have been discussing as is asset management.

SOME REALITIES

In summary, we have talked about a wonderful electronic portfolio scenario where all assets and liabilities and other financial and nonfinancial data are centrally controlled and managed. We have talked about magic "expert" system-type software that can analyze portfolios, suggest portfolio changes, and evaluate effects of changes on portfolio objectives and performance.

We have also talked about programs that can monitor past performance, make financial projections and budgets, and monitor current trends and changes in market and changes in the portfolio owner's situation that will "flag" the need to evaluate a possible change in portfolio structure. Finally, we have talked about the ability to immediately execute portfolio changes through a network linking all domestic and international financial instruments markets.

What could prevent all this from happening? There are many things. A number of years ago, with the advent of electronics funds transfer systems and hardware and the vast computer possibilities in terms of speed, convenience, and efficiency, it was projected that the United States would rapidly become a paperless society. All payments

140

Chapter Eight

of bills, invoices, and transfers between bank accounts would be handled automatically. This didn't occur over the short time it was expected to occur because of resistance by the public. The public had misgivings about the new system, and among other things, did not like being unable to have traditional hard copies, such as canceled checks, as evidence of completed transactions. It was erroneously assumed that the public would readily jump on the bandwagon and immediately accept electronic funds transfer. This assumption underestimated the public's resistance to change and the degree of "mistrust" or skepticism of new systems.

The same thing could occur with the portfolio management possibilities discussed herein: The idea could meet general public resistance. For secrecy purposes, people may not want to have all their assets under one roof. Or they might not want to have anyone in "central control" over their accounts and may be willing to accept lower yields, higher risks, and cumbersome bookkeeping and record keeping to avoid it. Also, people just might not believe that portfolio managers and computerized management programs are any better. They may feel they could do it on their own while saving management fees in the process. Some may be resistant to having their accounts grouped together for fear of access by tax or other regulatory authorities. Other unknown factors could prevent mass acceptance of mass implementation of sophisticated portfolio management techniques as well.

Government regulations may prove to be obstacles. They are already obstacles in the sense that the financial services industries of insurance, banking, and securities still are separated by law. Maintaining this separation to some degree will inhibit the development of a truly centralized and effective portfolio management process.

There are other realities to contend with as well—economic realities, for example. It may not be economically possible to market and implement this process quickly. The cost of computerization and the cost of research and development itself will be extremely high, and these costs must be recovered in a reasonable amount of time; otherwise, it just will not be economically feasible to undertake them.

There are also extreme situations such as war, political upheaval, economic depression, etc., which, although they should not dominate the planning process, might play an important inhibitive role should they occur.

CONCLUSION

All in all, we have seen a rapid explosion of financial products. Ingenious financial products have made portfolios more fungible and more easily convertible into other forms of assets, adding flexibility and liquidity to portfolios. Entry levels have been reduced so that these products can be brought to the mass market.

Technology has been exploding as well, providing us with the tools and software techniques to more easily organize and catalogue our portfolios and better manage them cost-effectively.

These events have brought us to the threshold of something potentially big and beneficial to everyone—the quick, easy, and scientific management of portfolios, large or small, through the use of sophisticated portfolio management techniques that once were available only to managers of large portfolios.

There is little doubt that this development will occur. It's just a matter of how soon and how broadly.

CHAPTER NINE

Financial Planning

Frederick B. Putney, Ph.D.

Fred Putney received his B.B.A. from the University of Washington in 1961 and his Ph.D. from Stanford University in 1968. He has been a faculty member of the Columbia University Graduate School of Business since 1968, and during the period 1970–1981, he also served as Deputy Vice President for the Health Sciences Campus of Columbia University. Since 1981, he has been an Adjunct Professor of Finance while pursuing his investment advisory activities at Brownson, Rehmus & Foxworth (of which he was a founder in 1969) and management consulting activities as a partner in The Riverside Group (of which he was also a founder in 1976). He is an active consultant and advisor to a number of leading industrial firms, financial institutions, and individuals.

Personal financial planning is something that all people do. Often, however, the planning that is done is anecdotal; that is, it is targeted at a specific decision and on an irregular and infrequent basis. What are the common instances in which an individual is involved with personal financial planning? Let's look at some of these more common situations:

- Purchase or refinancing of home—a major financing decision and buyer must file financial disclosure information for mortgage.
- Purchase of auto or renovation of home—a financing and investment decision that requires completion of financial disclosure forms and comparison of funding choices.

- Decision on voluntary retirement funding contributions such as IRA, Keogh, 401K, etc.—a tax, cash-flow investment, and wealth-building choice carried out at least annually.
- Determination of withholding rates and estimated taxes—requires annual tax planning based on earnings, investment results, etc.
- Purchase of life insurance.
- Purchase of long-term disability insurance.
- Funding children's education, annually or in advance.
- Selection of investments and investing.
- Payment of estimated taxes and filing tax return.

Often these situations involve a product or service sale or use by an institution, broker, or professional. Generally, the service provider requires selected financial information on the individual at a point-in-time or for the year past. Seldom is the data comprehensive, and seldom does it project the individual's situation forward.

True financial planning for the individual should be forward looking and comprehensive. Then individual decisions can be placed into the context of an individual's or family's situation so as to evaluate their impact on the future.

This chapter is directed at *comprehensive* financial planning for the individual or family to help the individual decide how much of what to purchase and when to purchase it, when to invest, etc.

Personal financial planning is more complex than financial planning applied to a business. It requires the effective use of all financial planning and analysis tools with which you are familiar. There are, however, three additional dimensions that add to the difficulty.

First, the time periods required to do an effective planning job are greater than we normally apply to the business world. That is, we must plan situations for 5, 10, 15, 20, or 30 or more years ahead. This exaggerates the problems of uncertainty.

Second, the long- and short-term planning must take into account many states of the world for the individual or family as an economic entity. These require consideration of a number of situations; for example, estrangement, illness, disability, or death of any member of the family. Planning with these possibilities requires both legal structures and financial packages that must be developed for the family to achieve objectives. Unplanned affairs force the family to accept the results of un-planned events and of the default options provided by statutory law and government-sponsored programs.

Third, personal financial planning is often highly emotional. The family's objective is the management of personal needs, expectations, and responsibilities. The discipline of financial planning emphasizes a rational, methodical, and objective process about items that individuals consider personal and private—and that often are not amenable to rational analysis.

This chapter provides an overview of the process, recommended steps, suggested goals for each of the decision analyses, and some examples of personal financial planning. The exercise is one that should be updated on an annual basis and when important changes occur in the family's life or the economy. The planning activity and the resultant plan are part of a process that should be continually updated as assumptions, needs, or situations change.

THE STARTING POINT—PERSONAL FINANCIAL STATEMENTS

One of the best starting points for the planning process is to create a set of personal financial statements: tax, cash flow, and balance sheet.

There are many formats for the development of these financial statements. A simple first step is to complete a retrospective analysis of last year. Many individuals develop such an analysis each year when doing their income taxes. The categories of revenues and expenses will vary with individual situations and whether the data base was created for tax planning or other applications.

The next step is to extract from a retrospective review of prior years the basic patterns of expense so that cash expense items may be projected into the future. Many of the expense streams must be individually estimated based on individual needs, situations, and life-style expectations and cannot be simply extrapolated from the past. From these decision rules, plus assumptions about inflation and earnings growth rates, pro forma cash-flow and balance-sheet statements can be constructed.

Often, the best way to create a set of financial statements is to start with a structured inventory of your financial situation. A simplified format of a hypothetical case is shown in Table 9-1 (pages 146, 147). It's almost anecdotal. It starts with personal information, benefits, and insurance; then it turns to a description of assets and liabilities.

The next step is to review last year's spending by categories. For example, in our hypothetical case set forth in Table 9-1, we now review spending and tax records for 1986, adjust for changes we are aware of for the current year, and then complete the bottom section of Table 9-2 (pages 148, 149). Notice the notes to the right of the numbers. Each individual should select the appropriate projection rule for each factor of expense. Some suggestions are made in Table 9-2 for a family that has a stable personal life-style.

Now we want to complete the Income section of Table 9-2. Some of these are asset determined, and others are earnings projections from salaries, bonuses, consulting, etc. Normally there will be variability in projecting pay or bonus increases. Often a prudent rule is to use a growth rate. This is validated by recent (2-3) years results plus a judgment about the future. If the amount of uncertainty is large *or* discretionary cash flow is small, it could be wise to do a conservative case alongside the expected case to determine how sensitive cash flow is to such changes.

We can now turn to Table 9-3 (page 150), which is the forming of a balance sheet or net worth statement. As shown in Table 9-3, this form organizes the anecdotal information shown in Table 1 into a standard accounting format.

We now have completed our basic inventory and created a cash-flow statement and balance sheet for 1987. This organized information can now be used to answer current questions:

- Do we have enough liquidity (cash and marketable securities) to meet contingencies?
- Do we have enough life insurance to maintain the family life-style in case of death of the breadwinner?
- Do we have enough disability coverage to maintain the family life-style during disability?
- Do we have free cash flow after paying family costs, taxes, etc., to afford a vacation, to pay fully for children's education, etc.?

TABLE 9-1. *Personal Financial Planning Hypothetical Profile—Married.*

Age of Breadwinner: 47
Age of Family Members: Spouse   44
                                Daughter 17
                                Son   15
                                Son   11

Health: Excellent for all
Employment Status: Employed 20 years, 7 with current employer
Residence: Westchester County, New York State
Compensation History:
    Current Salary: $86,300
    Last Five Years' Salary Growth Rate: 10%
    Profit-Sharing Bonus: 0–20% of base-year compensation paid on January 15 of succeeding year. Average bonus over last 5 years is 9%.

Pension Program: Employer pays 10% of first $45,000 compensation to vested pension trust and 5% of compensation for base salary beyond $45,000. Plan is a defined contribution plan.

Cumulative vested pension benefits from this and prior employers is $70,000; which is 50% invested in bonds, 50% in diversified common stock portfolio.

401K program started 7/1/84 by employer. First 5% of salary of voluntary contributions is matched at 3% by employer.

Benefits:
    Medical: Fully paid family extended 120-day BC/BS policy through employer-paid group plan. Major medical insurance through employer-paid group plan that has a complementary deductible of $100, a limit per disease/incident of $50,000, and family limit of $500,000.

    Insurance: 1. Whole life policy in its twenty-fourth year, $30,000; Cash surrender value—$9,550.
    2. Group term insurance through employer up to one-and-a-half times base compensation. Current enrollment at $131,800.
    3. Declining balance term insurance in its fifth year of 25 years. Stated value of $100,000; death benefit currently $69,600.
    4. Whole life insurance policy of $25,000 in its tenth year. Cash surrender value—$3,250.
    5. Automobile liability coverage of $100,000/ 300,000 (includes second-car rider).
    6. Employer paid group disability benefits with a $2,000/month maximum for complete disability

TABLE 9-1. *(Cont.)*

plus full payment and maintenance of BC/BS,
major medical, and group term insurance.

7. Homeowner's policy for:

General Liability	$100,000/300,000
Fire, etc.	120,000
Theft and Personal Effects	30,000

Assets:

Home (joint tenancy):	Purchase price five years ago	$105,000
	Est. current market value	135,000
	Mortgage 25 years @8%	65,000
	Current Principal	60,412
Automobiles:	Two; one 2 years old, one 6 years old	
	Estimated value	6,000
Furnishings, art, and personal effects:		50,000
Savings Account Balance:		
	One—1-year certificate at 6.0%	15,000
	One—Super Now Account at 5.8%	15,000
Common Stock:	Current Market	41,000
	Yield	3.1%
Bonds:	25 Utility Bonds at par 9%	25,000

Other: 50% partnership interest in recreation
condominium at shore (purchased two
years ago)

Market value	96,000
Purchase price	80,000
25-year mortgage @9%	65,500
Furnishings	9,000

Rented 25 weeks per year and used by
each 50% partner one week each year
for vacation.

Average net cash flow per month to
maintain property is $300 per month
for each 50% partner.

Provides loss for tax purposes of
$1,700 this year, and such loss is
expected to decline by $400–$500 each
year. Cash maintenance cost is also
expected to increase by 10% per year.

Business Interests: Partnership interest of 5% in a local fast-food
franchise. Estimated share of undistributed
partnership equity is $6,500. Provides loss for
tax purposes of $1,800 in 1986 with a net cash
flow to you of $600. Net cash flows to you per
year are expected to increase 15% per year, and tax
losses to decrease at 20% per year. By 1992 it is
expected that taxable income from your share of the
partnership will be $1,200 with a net cash flow to
you of $1,900 (unless there is refinancing).

TABLE 9-2. *Financial-Planning Worksheet—Pro Forma Cash-Flow Worksheet: 000 omitted (Example figures from hypothetical case).*

Item	1987	1988	1989	1990	1991
Income					
Salaries: Breadwinner (including bonus) Spouse	100.8	Projected at assumed growth rate and market rates			
Consulting Fees	8.0	Individual item based on attainable plan			
Dividends	1.2	Function of investment portfolio			
Interest	6.2	Function of investment portfolio and market rates			
Distributions from Investment:					
Real Estate (Partnership)	0.2	Should change with existing and future investment program assumptions			
Business Interests	0.9				
Other	—				
Capital Gains:					
Real Estate	—	Specific properties			
Marketable Securities	—	Gains/losses are a function of portfolio management			
Trusts	—	Function of investment program & trust provisions			
Other	—				
Royalties	—	Result of specific investments or publications			
Notes Receivable	0.0	Function of investment program			
Total	117.3				
Expenses					
Food and Household Items	12.6	Projected at price index plus lifestyle assumptions			
Entertainment and Travel	11.0	Projected at price index plus lifestyle assumptions			
Clothing and Misc. Personal	9.1	Projected at price index plus lifestyle assumptions			
Transportation	4.7	Projected at energy price index			
Utilities	3.1	Projected at energy price index			
Mortgage and Loan Princ. & Int.	6.0	Specific contracts			
Medical	2.8	Projected at health price index			
Dental	1.6	Projected at health price index			
Charities	1.2	Discretionary			

TABLE 9-2. (Cont.)

Item	1987	1988	1989	1990	1991
Education	17.5	Function of age of children and education expectations			
Insurance Premiums (incl. Dividends)	2.2	Function of policies in effect and changes in insurance			
Taxes—Federal (Inc. & S.S.)	26.0	Derived expense based on ap-			
State and Local	3.9	plication of 1986 tax law, state,			
Property	3.1	city, etc., tax schedules applied to expected taxable income			
Total	104.8				
Increase in Cash	12.5				
Use of Cash					
Investments	4.7	Function of net cash flow and borrowing			
Cash Balance Change	7.8	Liquidity choice			

Also, when reasonable projections are made by preparing project-ed cash-flow statements and balance sheets for the next 5 to 10 years, we can now evaluate different investment and spending plans for feasi-bility and the achievement of our financial goals.

There are five overtly managed decision programs that determine the shape of a financial situation for the future and an estate at various points in time. These are:

1. Earnings/life-style program.
2. Income tax planning and base case.
3. Insurance.
4. Investment and financing program.
5. Estate planning.

These decision programs are highly interdependent. They are also subject to external changes, such as market factors, tax rules, insurabili-ty, and legal status (marital status, state of residence, etc.).

A brief overview of these five decision programs follows.

TABLE 9-3. *Financial-Planning Worksheet—Pro Forma Balance Sheet (Example figures from hypothetical case).*

Item	1987	1988	1989	1990	1991
Assets					
Cash	$ 4,000	Derived figure from cash flows projections			
Savings Accounts	77,000				
Marketable Securities					
Common Stock	55,000				
Bonds	25,000				
Mutual Funds	—	Should change, based on investment program			
Accounts & Loans Rec.					
Real Estate					
Residence	161,000				
Other	49,000				
Business Interests	10,000				
Home Furnishings	29,000	Choice amount based on use of			
Personal Effects	18,000	cash and food and household item budget			
Cash Value of Life					
Insurance	13,000	Based on policy schedules			
Employer Benefits	120,000	Based on employer retirement plan			
Miscellaneous	12,000	Including automobiles			
Total Assets	$573,000				
Liabilities					
Accounts Payable	$	Derived from cash flow projections and investment program			
Notes Payable	—				
Mortgages	93,000	Based on amortization schedule of mortgages in effect			
Insurance Loans	—	Discretionary and related to			
Other Debts	—	investment program			
Pledges to Charities		Discretionary			
Taxes Payable	—				
Total Liabilities	$ 93,000				
Net Worth	$480,000	Derived			
Face Value of Insurance					
Policies	$264,000	Adjusted by employer plans and individual choice			
Gross Estate	$ 744,000				

I. Earnings/Life-Style Program

Goals: The goals of an earnings/life-style program will vary from individual to individual. For illustrative purposes we assume them to be:

1. To provide an attractive residential environment for you and your family.

2. To provide for current consumption levels that allow you an attractive standard of living.

3. To provide desired medical and dental services to you and your family to maintain the best health possible, given personal endowment and life-style.

4. To provide educational opportunities for you, your spouse and children to the level desired.

5. To provide the entertainment, recreational, and leisure activities commensurate with your choice functions as to investment, current consumption, and estate desires.

6. To assure that these basic desires are satisfied in a manner commensurate with expected income levels and your attitude toward risk.

7. To minimize unnecessary taxes on income and wealth.

8. To set your expectations and desires on realistic estimates of income based on attainable performance, market, and economic factors.

9. To structure needs and expenses to maintain flexibility to adapt to changing conditions while providing for basic life needs.

10. To maximize the probability of attainment of estate, retirement, and survivor benefits goals.

There may be other goals unique to an individual or a family, and there may be substantial weighting of some goals over others. Whatever the goal set, the first logical step is to project your income, expense, and asset base into the future, doing nothing about investments other than what is currently being done (using the current tax laws to project future taxes).

Operating expense items should be projected in view of inflation projections. A good index to use would be the average of the last few years' inflation projected into the future.

Other costs such as residence costs should be developed from expected cost data. If you are buying or selling a residence, these costs should be projected to the time of change or acquisition based upon expected market factors. Special items such as educational expenses for children are based on projected costs for the type of education projected and for the period of time during which the children will be in school or college.

With these projections, which we will call a base case, you can now test your life-style goals to see which, if any, can be achieved by taking the conservative approach of continuing to do what you have been doing. Upon review of the base case, you may discover that your tax burden is growing (and rather high) and that you have cash-flow problems. You might also discover that your pension funding is either inadequate or so large that it will push you into the new 15% excise tax.

One of the methods of achieving your goals over time is through an effective investment program. After all, investment is nothing other than the *deferral* of consumption. In exchange for that deferral, you hope to achieve an after-tax return that rewards that deferral by the substantial achievement of your family's financial life-style goals.

A word of caution is required. All investments have risk and you *must* differentiate between investment and speculation. Leave the speculation to risk seekers or risk takers. Develop a long-range investment plan utilizing reasonable rates of return based on recent history in the financial markets.

Table 9-4 (pages 154, 155) shows reasonable expected rates of return over the long haul for different types of assets, assuming a business cycle level of inflation in the 4%-6% zone. This set of arbitrary expected rates is based on many studies and benchmarks and is included only to provide an estimated guide. The reader should carefully check market data bases to validate his or her own expected rate of return and to review carefully specific chosen investments. Many good professional services are available publicly or by subscription that will provide excellent data on expected rates of return for specific investments and their track record.

Table 9-4 provides columns for you to fill in your dollars and percent of investments by type from your work sheets shown in Table 9-3. The expected return before- and after-tax columns provide arbitrary sample expected (mean) annual rates of return given recent history.

Note, however, that as you move down the page, the investments become less liquid (convertible immediately to cash) and more risky. Some investments, like those shown in the category of *Other Investments,* should be undertaken only if:

- You are in the combined marginal tax bracket of 35% in 1987 and 33% thereafter.
- You have adequate free cash flow.
- You can "afford" to lose the entire investment.
- You have taken care of all of your basic life-style needs.
- You have good tax and investment counsel.

The *Retirement Plan* category of investments may be invested in very liquid instruments such as U.S. Treasury bonds, etc., but because of the tax-qualified plan, you cannot use the money for current use without penalty. Read your retirement plan documents carefully and, if necessary, seek guidance from your employee benefits office or tax counselor.

Now, with a data base like Table 9-4 giving basic information and showing expected market rates of return, we can focus our attention on developing an Investment and Financing Plan. The rates of return in Table 9-4 can serve as a selection guide, plus a basis for projecting a financial plan into the future.

II. Income Tax Planning and the Base Case

We are now in position to make the base case projections using our sample data shown in Tables 9-1–9-4. We will first model the income and spending flows for our hypothetical family. This is shown in Table 9-5 (pages 156, 157). Notice we have displayed only the years 1987-1991 and 1996 to minimize the clutter on the page. (We could show all years if the intervening years are important.)

Table 9-5 is organized into three models. Number 1 is for earnings streams of the family showing gross pay before deductions. Number 2 shows the personal spending pattern broken down into categories from the data supplied, plus FICA (and other tax) payments and exemptions for tax purposes. Number 3 shows the anticipated college costs for the three children.

TABLE 9-4. Investment Profile Work Sheet.

Types of Investments (General)	$ Investments	% of Investments	Expected* Return Before Tax	Expected* Return After Tax	Expected Rate of Return for Holding Period
Liquid or Marketable Securities					
Savings Certificates			6.5%		
Money Market Instruments			6.0%	4.5%	
Mutual Funds (Professionally Managed Portfolios)			12.0%		$\beta = 1.0$
Taxable Bonds			8.5%		Grade A
Tax Exempt Bonds				6.75%	Grade A
Common Stock			13.0%		$\beta = 1.2$
Residential Investments					
Home					
Land					12-year holding period average leverage
Furnishings				5%	Not applicable
Other Investments**					
Real Estate: Commercial				14–20%	After tax (with leverage)
Residential				12–20%	
Business (various)					Variable
Tax Shelters e.g.,					
Real Estate Limited Partnerships				12–20%	After tax (with leverage)
Oil & Mineral				12–18%	

TABLE 9-4. (Cont.)

Types of Investments (General)	$ Investments	% of Investments	Expected* Return Before Tax	Expected* Return After Tax	Expected Rate of Return for Holding Period
Cash Crops					
Others				25–50%	Before tax
Venture Capital					Various, depending on investment vehicles
Retirement Plan Investments (vested)					
IRA					
Keogh Plan					
SRA					
401K Plans & Thrift Plans					
Deferred Compensation					

*Figures are arbitrary sample rates of return assuming 4%–6% long term inflation and risk/return performance similar to the last 10 years.

**Assumes 33% marginal tax bracket including state taxes.

TABLE 9-5.

Asset Detail
($000)

#1 Earned Income-Salary/Bonus
8% Appreciation

	1987	1988	1989	1990	1991	1996
1. Salary	93.2	100.6	108.7	117.4	126.8	186.2
2. Consulting	8.0	8.6	9.3	10.0	10.8	15.9
3. Social Security Income (Cash)	0.0	0.0	0.0	0.0	0.0	0.0
4. Bonus (9% of Previous Year's Salary)	7.6	8.4	9.1	9.8	10.6	15.5

#2 Personal Property & Spending
2% Appreciation of Value, 6% Appreciation in Expense

	1987	1988	1989	1990	1991	1996
1. Number of Exemptions in Each Year	5.0	5.0	5.0	5.0	4.0	3.0
2. Mark. Val. of Personal Assets at Year End	59.4	60.6	61.8	63.1	64.3	71.0
3. Durables & Residence Spending	0.6	0.6	0.7	0.7	0.8	1.0
4. Food & Clothing	20.6	21.8	23.1	24.5	26.0	34.8
5. Vacation & Travel	11.0	11.7	12.4	13.1	13.9	18.6
6. Personal Spending –Transportation	4.7	4.9	5.2	5.5	5.9	7.9
7. Other Basic Living Costs–Utilities	3.1	3.2	3.4	3.6	3.9	5.2
8. Medical & Dental Expense (Cash, formula)	4.4	4.7	5.0	5.3	5.6	7.5
9. Debt-Charity	0.0	0.0	0.0	0.0	0.0	0.0
10. Ded. Charitable Contributions (Cash, B/1)	1.2	1.3	1.4	1.5	1.5	2.1
11. Insurance Premiums (Cash)	2.2	2.4	2.5	2.7	2.9	4.1
12. Social Security Taxes —FICA (Cash)	3.2	3.3	3.5	3.7	3.8	4.9

TABLE 9-5. *(Cont.)*

| | #3 Educational Spending—(3X) 8% Appreciation | | | | | |
	1987	1988	1989	1990	1991	1996
1. Education Spending —Daughter	17.5	18.9	20.4	22.0	0.0	0.0
2. Education Spending —Son	0.0	0.0	20.4	22.0	23.8	0.0
3. Education Spending —Son	0.0	0.0	0.0	0.0	0.0	35.0

The reason for showing each of these models (or assets) is that we can see detailed information for each decision area or asset. When we combine these, as you will see later, we will then have a total picture. This allows us to change different assumptions at each asset or stream level, add or delete an item, add or delete an asset, and then recombine all of the assets to get the total picture.

Tables 9-6, 9-7, and 9-8 (pages 158–163) show the asset models for our hypothetical family's assets. For example, Table 6 shows:

- Residence—Asset 4.
- Marketable Securities and Miscellaneous Stock—Asset 5.
- Marketable Securities and Bonds—Asset 6.

These models show market value, cost basis for tax purposes, dividend flows, reinvestment, mortgage balance, principal and interest payments, etc., given the stated assumptions.

Tables 9-7 and 9-8 show similar information for each of the other assets indicated for our hypothetical family.

When each of the detailed asset models is complete, we can then combine them into a set of aggregate financial statements for our hypothetical family. The first item to calculate is the income tax burden for each of the years. The reason this step is the first one is that you cannot determine net cash flow until you have calculated the tax bill for each year.

TABLE 9-6.

Asset Detail
($000)

#4 Residence—Westchester County, NY
5% Appreciation

	1987	1988	1989	1990	1991	1996
1. Year-End Market Value	160.8	168.8	177.3	186.1	195.4	249.4
2. Cost Basis	105.0	105.0	105.0	105.0	105.0	105.0
3. Year-End Mortgage Balance	56.5	54.9	53.2	51.4	49.4	36.8
4. Annual Mortgage Interest	4.6	4.5	4.3	4.2	4.0	3.1
5. Annual Principal Paydown	1.4	1.6	1.7	1.8	2.0	2.9

#5 Marketable Securities—Misc. Stock
10% Appreciation, 2.5% Yield

	1987	1988	1989	1990	1991	1996
1. Market Value at Year End	54.6	60.0	66.0	72.6	79.9	128.7
2. Value Move Forward 1 Year, for Div. Comp.	49.6	54.6	60.0	66.0	72.6	117.0
3. Noncash Dividend Income (Reinvested)	0.0	0.0	0.0	0.0	0.0	0.0
4. Dividend Income (Cash, Tax)	1.2	1.4	1.5	1.7	1.8	2.9

#6 Marketable Securities—Bonds
0% Appreciation, 9% Yield

	1987	1988	1989	1990	1991	1996
1. Market Value at Year End	25.0	25.0	25.0	25.0	25.0	25.0
2. Value Move Forward 1 Yr. for Div. Comp.	25.0	25.0	25.0	25.0	25.0	25.0
3. Taxable Interest Income (Cash)	2.2	2.2	2.2	2.2	2.2	2.2

TABLE 9-7.

Asset Detail
($000)

#7 Real Estate Investment—Condo
5% Appreciation

	1987	1988	1989	1990	1991	1996
1. Market Value at Year End	48.6	51.1	53.6	56.3	59.1	75.4
2. Cost Basis	28.4	25.9	23.3	20.8	18.3	5.6
3. Year-End Mortgage Balance	36.6	35.8	35.0	34.1	33.1	26.5
4. Interest Expense	3.3	3.3	3.2	3.1	3.0	2.5
5. Annual Principal Paydown	0.7	0.8	0.8	0.9	1.0	1.6
6. Cash Investment— Asset Acquisition	0.8	0.8	0.8	0.8	0.8	0.8
7. Rental Income	6.8	7.3	7.8	8.4	8.9	12.5
8. Expenses	1.8	2.0	2.1	2.3	2.4	3.4
9. Rent Less Interest & Expenses	0.1	0.5	0.8	1.2	1.7	4.3
10. Depreciation— Structure & Furnishings	3.4	3.4	3.4	3.4	3.4	3.4
11. Noncash Ordinary Income (–Expense)	– 1.7	– 1.3	– 0.9	– 0.4	0.1	3.3

#8 Partnership—5% of Franchise

	1987	1988	1989	1990	1991	1996
1. Cash Investment— Asset Acquisition	0.0	0.0	0.0	0.0	0.0	0.0
2. Noncash Ordinary Income (–Expense)	– 0.9	0.0	0.6	1.2	1.3	2.1
3. Cash (Capital) Distributed, W/Drawn	0.9	1.0	1.4	1.9	2.1	3.4
4. Cost Basis at Year End	– 1.8	– 2.9	– 3.7	– 4.4	– 5.1	– 10.3
5. Market Value at Year End	9.9	11.4	13.1	15.0	17.3	34.8
6. Long Term Cap. Gain (–loss) (Noncash)	0.0	0.0	0.0	0.0	0.0	0.0
7. Tax Preference Income	0.0	0.0	0.0	0.0	0.0	0.0

TABLE 9-7. (Cont.)

	#9 Nonmarketable Securities—Acct Rec 0% Appreciation, 0% Yield					
	1987	1988	1989	1990	1991	1996
1. Market Value at Year End	0.0	0.0	0.0	0.0	0.0	0.0
2. Cash (Capital) Distributed, W/Drawn	0.0	0.0	0.0	0.0	0.0	0.0

To simplify the model, we have assumed here that taxes are fully paid in the taxable year by withholding or estimated payments made prior to December 31 of each year. In reality, you may have a tax refund due in the following year or a final payment due in April of the following year, depending on the accuracy of your withholding and estimated payments.

However, the kind of model shown in Tables 9-9–9-11 is a *long-term planning* model, not an accounting model. For year-end tax planning you should use a one-year accounting model to time and calibrate payments. Remember the basic guide in taxes is to withhold or pay estimated taxes equal to last year's taxes or 90% of this year's expected liability during the year to avoid penalties.

Now, let's turn to Table 9-9 (page 164). This is a very simplified summary of the 1040 form showing the components on the tax return (rounded to the nearest thousand). The purpose of this form is to get an estimate of state and federal income taxes by year. Notice the title of each item; then, in brackets, there is a number. For example, in line one we have *Salary [1]*. This stands for salary, bonus, and consulting income as detailed in asset #1. To understand where that number came from, you would have to refer to asset #1 as shown in Table 9-6.

At the bottom of the page, you will see the two different methods of tax calculation—table and alternative minimum tax. This computer model will calculate both methods and select the correct one to be shown in the statement above. In this case, for 1987, the tax-table method is the correct one; the tax is $23,000, and it is shown above as the *Federal Income Tax*. This places our family in the 35% marginal federal tax bracket for 1987 and 33% thereafter. With state taxes this produces an aggregate marginal tax of approximately 39% for our sample case.

It should be noted that because our family has very little preference type of income (deductions), they are in no jeopardy of invoking the alternative minimum tax.

We can now turn to Table 9-10 (pages 165, 166). This is the key planning statement! Our hypothetical family had a savings account balance of $74,000 as shown in Table 9-1. The cash statement starts with the beginning balance of cash and money markets, in this case $74,000. Notice in Table 9-10, the first line shows a cash balance at 1987 (beginning of the year) of $74,000.

The next category shows gross income flows. Here again you will see the title followed by a number in brackets. The number in brackets will refer you to the appropriate detailed asset(s) shown in Tables 9-6–9-8. The third line on our sample case shows *Interest on Excess Cash (6%)*, which automatically reinvests excess cash at a 4% after-tax rate. Likewise, if cash flow were negative, there would be an expense item called *Interest Expense on Cash Deficits*. This automatic feature of the computerized planning model allows the planner to "see" the impact of a planning program on cash flow and borrowing.

The next category shows family spending flows detailed by type and category. Notice the inclusion of taxes that were already calculated in the tax statement shown in Table 9-9. Mortgage payments are shown in two places—the interest expense is shown in the spending group, and the principal pay down is shown in the next group, called *Change in Debt*.

The difference between *Income* and *Spending* is shown as *Net Operating Cash Flow*. For example, in 1987, *Income* was $116,000; *Spending* was $102,000; and *Net Operating Cash Flow* was $14,000. Indeed, throughout the planning period, our hypothetical family has between $39,000 and $<2,000> *Net Operating Cash Flow*. In other words, they are well positioned to pay off debts and invest annually but must watch the years with negative cash flows.

The next group shows *Change in Debt,* and in this case it shows the scheduled pay down of principal on their two mortgages, one for their residence (asset #4) and one for the condominium (asset #7).

The *Asset Transactions* group shows pay-ins and distributions from all investments. Some of these, such as the 401K, are annual decisions. Others, such as the condo and partnership, are committed flows that probably cannot be changed in the near term.

TABLE 9-8.

	Asset Detail ($000) #10 Life Insurance					
	1987	1988	1989	1990	1991	1996
1. Insurance—Death Benefit Year-End, Whole Lf.	30.0	30.0	30.0	30.0	30.0	30.0
2. Insurance—Cash Value at Year End	9.6	10.0	10.5	11.1	11.6	14.8
3. Insurance—Death Benefit Year End, Group Term	139.8	153.7	169.1	186.0	204.6	329.5
4. Insurance—Death Benefit, Declining Term	69.6	65.9	62.1	58.2	54.2	33.2
5. Insurance—Death Benefit Year End, Whole Lf.	25.0	25.0	25.0	25.0	25.0	25.0
6. Insurance—Cash Value at Year End	3.3	3.5	3.6	3.8	4.0	5.1

	#11 Pension Program—Defined Contribution 10% Appreciation					
	1987	1988	1989	1990	1991	1996
1. Calculation Wage Base	45.0	45.0	45.0	45.0	45.0	45.0
2. Emplr. Contrib. Below Cal. Wage Base	4.5	4.5	4.5	4.5	4.5	4.5
3. Salary Above Calculation Wage Base	48.2	57.5	67.7	79.0	91.4	174.7
4. Employer Contribution Above Cal. W.B.	2.4	2.9	3.4	4.0	4.6	8.7
5. Total Employer Contribution	6.9	7.4	7.9	8.5	9.1	13.2
6. Annual Contributions—Fixed Income Fund	3.5	3.7	3.9	4.2	4.5	6.6
7. Market Value—Fixed Income Fund	44.9	48.6	52.6	56.9	61.5	90.4
8. Annual Contribution—Marketable Sec. Fund	3.5	3.7	3.9	4.2	4.5	6.6
9. Market Value—Marketable Securities Fund	44.9	48.6	52.7	57.0	61.6	90.6
10. Market Value at Year End: Retirement Fds.	89.8	97.2	105.3	113.8	123.0	181.0
11. Pension Income	0.0	0.0	0.0	0.0	0.0	0.0

TABLE 9-8. *(Cont.)*

	#12 401K Profit Sharing Plan 12% Appreciation					
	1987	1988	1989	1990	1991	1996
1. Deductible Employee Contribution 401K	4.7	5.0	5.4	5.9	6.3	7.0
2. Cash Investment— Employee Contribution	0.0	0.0	0.0	0.0	0.0	0.0
3. Market Value at Year End 401K	31.0	42.3	55.5	70.9	88.7	227.3
4. Cost Basis at Year End, 401K Plan	0.0	0.0	0.0	0.0	0.0	0.0
5. Market Value of Annuity at Year End	0.0	0.0	0.0	0.0	0.0	0.0
6. Pension Payout— 401K, Nontaxable	0.0	0.0	0.0	0.0	0.0	0.0
7. Pension Income(P.S.I) (cash)—401K	0.0	0.0	0.0	0.0	0.0	0.0

The combination of *Change in Debt* and *Asset Transactions* is shown in the line *Net Capital Transactions*. For example, in 1987 the net effect is an outflow of about $7,000, declining to $5,000 in 1996. Given the net operating cash flow less the net capital transactions, we can now determine net cash flow for the year. For example, this is $7,000 in 1987. The resultant cash balance at the end of 1987 is $81,000, which now becomes the beginning cash balance for 1988.

Clearly the family has the ability to pursue additional investments given the large cash balance.

Table 9-11 (pages 168, 169) shows the projected year-end balances of all assets and liabilities for our hypothetical case. The format is like a regular balance sheet, except the groupings are slightly different. The assets are grouped into categories with personal assets (home, personal property, and cash value of life insurance) grouped together at the bottom. With total assets of $573,000 and liabilities of $93,000 in 1987, our hypothetical family has a net worth of $480,000. That net worth is projected to increase to $1,167,000 by 1996, but when adjusted for 5% inflation, that 1996 net worth is adjusted to $752,000 in 1987 dollars.

TABLE 9-9.

| | Tax Statement ($000) | | | | | |
	1987	1988	1989	1990	1991	1996
Salary [1]	109	118	127	137	148	218
Dividend Income [5]	1	1	2	2	2	3
Interest Income [6]	2	2	2	2	2	2
Other Taxable Income [7 8]	– 3	– 1	0	1	1	5
Deductible Retirement Savings [12]	– 5	– 5	– 5	– 6	– 6	– 7
Adjusted Gross Income	104	115	126	136	147	221
Personal Exemptions	10	10	11	11	9	9
State & Local Income Taxes	7	7	8	9	10	15
Interest Expense [4]	3	2	1	0	0	0
Contributions [2]	1	1	1	1	2	2
Zero Bracket Amount	0	0	0	0	0	0
Net Itemized Deductions	11	10	10	11	12	17
Taxable Income	83	95	105	114	126	195
Federal Income Tax	23	24	27	30	33	56
State & Local Income Taxes	7	7	8	9	10	15
Total Income Tax	30	31	35	39	43	71
Tax Details:						
Tax Table	23	24	27	30	33	56
Alternative Minimum Tax	13	15	17	20	22	41
Income Averaging	0	0	0	0	0	0

The last two lines on the balance sheet are included for planning purposes. First is the line *Debt as a percent of net worth.* This is shown to get a feel for the degree of leverage used by our family. For example, in 1987, debt is 19.4% of net worth, and it declines to 5.4% by 1996. This percentage relates to the ability of the family to take on more debt as a part of an investment program.

The last line shows the face value of life insurance. When this amount is combined with net worth, you can obtain the size of the gross family estate. This is useful in determining the adequacy of life insurance coverage to provide for survivors in the case of death of the breadwinner.

TABLE 9-10.

	Cash Statement ($000)					
	1987	*1988*	*1989*	*1990*	*1991*	*1996*
Cash Balance as of January 1	74	81	91	83	74	183
Income						
Salary [1]	109	118	127	137	148	218
Interest Income [6]	2	2	2	2	2	2
Interest on Excess Cash (6.00%)	4	4	4	4	4	11
Dividend Income [5]	1	1	2	2	2	3
Total Income [5]	116	125	135	145	156	234
Spending						
Federal Income Tax	23	24	27	30	33	56
State & Local Income Tax	7	7	8	9	10	15
Social Security Tax [2]	3	3	3	4	4	5
Interest Expense [4]	5	4	4	4	4	3
Medical & Dental Expenses [2]	4	5	5	5	6	7
Contributions & Gifts [2]	1	1	1	1	2	2
Basic Living Expenses [2]	24	25	27	28	30	40
Durables & Residence [2]	1	1	1	1	1	1
Education Spending [3]	17	19	41	44	24	35
Vacation & Travel [2]	11	12	12	13	14	19
Insurance Premiums [2]	2	2	3	3	3	4
Other Personal Spending [2]	5	5	5	6	6	8
Total Spending	103	108	137	148	137	195
Net Operating Cash Flow	13	17	− 2	− 3	19	39
Change in Debt						
Residence—Westchester County, NY [4]	− 1	− 2	− 2	− 2	− 2	− 3
Real Estate Investment— Condo [7]	− 1	− 1	− 1	− 1	− 1	− 2

TABLE 9-10. (Cont.)

	1987	1988	1989	1990	1991	1996
Asset Transactions						
Real Estate Investment—						
Condo [7]	– 1	0	0	0	1	3
Partnership—5% of						
Franchise [8]	1	1	1	2	2	3
Nonmarketable Securities—						
Acct. Rec. [9]	0	0	0	0	0	0
401K Profit Sharing						
Plan [12]	– 5	– 5	– 5	– 6	– 6	– 7
Net Capital Transactions	– 7	– 7	– 7	– 7	– 6	– 6
Net Cash Flow	6	10	– 9	–10	15	33
Cash Balance as of						
December 31	80	90	81	71	86	216

Now, with these three basic projected base case statements (Tables 9-9–9-11), we have the background data for addressing the planning issues of our hypothetical family. Some preliminary observations can be made:

1. They have ample cash flow and cash balances to handle contingencies and provide for an incremental investment program.
2. They are in the combined 33% marginal tax rate and therefore could benefit from some more tax advantaged investments.
3. Their net worth is substantial and growing, and with modest debt levels, they could undertake some additional debt if associated with investments.

Translated, this states that they have net investment capacity, cash-flow availability, and unused debt capacity. But before you jump off into an investment program, the adequacy of insurance coverage to handle various contingencies should be evaluated. A necessary step before developing an investment program is to review the adequacy of all insurance to cover various contingencies.

III. The Insurance Program

An individual deals with a variety of insurance coverages. These break down into three groups:

1. Health—Hospitalization, physician/outpatient care, dental, major medical.
2. Income Substitute—Life, disability.
3. Property and Casualty—Automobile/marine/aviation, homeowner's, flood, personal property, general liability, buy/sell coverages.

Insurance transfers financial risks on life, property, income, and avoidance of obligations to others. This transfer is made by contract with an insurer for a fee.

Your insurance strategy should be to provide the kind and amount of insurance you need given your financial situation, your attitude toward risk, and the cost of insurance. You should avoid *overinsuring*, i.e., insurance coverage for small potential losses that you could cover out of income or savings without jeopardizing your life-style. You also want to avoid *underinsuring*—if your claim limits are too low you are not protected against substantial or catastrophic losses.

You should determine the kinds and amounts of insurance that you need at various points in your life and then seek insurance contracts that meet your needs. You should not wait to be sold insurance by an insurance agent.

For each type of insurance, there are some simple rules to help you determine the amount of insurance coverage desirable. These are discussed as follows:

Health Insurance is probably the most common form of insurance. A family purchases a policy of coverage (most often paid by an employer) that funds eligible costs when a family member requires medical services. Most policies are complex and should be read carefully. Medical bills for accidents or illnesses can be staggering, so every family should review their coverage as to comprehensiveness (the extent of coverage of services) and as to limits. Generally, you will need either a comprehensive HMO-type package or a combined hospitalization-and-physician-services package plus a major-medical portion with a large upside limit. The idea is to cover the major expenses by insurance, leaving some minor charges, deductibles, and co-pay costs to the family.

TABLE 9-11.

	Projected Year-End Balance Sheet ($000)					
	1987	1988	1989	1990	1991	1996
Assets						
Cash & Fixed Income						
Cash/Checking Accounts	15	15	15	15	15	15
Cash—Reinvested at (6.00%)	66	76	68	59	74	203
Subtotal	81	91	83	74	89	218
Investments						
Real Estate Investment— Condo [7]	49	51	54	56	59	75
Marketable						
Marketable Securities— Misc. Stock [5]	55	60	66	73	80	129
Marketable Securities— Bonds [6]	25	25	25	25	25	25
Subtotal	80	85	91	98	105	154
Nonmarketable						
Partnership—5% of Franchise [8]	10	11	13	15	17	35
Nonmarketable Securities— Acct. Rec. [9]	0	0	0	0	0	0
Subtotal	10	11	13	15	17	35
Retirement Funds—Self-Managed						
401K Profit Sharing Plan [12]	31	42	56	71	89	227
Retirement Funds—Contract Pension Program—Defined Contribution [11]	90	97	105	114	123	181
Personal						
Personal Property [2]	59	61	62	63	64	71
Residence [4]	161	169	177	186	195	249
Cash Value of Life Insurance [10]	13	13	14	15	16	20
Subtotal	233	243	253	264	275	340
Total Assets	574	620	655	692	757	1230

TABLE 9-11. (Cont.)

	1987	1988	1989	1990	1991	1996
Liabilities						
Residential Mortgage [4,7]	93	91	88	86	83	63
Personal Property						
& Spending [2]	0	0	0	0	0	0
Total Liabilities	93	91	88	86	83	63
Net Worth	481	529	567	606	674	1167
Net Worth in 1987 Dollars						
(5.00%/year)	481	505	514	524	555	752
Debt as a % of Net Worth	19.4	17.1	15.6	14.1	12.2	5.4
Insurance Death Benefit [10]	264	275	286	299	314	418

Dental coverage is less prevalent than medical coverage but is now available through many employer and union plans. These generally cover basic services and have low limits on orthodontic work and special services.

The key planning issue many people face is the evaluation of major medical coverage and limits. You always want to make sure the big bills will be covered. This is also true for social security and Medicare, where supplemental coverage is often prudent and necessary.

Income-substitute insurance covers two basic types of insurance. The first is life insurance.

The role of life insurance is often not fully understood. Its function is to provide to survivors substitute income that is necessary to achieve the life-style goals of the survivor's family at a specified level. There are three basic questions one should ask about life insurance:

1. How much coverage is required?
2. What type of coverage should be used?
3. What is the cost of such coverage?

The first step in the planning of life insurance coverage is to determine the *amount of coverage* desired. Based on a projected financial plan, it is possible to forecast the level of income needed to maintain the family at a reasonable life-style level. Commonly, planners use 75% of forecasted life-style expense with the breadwinner alive as a base need for the surviving family. Next, determine the noninsurance-based assets and the entitlements available to the surviving family to determine how much of the need can be satisfied from income from investable assets plus entitlements. From this, calculate family income needs. With that income need defined, calculate the present value of an annuity equivalent that provides the necessary income. This present value is the amount of life insurance coverage needed.

For example, in the hypothetical case shown in Tables 9-9–9-11, our family had a net worth in 1987 of $481,000 plus life insurance of $264,000. We can now calculate, as shown in Table 9-12, the amount of coverage actually needed to maintain the family. The additional amount of coverage could vary from $125,000 to $181,000, depending on your assumption about rate of return on investments and the desire to provide a fund to cover lost social security income after the children reach age 16.

A simplified "rule of thumb" table is constructed below, based on some guess work and averages common to the insurance business.

Rule of Thumb Insurance Coverage (Assuming total survivor income @75% of projected living expenses for family)

Age of Insured	Insurance Coverage as a Multiple of Salary
25-30	4.5-5.0
30-35	4.0-5.0
35-40	3.5-4.0
40-45	3.0-3.5
45-50	2.5-3.0
50-55	2.0-2.5
55-60	1.5-2.0
60-65	1.0-1.5
65	1.0

The next step is to determine what type of coverage you should have. There are two basic types of insurance coverage—term insurance and ordinary life insurance. In general, term insurance is pure insurance with no built-in savings program—that is, there is no residual value. Ordinary life insurance (whole life or "straight life," universal life, life paid

TABLE 9-12.

1. Investable Assets		
Cash & Marketable Securities	$161,000	
Other Assets	59,000	
Death Benefits from Deferred Compen-		
sation and Retirement Plans	121,000	
Employer Provided Life Insurance	139,800	
Subtotal	480,800	
Less: Mortgages	93,000	
Final Expenses	20,000	
Available Assets		$367,800
2. Average Annual Family Living		
Expenses (75% of basic expenses)		31,500
3. Estimated Income from Investable		
Assets (use 5% real return)	13,390	
Entitlements (est. for limited		
period)	14,400	
TOTAL		27,790
4. GAP		3,710
5. Add Children's Education Fund	150,000	
Widows' Retirement Fund	100,000	
		250,000
6. Necessary Insurance ($250,000 + PV		
of $3,710 for life)		305,000
7. Less: Self-Pay Insurance Carried		124,000
8. Additional Insurance Needed		$181,000

up at 65, 20 payment life, etc.) has a built-in savings and investment component: insurance is purchased either individually or through a group. Individual contracts have the highest commission and distribution costs but also may have a lower risk class cost, so comparative shopping pays rewards in reduced overall costs.

There is a wide variety of contracts for term insurance as well as for ordinary life insurance. Some of the more standard ones are:

Term Insurance

Declining Term: provides annual insurance (face value) in a decreasing amount to a specified date at a given annual premium.

Level Term: provides annual insurance (face value) until termination date or specified age for a given annual premium.

Renewal Term: provides annual insurance (face value) during a specified term at a given rate for the term but can be renewed (without prequalification) for another term at the then-age-adjusted and risk-class term rate.

Convertible Term: is term coverage that can be converted to ordinary life under specified rules during the term of the policy.

Ordinary Life

Whole Life: is a face value insurance contract that accrues a cash value that will fully fund the insurance coverage at some future date; that is, it builds up an investment account and in the interim provides term coverage for the difference between cash value and face value. Typically, there is an annual fixed premium based upon age at enrollment.

20-Pay Life: is the same as straight life, except that insurance is fully funded by the twentieth year by the investment buildup.

20-Year Endowment: is similar to the above, and the most expensive as it provides full funding of the face value under more restrictive and conservative rules.

Universal Life: is insurance with an imbedded investment account that has a base guaranteed ratio of return (usually 4%-6%). Investment income varies with market rates and investment product choices.

Life Paid Up at 65: is similar to the above but is fully funded by age 65 and requires no more premium payments beyond that age.

Retirement Income: is a fully funded annuity contract with an insurance component.

Two items are of concern in planning your life insurance. First, make sure you have some of your insurance needs met separately from employer-based plans as your employment situation can change. Second, and most important, protect your insurability with renewal, conversion, and permanent insurance options. Make sure that your future health does not disqualify you from needed insurance coverage.

TABLE 9-13. Sample Insurance Policies' Cost Per Year—$25,000.

	Male Age at Contract		
	35	40	45
Term Policies			
Declining Term to 65	98.00	121.50	153.75
5/Year Renewable & Convertible	77.25	106.25	165.50
Level Term to 65	244.00	294.50	354.00
Declining Term to 100	213.75	272.50	355.25
Level Term to 75	325.00	402.25	500.00
Ordinary Life Policies			
Whole Life (Straight Life)	438.75	539.25	661.00
20-Pay Life	637.50	743.75	870.00
20-Year Endowment	1050.00	1080.00	1125.00
Retirement Income @65 @$250/month	950.00	1193.50	1637.50

The third step deals with the cost of coverage. In general, group coverage through your employer is the most accessible. Generally, you want to use this source to the maximum even if supplemental coverage in an employer's plan is paid for by you, unless you can obtain individual term coverage at a lower rate. Shop around, as individual term policies may be cheaper per dollar of coverage.

Table 9-13 shows representative annual costs for various policies with a face value of $25,000 purchased on an individual contract.

Although these rates will vary between companies and as investment markets change, the relative values stay fairly constant. It is obvious that the savings and investment aspect of an ordinary life policy increases its annual and lifetime costs substantially compared to term policies. The attributed investment buildup must offset the higher cost.

One evaluation of the cost of straight-life coverage and the effectiveness of the insurance company as your investment manager is shown in the following tables. Table 9-14 (page 174) shows the adjusted costs per $1,000 of insurance. Table 9-15 (page 174) shows the relative investment performance of the insurance company compared to investing the cash value at 10% per year.

The tables show that the return on the investment portion of the insurance program is significantly less than 10%.

TABLE 9-14. *Whole-Life Policy Annual Cost Per $1,000 of Coverage—$10,000 Whole Life Policy at Age 25.*

Age	Premium	Insurance	Cash Value	"Pure" Insurance	Actual Cost/$1,000
25	167	10,000	0	10,000	$16.70
30	167	10,000	490	9,510	17.58
35	167	10,000	1270	8,730	19.13
40	167	10,000	2000	8,000	20.87
45	167	10,000	2790	7,210	23.19

TABLE 9-15. *Savings in Whole Life* Compared To Investment at 10% on Cash Value.*

$100,000 Policy @ Age 25			$100,000 Policy @ Age 35		
Age	Cash Value	Invest @ 10%	Age	Cash Value	Invest @ 10%
30	5,370	7,982	30	—	—
35	15,210	20,862	35	—	—
40	28,320	41,264	40	7,770	11,545
45	46,090	73,341	45	21,490	29,338
50	69,900	123,726	50	39,420	56,726
55	101,600	202,814	55	63,230	98,766
60	143,390	326,974	60	94,500	163,235
65	196,970	521,886	65	134,590	262,736

* Assumes reinvestment of dividends

Employer-paid term insurance is the most accessible form of life insurance. Usually, employers pay for some of the coverage up to a given multiple of salary. Some programs allow you to buy additional coverage beyond the amount paid for by your employer up to a limit. The supplemental insurance is usually paid by you with after-tax dollars through payroll deduction. Term insurance paid by the employer for the benefit amounts over $50,000 may cause you to have "imputed income" reported on your W-2. The scheduled cost of coverage over $50,000 paid by the employer is reportable as income because the employer paid the premium and therefore gave "value."

The IRS uses a standard table to calculate the imputed value of the premium paid on your behalf for insurance more than $50,000. The table below gives an approximate estimate of the "imputed" income per thousand of insurance more than $50,000 for several age groups.

Imputed Value of Insurance Premiums (for employer-paid term insurance coverage more than $50,000).

Age	Rate/$1,000 Coverage
Under 30	$ 0.96
30–34	1.08
35–39	1.32
40–44	2.04
45–49	3.48
50–54	5.76
55–59	9.00
60–69	14.04

Disability Insurance is the second kind of income replacement insurance held in case of major illness or disability. Some disability coverage is provided (to those eligible) through the social security system. The approximate maximum social security family disability coverage is about $1,479 per month (in 1987) and can start after five months of disability. In addition, many companies provide supplemental and long-term disability coverage.

Employer coverages are typically by formula as a fraction of your salary up to a maximum amount per month. Most such plans are offset by the social security disability coverage, and thus the coverage is only up to the limit of the highest coverage. If the employer pays the cost of the disability policy, the disability benefits are taxable income to the recipient. If the policy is paid for by the insured, then the benefits come without federal income taxation.

There are two basic kinds of disability insurance. The first is physical or functional disability where physical function forms the basis of compensation under the insurance coverage. This is the most common type of disability coverage and is the least expensive per dollar of coverage either in group or in individual programs. The second type of coverage provides for a definition of disability in terms of income-generating capacity in the insured's chosen field. This is more complex and the costs of such coverage are substantially higher.

Another factor of importance in disability insurance is continuation of basic health benefits, retirement funding eligibility, etc. If disabled,

TABLE 9-16.

Requirements Calculation		
Basic living expense	$42,000	
Home mortgage and other loans	6,000	
Ongoing expense		$48,000
Employer group disability & social security		24,000
Shortfall to come from invested assets and supplemental disability		24,000
Real income on invested (nonretirement) assets		11,000
Net supplemental disability insurance required		$13,000
Additional monthly benefit required		$ 1,083

you often need to maintain your family coverages and eligibilities. This is done either by waiver-of-premium for the specific policy or paid for by the disability coverage.

A major issue on disability coverage is the *proratability* of the benefits. Only if the coverage provides for prorating will the insured be able to continue benefits while working at partial functioning levels. Many policies do not provide for prorating benefits.

Table 9-16 is an example calculation of the disability coverage needed by our hypothetical family from Tables 9-9–9-11.

Thus, our hypothetical family could use up to about $3,083 per month disability coverage rather than the $2,000 per month provided by the employer plan plus social security.

The next category of insurance is the property and casualty group of insurance coverages, the most common of which are briefly discussed as follows.

Automobile Insurance. Most automobile insurance contracts are a bundle of basic insurance contracts. The two basic components (endorsements) of automobile policy are *collision* and *general liability.* The rules, rates, and types of coverage vary from state to state and are different depending on whether the state is operating under a "no-fault" law.

Collision coverage insures you and others for damage to property and covers repair bills. It is the costliest portion of the policy (in part because we wrinkle a lot of fenders). Most such endorsements allow for a *deductible* amount (the amount you are self-insuring). The higher the deductible, the lower the premium. Deductibles usually are available at $25, $100, $200, $500, and $1,000. Most higher income people could easily afford a $500 to $1,000 loss and should take one of the higher deductible amounts for substantial annual cost savings.

The second major endorsement is *general liability* coverage, which is quite inexpensive. This coverage is designed to protect you financially from liability incurred as a result of carelessness or action that causes injury, pain, or suffering to others. Here you want to have coverage in proportion to your assets, earning power, and the types and amounts of recent liability settlements in your area. You should coordinate the upper range of this coverage with any umbrella general-liability policy.

Common additional endorsements include comprehensive, uninsured motorists, medical payments, and towing.

Comprehensive coverage generally relates to damage to your vehicle due to fire, wind damage, vandalism, etc. Again, there is a deductible option similar to collision. This coverage tends to be fairly expensive coverage, so you should lean toward higher deductibles if you wish to include this.

Uninsured-motorist coverage provides insurance protection against liabilities and damages caused by an uninsured motorist. This can obviate (depending on state law) the need to sue your own insurer to receive coverage or compensation.

Medical payments coverage is specific coverage for medical costs associated with an accident. It is usually necessary given the high cost of medical care. Your own health insurance and general liability policies seldom provide such coverage, although in some states there is an overlap.

Towing coverage covers cost of towing. Make sure that you do not duplicate other coverage, such as automobile club membership.

As a general rule, you should coordinate your homeowner's general liability and automobile policies to avoid overlapping coverage or gaps in coverage. Your insurance agent should be able to help you with such coordination.

Homeowner's Insurance. Homeowner's insurance is, like automobile coverage, a comprehensive package of different types of insurance covering property and general liability.

Homeowners have a choice among several insurance packages. All packages include protection against liability claims (with a minimum limit of $25,000). Also included are protection against loss from physical damage by fire, theft, windstorm, hail, explosion, riot or civil commotion, aircraft and vehicles, smoke, vandalism and malicious mischief, and the breakage of glass. These are the typical named perils in *basic form (HO-1)* coverage.

The *broad form (HO-2)* coverage adds protection from losses from falling objects; weight of ice, snow, and sleet; collapse of building; sudden breakage of heating or plumbing system or of an appliance; freezing of plumbing, heating, and air conditioning systems; and sudden injury from electrical appliances or wiring.

The *comprehensive form (HO-5)*, sometimes called the "all-risk" coverage, insures against property damage from everything *but* flood, earthquakes, war, nuclear accident, and whatever else your particular policy *excludes*. The comprehensive form (HO-5) provides the most complete coverage but is also the most expensive.

The most commonly used homeowner's coverage is a package called the *special form (HO-3)*. It is less expensive than the HO-5 form and gives comprehensive or all-risk coverage on your dwelling but less complete coverage on your personal property. Typically, it uses a formula that provides coverage of your personal property up to 50% of the amount of coverage for the dwelling, excluding silver, jewelry, furs, art, and collectibles. If you have such items and use the HO-3 policy, you will need supplemental coverage for such items.

Whichever package you choose, be sure that your home is insured for *at least 80% of its replacement value.* That is the magic number that ensures full reimbursement for a partial loss, without regard to depreciation. With a total loss, you will be covered up to the face amount of the policy. Most insurance claims are for a partial loss. Without the *minimum* 80% coverage, you may not receive enough cash to pay for repairs or replacement of personal property damaged. The example below shows how this works.

EXAMPLE

Home replacement value	$ 80,000
Home market value	100,000

Minimum insurance to meet 80% rule	$ 64,000
Assume policy with $100 deductible Assume a fire with $5,000 damage	
A. If coverage $\geq$ $64,000, your payment =	$4,900
B. If coverage < $64,000, say, $40,000, you would collect the greater of $[(40/64) \times \$5,000] - \$100 =$	$3,025
or	
Replacement cost – depreciation—say	$2,000

For property damage, it is important that you be able to document the items of personal property and their value. Accordingly, you should retain receipts that aid in establishing these values and keep them somewhere else. As a further suggestion, if you have access to a video recorder and video camera, you should tape a tour through your home (including closets and drawers) to aid in documenting the inventory of your losses. Again the tape should be kept in another location. Photographs may also be used to aid in such record keeping.

Most Common Homeowner's Policy Types:
> HO-1—Basic coverage.
> HO-2—Broad form.
> HO-3—Special form.
> HO-4—Tenant's form equivalent to renter's HO-2.
> HO-5—Comprehensive form.
> HO-8—Special coverage—useful for unique or historic facilities.

Personal excess general liability coverage beyond that provided in your homeowner's or automobile policy may be advised given your position or the size of your asset base. This type of insurance is relatively cheap to purchase at the $1 million to $5 million level and often can be purchased as a rider on top of your general automobile or homeowner's policies.

Now once you have satisfied the insurance coverage needed, you are in a position to develop the incremental investment and financing plan. This is the key area in which the financial planning contributes to the achievement of your goals and adds to your real net worth.

IV. Investment And Financing Plan

Goals. The goals of a typical investment program are assumed to be:

1. To accumulate wealth to meet desired estate, retirement, or future income/consumption goals.
2. To attain the highest rate of return commensurate with the level of risk acceptable.
3. To provide for liquidity needs in times of emergency.
4. To provide for specific life-style/educational needs at specific periods of time in the future.
5. To minimize dependence on salaried income sources in the future.
6. To attain the special goals of each family situation.

Approach. The first step is to develop a complete profile of your investment program at present. A sample work sheet was shown in Table 9-4 above with arbitrary sample rates of return indicated. The next step is to develop an estimated cash-flow work sheet that combines the cash flows from your existing investment portfolio and your pro forma operating cash-flow statement. This provides you with an estimate of net cash flows that are available for future investment (or net cash drains) before consideration of financing plans. This step was shown in Table 9-10 for our hypothetical family.

Each of the types of investment opportunities allow leveraging through either general or specific types of debt; for example, real estate mortgages and marketable securities/margin borrowing. Based on the type and the specific investment choices, the financing plan will interact closely with the investment plan.

Before you undertake any class of investments or a specific investment, you should have carefully assessed your basic living needs, existing obligations, special needs (for example, education for your children), investment servicing requirements, adequacy of your estate structure and size, disability coverage, sensitivity of investments to various risks, and your own attitude toward risk. There are several risk types about which you should be concerned: liquidity risk, risk as to return, and risk as to principal.

A sample investment program for a hypothetical situation is shown in Table 9-17 (page 182). Here it is assumed that such investments are appropriate to the individual goals, needs, and risk assessment. Also, it assumes a capacity for incremental net borrowing or draw down of cash over a five-year period of $86,400.

Note that the format provides only net cash flows for each investment plus an estimated taxable gain or loss. The latter is necessary to estimate the effect such investments will have on the operating pro forma where taxes are projected. Caution must be used in estimating the tax effects of such investments on the total portfolio. (The alternative minimum tax may also be important in evaluating the tax impact as are the new phase-in rules from the 1986 tax law.)

Tables 9-17 and 9-18 (page 183) set the framework for developing a five-year investment plan for our hypothetical sample case. Using the data from Table 9-11 (the base case projected balance sheet) for our client, we ended up with an asset mix for 1987 and 1991 as shown in Table 9-19 (page 183).

Using the guides in Tables 9-17 and 9-18, we can modify the asset mix currently in 1987 and for investments during the period 1987-1991 to increase the rate of return and to move the asset mix toward the desired rate level. In asset selection, we should be concerned about tax effects and risk level, and choose those combinations that yield the best after-tax rate of return for a given (and acceptable) level of risk.

Given the 1986 tax law restraints on tax shelters and the interest deduction limitation, one approach is to use some of the borrowing power against the primary residence (up to the cost base plus any educational borrowing). In this case, we will increase mortgage borrowing on the house to $105,000 (the historical cost base of the house) thus freeing up an additional $50,000 for our new investment program. Second, we will use the cash and money market balance to deploy the resources to other investments. Third, we will utilize the full $7,000 voluntary contribution on the 401K and the full 20% allowed on the Keogh Plan. Here a caution is required; that is, one must watch the Section 415 Aggregate Cap in the IRS Code that allows only up to 15% of compensation and up to $30,000 funded in qualified plans annually.

TABLE 9-17. *Investment Profile Work Sheet Assumes 5% Inflation, New York State Residence.*

Types of Investments (general)	Expected Total Return Before Tax*	Expected Total Return After Tax*	Comments
Liquid or Marketable Securities			
Savings Certificates	5.0%	3.1%	
Money Market Instruments	5.5%	3.5%	
Mutual Funds (professionally managed portfolios)	12.0%	8.6%	β = 1.0
Treasury Bonds	7.0%	5.0%	
Taxable Bonds	9.0%	6.0%	
Tax Exempt Bonds		6.5%	Gr. A (hi. mrgn. brkt.)
Common Stock (growth)	13.5%	9.8%	β = 1.2
Common Stock (H Yield)	12.0%	8.4%	β = ≤.8
Residential Investments			
Home (Equity			12-year holding period average leverage
Land Portion)		9.0%	
Furnishings			
Other Investments			
Real Estate: Commercial		5–10%	Aft. tax (w/o leverage)
Residential		6–12%	
Business (various)			Variable
Tax Shelters (e.g.)			
Real Estate Ltd. Partnerships		12–20%	Aft. txs. (w/ leverage)
Oil & Mineral		12–18%	
Cash Crops			
Others			
Venture Capital		16–35%	After tax
Retirement Plan Investments (vested)			
IRA			Various depending on investment vehicles
Keogh Plan			
401K Plans			
Deferred Compensation			

*Figures are arbitrary sample rates of return, based upon rates in force 12/86 and assumes 1986 Tax Law.

TABLE 9-18. *Asset Allocation Grid.*

	Before-Tax Inflation Adjusted Return	Best Suited for		% of Investment Assets Unconstrained Target Planning Range
		Tax Qual. Funds	Self-Mgmt. Funds	
Financial Instruments				
Taxable Money Markets	+ 0–1%	x		2%–5%
Tax Exempt Money Markets	– 1–1%		x	
Treasury Bonds	+ 0–2%	x		
Municipal Bonds	+ 0–1.5%		x	15%–30%
Corporate Bonds	+ 2–4%	x		
Mortgages	+ 3–5%	x		
Common Stocks				
—low yield	+ 7–9%		x	
—index equiv.	+ 6–9%		x	30%–50%
—high yield	+ 4–6%	x		(0%–10% foreign)
Foreign Stocks	+ 5–9%	x		
Other Assets				
Real Estate				
—unleveraged	+ 1–4%	x		10%–25%
—leveraged	+ 6–9%		x	
Minerals	+ 3–8%		x	
Collectibles	+ 8–12%		x	0%–10%
Businesses	var.		x	

TABLE 9-19. *Asset Mix: Sample Case—Base Case Run.*

	1987		1991	
	$	%	$	%
Cash & Equivalents	81,000	19%	89,000	15%
Fixed Income	70,000	17%	87,000	14%
Common Stock	131,000	31%	231,000	38%
Real Estate (Net)	117,000	28%	171,000	28%
Other	23,000	5%	33,000	5%
	$422,000	100%	$611,000	100%

TABLE 9-20. *Proposed Incremental Investment Plan.*

	1987	1988	1989	1990	1991	Total
Tax Qualified Plans						
401K (Common Stock)	700	756	816	882	952	4,106
Keogh (Common Stock)	1,600	1,720	1,866	2,016	2,177	9,379
Tax Advantaged Investments						
Real Estate	25,000					25,000
Oil and Gas		25,000				25,000
Fixed Income						
Municipal Bonds	25,000	1,750	1,872	2,004	2,144	32,770
Common Stocks	50,000	2,500	2,800	3,136	3,512	61,940
Total Required	102,300	31,726	7,354	8,038	8,785	158,195
Sources						
Home Mortgage	50,000					50,000
Sale of Taxable Bonds	25,000					25,000
Cash Pool*	27,300	31,726	7,354	8,038	8,785	83,195
Total	102,300	31,726	7,354	8,038	8,785	$158,195

*Notice that $19,000 comes from reduced tax dollars due to the higher interest deductions.

Thus, by the combination of the above moves, we can invest $158,195 incrementally for the period 1987-1991 while maintaining a cash balance of at least $20,000 for liquidity and flexibility. This is shown in more detail in Table 9-20. Notice the source of funds:

Borrowing on house	$50,000
Sale of taxable bonds	25,000
Reduced taxes	19,000
Existing cash balance	64,195
	$158,195

As a part of your investment program, you should develop a financing plan that is commensurate with your attitude toward risk, the riskiness of the investments, your liquidity needs, and the capacity of your estate and benefits program to maintain investments without forced liquidation.

The sources of credit should be familiar to you. In addition, most life insurance (other than term) policies have loan provisions, most brokerage firms provide the availability of margin borrowing on eligible accounts, and certainly mortgage and other types of financing are available to qualified individuals for real estate. With the 1986 Tax Law, you must be mindful of the new limiting rules on interest deductions.

You should analyze the impact that use of credit has on your pro forma balance sheet and develop guides as to the amount of leverage, risk, and liquidity desired or possible for your needs. In addition, careful sensitivity analysis should always be undertaken with each investment program and financing plan to test sensitivity of returns and cash flows to optimistic, expected, and pessimistic economic situations.

We can now see the effect of this investment program on our hypothetical family. Tables 9-21–9-23 (pages 187–191) show the same planning statements as before, except we have now included the investment plan shown in Table 9-20 to see whether it makes sense and whether there will still be enough cash available to fund ongoing expenses and increasing educational costs.

Table 9-21 shows the revised tax statement. Notice that projected federal income taxes for the period 1986-1991 are now a total of $123,000 as compared to $137,000 in the old base case. With state tax reductions, this provides about $19,000 to fund part of the investment program, whose total cash commitment is $158,195.

The cash flow statement is shown in Table 9-22. Notice that with the expanded level of investment we now have, there is still ample cash flow and balances to fund expanded education costs. Indeed, the sum of the net cash flows for 1987-1991 is ($33,000) as compared to the base case of $150,000. When this is combined with beginning cash balances, we can keep the cash balance above $20,000 at all times.

Table 9-23 shows the revised balance sheet reflecting the impact of the investment program. Notice that the net worth at 1991 has increased from $675,000 to $742,000, and by 1996 the increment is even larger. The debt burden has actually been increased in relation to net worth. For example, debt as a percentage of net worth is 17.8 in 1991 with the investment program, versus 12.2 in the base case. But at age 52, carrying 17.8% debt to net worth is not a very burdensome load.

Thus the value of an investment program can be tested:

- For tax efficiency.
- For what it does to cash flow.
- For the impact on leverage and for the key.
- For its increment to net worth.

Another aspect of an investment program is its distribution by investment type and the expected rate of return as well as liquidity. In Table 9-4 early in this chapter and in Table 9-18 above, we set forth the expected rates of return by types of investment. We could ask the question: How are our assets allocated for this hypothetical case? Indeed, this is one of the key long-term planning decisions, that is, how to allocate our assets by asset type, risk, and expected return as well as liquidity.

Using Table 9-23 as a data base, let's look at the "planned" asset allocation for the year 1991. Table 9-24 (page191) summarizes the allocation of nonpersonal assets into their categories.

The heavy concentration in real estate is offset by a rather high liquidity level. Planning targets are a function of age, tolerance of risk, and the need for liquidity as well as the overall asset level. These targets should be managed (that is, set) and then investments selected to achieve that allocation. Obviously, all the issues such as diversification apply in that even within a category you would want more than one holding to avoid having all the eggs in one basket.

Now, let's assume that these targets and the outlined investment program make sense for our hypothetical family. We now face the problem of selecting the specific investments and choosing the means of implementation. Here you need to turn to the market to select specific investments and channels. These are discussed in the other chapters of this book and, as well, there are a variety of information sources. Compare the commission costs, track records, etc., of each alternative and select those you are comfortable with.

Remember that as you get into complicated and tax sensitive investments, it pays to get good advice from tax or investment counsel to interpret the issues as they relate to you.

One last item that we have not discussed is your estate plan beyond your insurance coverage. Because the tax laws have changed since

TABLE 9-21.

	Tax Statement ($000)					
	1987	1988	1989	1990	1991	1996
Salary [1]	109	118	127	137	148	218
Dividend Income [5 15]	3	3	3	4	4	7
Partnership Income [13]	0	0	2	3	4	2
Taxable Capital Gain (loss) [15]	1	1	2	2	2	4
Other Taxable Income [7 8]	−3	−1	0	1	1	5
Deductible Retirement Savings [12 14]	−7	−8	−8	−9	−9	−14
Adjusted Gross Income	103	113	125	137	150	222
Personal Exemptions	10	10	11	11	9	9
State & Local Income Taxes	6	7	7	8	9	14
Home Mortgage Interest [4]	7	9	9	9	9	8
Contributions [2]	1	1	1	1	2	2
Medical & Casualty Loss Deductions [2]	0	0	0	0	0	0
Zero Bracket Amount	0	0	0	0	0	0
Net Itemized Deductions	16	17	18	19	20	25
Taxable Income	78	86	97	108	121	188
Federal Income Tax	20	21	24	27	31	53
State & Local Income Taxes	6	7	7	8	9	14
Total Income Tax	26	28	32	36	40	67
Tax Details:						
Alternative Tax Calculations						
Tax Table	20	21	24	27	31	53
Alternative Minimum Tax	11	13	16	18	21	39
Income Averaging	0	0	0	0	0	0
Long Term Capital Gain (Loss) [15]	1	1	2	2	2	4

TABLE 9-22.

	Cash Statement ($000)					
	1987	1988	1989	1990	1991	1996
Cash Balance as of January 1	64	66	46	33	20	99
Income						
Salary [1]	109	118	127	137	148	218
Interest on Excess Cash (6.00%)	3	2	1	1	1	6
Dividend Income [5]	1	1	2	2	2	3
Total Income	113	121	130	140	151	226
Spending						
Federal Income Tax	20	21	24	27	31	53
State & Local Income Tax	6	7	7	8	9	14
Social Security Tax [2]	3	3	3	4	4	5
Interest Expense [4]	2	0	0	0	0	0
Interest on Qualified Mortgage [4]	7	9	9	9	9	8
Medical & Dental Expenses [2]	4	5	5	5	6	7
Contributions & Gifts [2]	1	1	1	1	2	2
Basic Living Expenses [2]	24	25	27	28	30	40
Durables & Residence [2]	1	1	1	1	1	1
Education Spending [3]	17	19	41	44	24	35
Vacation & Travel [2]	11	12	12	13	14	19
Insurance Premiums [2]	2	2	3	3	3	4
Other Personal Spending [2]	5	5	5	6	6	8
Total Spending	104	110	139	149	137	196
Net Operating Cash Flow	9	12	− 9	− 10	13	30
Change in Debt						
Residence—Westchester County, NY [4]	49	− 1	− 1	− 1	− 2	− 3
Real Estate Investment— Condo [7]	− 1	− 1	− 1	− 1	− 1	− 2
Asset Transactions						
Real Estate Investment— Condo [7]	− 1	0	0	0	1	3
Partnership—5% of Franchise [8]	1	1	1	2	2	3
Real Estate Investment [9]	2	2	2	2	2	3

TABLE 9-22. *(Cont.)*

	1987	1988	1989	1990	1991	1996
401K Profit Sharing Plan [12]	− 5	− 6	− 6	− 7	− 7	− 11
Oil & Gas [13]	0	− 25	3	4	5	3
Keogh [14]	− 2	− 2	− 2	− 2	− 2	− 3
New Investment in Marketable Sec. [15]	− 50	0	0	0	0	0
Net Capital Transactions	− 7	− 31	− 4	− 3	− 2	− 5
Net Cash Flow	2	− 20	− 13	− 13	11	25
Cash Balance as of December 31	66	46	33	20	31	123

1981, there are a number of changes in the way estate planning is structured. As the size of your gross estate becomes larger than $600,000, you should consult with an estate planning counsel on the best methods of structuring your wills and trusts, owning assets, naming of beneficiaries, etc. These issues will have a profound effect on whether your resources are able to carry out your estate plan and goals under various contingencies.

TABLE 9-23.

	Projected Year-End Balance Sheet ($000)					
	1987	1988	1989	1990	1991	1996
Assets						
Cash & Fixed Income						
Cash/Checking Accounts	15	15	15	15	15	15
Cash—Reinvested at (6.00%)	51	31	18	5	16	108
Subtotal	66	46	33	20	31	123
Investments						
Real Estate Investment— Condo [7]	49	51	54	56	59	75
Oil & Gas	0	22	24	24	23	12
Subtotal	49	73	78	80	82	88
Marketable						
Marketable Securities— Misc. Stock [5]	55	60	66	73	80	129
Marketable Securities— Bonds [6]	27	29	31	33	35	49
New Investment in Marketable Sec. [15]	53	59	66	74	83	147
Subtotal	134	148	163	180	198	325
Nonmarketable						
Partnership—5% of Franchise [8]	10	11	13	15	17	35
Real Estate Investment [9]	25	27	29	31	33	46
Subtotal	35	38	42	46	50	81
Retirement Funds— Self-Managed						
401K Profit Sharing Plan [12]	33	46	62	80	102	272
Keogh [14]	2	4	6	9	12	40
Subtotal	35	50	68	89	114	312
Retirement Funds—Contract						
Pension Program—Defined Contribution [11]	90	97	105	114	123	181

TABLE 9-23. (Cont.)

	1987	1988	1989	1990	1991	1996
Personal						
Personal Property [2]	59	61	62	63	64	71
Residence [4]	161	169	177	186	195	249
Cash Value of Life Insurance [10]	13	13	14	15	16	20
Subtotal	233	243	253	264	275	340
Total Assets	642	696	742	793	874	1450
Liabilities						
Residential Mortgage [4,7]	141	139	137	134	132	115
Personal Property & Spending [2]	0	0	0	0	0	0
Total Liabilities	141	139	137	134	132	115
Net Worth	501	557	605	659	742	1335
Net Worth in 1987 Dollars (5.00%/Year)	501	530	549	569	610	861
Debt as a % of Net Worth	28.2	25.0	22.6	20.4	17.8	8.6
Insurance Death Benefit [10]	264	275	286	299	314	418

TABLE 9-24. ($000 omitted).

Type	Self-Managed	Tax-Qualified Plans	Total $	Total %
Cash & Equivalents	$ 31	$	$ 31	5%
Fixed Income	35	61	96	14%
Common Stock	163	176	339	50%
Real Estate (Leveraged)	155		155	23%
Oil & Gas	23		23	3%
Other	33		33	5%
	$440	$237	$677	100%

PART FOUR

Marketing

CHAPTER TEN

Delivering Financial Products and Services to the Consumer

J. Bud Feuchtwanger

J. Bud Feuchtwanger is President of The Feuchtwanger Group. In this capacity he is a consultant to commercial/savings banks, S&L's, insurance companies, and securities firms on retail products and their distribution. He is a director of the Inter-Financial Association, a member of The New York Society of Security Analysts, and President of U.S. Financial Products Corporation.

He is a frequent speaker at industry conferences and seminars, has written articles for many financial services publications, and published books on retail securities in banking. Mr. Feuchtwanger is a graduate of Brown University with a degree in economics.

Delivery, or how one gets products and services to the user, is one of the most important parts of marketing. It is not possible to be a successful marketer of financial services unless you have a complete understanding and mastery of delivery.

Although delivery is one part of the marketing process, the two words are often interchanged. For example, direct mail is a delivery system and it is also marketing—direct-response marketing. The purpose of using the term *delivery* is to help executives to organize the process of getting a product or service into consumers' hands efficiently and to differentiate this process from product development, pricing and packaging.

We all know of fine products that filled a need, were priced well, packaged in a convenient form, but were not successful because they weren't marketed or delivered effectively.

A good example of not fully understanding the most effective delivery of a product is the bank-sponsored asset management account. For most banks, the marketing results have been disappointing enough to be considered a failure. Banks marketed the account on a passive sales basis and made the wrong assumptions as to why Merrill Lynch was so successful.

The results were exorbitant account-acquisition costs per account—$600 for some, $2,000 for most. To add insult to injury, the accounts that were opened at banks were used more as interest-bearing checking accounts than as a source of loans, securities transactions, etc. Was *delivery* of the product ineffective, or was it just that Merrill Lynch and the other brokers had already signed up most of the people who were interested in the service?

It was probably a combination of three factors:

- The securities firms had already signed up those customers interested in the service.
- Securities firms used their commissioned sales forces to solicit accounts, while banks relied on direct mail, which is relatively passive when compared to a sales force. And direct mail doesn't lend itself to explaining complicated products like asset management.
- Many large banks have had an obsession with putting all of a customer's accounts on one statement, thinking this is what the customer most wanted. In reality, these consolidated statements were so complicated that it took an accountant to understand them. Secondly, the package of services involved was fixed, whereas many customers may have wanted to pick and choose which accounts were to be consolidated.

When we discuss delivery, bear in mind the difference between the passive forms (the branch) and the active ones (telemarketing, incentive compensation, direct-sales force) and traditional advertising, which falls in between. It is vitally important to understand the differences in effectiveness, cost, and availability when choosing the most effective delivery system(s). It is also important to remember that, contrary to popular belief, a product or service can often be delivered in more than one way at the same time.

Deregulation increased the importance of delivery. Deregulation has brought new competitors into almost every facet of financial services. Those companies that enter another industry tend to be the most aggressive and innovative (that is, banks into insurance, mutual funds, securities; securities firms into banking and insurance). They bring the latest technologies and techniques with them. This is one reason for the rapid expansion of electronic technologies.

Electronics provide instant information in enormous quantities, and cost benefits such as reduced personnel costs, customer conveniences, and broader, faster distribution. A bank or securities firm's customers can now get up-to-the minute information on their account or even cash from practically anywhere in the world.

There is a great temptation to look upon electronics as a revolution in distribution, but a more accurate assessment may be that electronic delivery used in conjunction with other methods of delivery is the revolution. The customer service person who has instant access to a customer's accounts may keep customers happy because of the attitude and service of the customer service person as well the information provided. It is more than likely that another form of distribution brought the customer to the institution in the first place.

There is a realization that financial service companies risk losing touch with their customers if they only deal with them electronically and through other nonpersonal methods of distribution. "High-touch," personal, one-to-one contact with customers has come back into vogue. A good example of its effectiveness may be what has happened to community banks. A few years ago, many experts were predicting the demise of community banks because the big, "more efficient and more progressive" ones would take all the customers, particularly the more affluent.

It hasn't happened. In fact, community banks have shown remarkable resiliency (community bankers probably don't think it's so remarkable) and have actually prospered. The number of community banks has remained relatively stable, while the intermediate and larger ones gobble each other up. New community commercial- and savings-banks formations have averaged 300 per year over the past few years. Obviously, many entrepreneurs see an opportunity to distribute financial services profitably at the local level. Community banks sell personal service, friendship, and often a first-name relationship. That appears to be a very strong method of distribution. More on this later as we discuss Citibank's efforts to distribute electronically on a national basis.

Delivery systems can be classified by:

- Face-to-face contact—insurance agents, bank platform officers, financial planners.

- Telephone—discount or full-service brokerage, municipal bond sales, insurance agents who set up appointments, further explanation of complicated products.

- Electronics—ATM's, home brokerage and banking, videotext.

- Direct-response marketing—credit cards and now most other financial products.

- General advertising—now more often targeted to particular population segments.

Personal vs. nonpersonal delivery:

Electronics and direct-response marketing are impersonal delivery systems. However, leads generated by direct response can be followed up with personal contacts, telemarketing, or more direct mail.

The telephone as a delivery system is considered personal because our society accepts the telephone as being an integral part of day-to-day personal contact.

Other methods of classifying delivery are by where or by whom the product or service is introduced to the customer:

Location	*By Whom*
Main office	Salaried personnel
Branch	Partially commissioned personnel
Mail	Fully commissioned sales personnel
Advertising	Outside vendor under contract
Telephone	
ATM	
At-home sales call	

Figure 10-1 shows a chart that was designed to help senior bank management determine how to distribute securities-related products. Notice that the chart encourages multiple methods of distribution.

FIGURE 10-1. *Securities-Related Distribution.*

	MAIN OFFICE	BRANCH OFFICE	DIRECT-RESPONSE MARKETING	TRADITIONAL ADVERTISING	SALARIED ACCT EXECUTIVES	REGULAR BANKING PERSONNEL	PARTIALLY COMMISSIONED	MARKETED BY OUTSIDE FIRMS UNDER CONTRACT
Investment Advice Generated by Outside Vendor, such as Valueline, S&P, or Argus.								
Financial Planning								
Insurance Products								
Asset Management Account								
Municipal Bonds–Retail								
Mutual Funds								
Nonpurpose Retail Loans Against Marketable Securities Held by Customers								
Trust Services								
Full Commission Brokerage								
Discount Brokerage								
Retail Investment Advisory Service on a Fee Basis for Small Accounts ($25,000-250,000) from Branches								

Effective delivery of financial products and services requires an understanding of the uses of combinations of distribution methods. Here are some examples:

Branches of securities and insurance companies are considered cost-effective and productive. But everyone recognizes that bank branches are too expensive to use as a passive delivery system to cash checks and take deposits. These "dumb" transactions can be done more efficiently by mail or ATM. In banking, much has to be done to broaden and upgrade the use of branches as a delivery network. The branch system will be most effective when used in conjunction with other methods of distribution—methods that bring the desired customers into the branch or create a telephone call to a sales/marketing person in a branch. For example, meet the insurance agent to sign a policy, open an investment management/trust account, discuss a mortgage, apply for a complex loan, talk to a financial planner, open a deposit account, execute a securities transaction, etc.

Discount brokerage (independent or bank affiliated) offers an excellent example of using a branch as the focal point of a two-part distribution system. Discount brokerage is a direct-response business. Customers are primarily solicited by direct mail, coupon ads, and statement inserts. Probably 95% of new customers either mail in their application or telephone the information to a broker who fills out the application. Customers rarely visit the brokerage office.

Based on this scenario, one would conclude that it is possible to have a national brokerage business from one office in a low-rent, out-of-the-way location. Not true. The most desirable customers (top 20%) and the remaining 80% prefer to deal with a broker in the geographical vicinity, perhaps a 25 mile radius.

It turns out customers have a "comfort" level that requires their brokers be accessible in case the customer ever needs to visit the broker. It is not sufficient to have a local telephone number tied to a broker hundreds of miles away or a nearby bank branch with no brokers present.

It costs approximately 50% less to solicit a customer when a broker is nearby than when the customer is required to call long distance with no possibility of personal contact. Understanding this concept is what made Quick & Reilly and Schwab so successful. Q&R was better at branching because Leslie Quick recognized that he didn't need to be in the high-rent district or on the ground floor. He just needed an accessible 500 square feet with a staff of two or three. All are supported by so-phisticated, successful, direct-response marketing campaigns.

Thus, one can see that discount brokerage really could be de-scribed as 75% direct-response marketing and 25% branching. Use one distribution system without the other and your success will be limited. With few exceptions, this is what has happened to the banking industry. A roaring bull market distracted them from their fundamental mistake of not branching discount brokerage.

The success of using both distribution systems is graphically dem-onstrated by Barnett Banks, which puts two professionals in carefully selected bank branches (they have over 20 brokerage branches). Results to date have been extraordinarily good. Because direct-response market-ing costs can be reduced by using local media and branch oriented mar-keting, the added personnel do not inflate costs. Barnett's *de novo* brok-erage subsidiary is quite profitable ($2.8 million pretax in 1986) and its profit margins in this area are among the highest in banking.

Where real estate rents are not out of line (as they are in many ma-jor cities), the best bank branch might contain fewer teller positions, but more ATMs, service phones, interactive CRTs, a sales oriented branch manager, an insurance agent, discount and/or full service broker, invest-ment manager/trust officer and possibly a travel agent. But it will not be enough to deliver these products only through personnel in the branch. Other methods of delivery must be combined with in-branch delivery or the insurance agent will starve and the discount broker won't open any new accounts.

Sears is attempting an unusual multiple distribution of its family of financial services, with its stores (branches) as the "anchor" distribution. Sears supports this method of distribution with traditional advertising, direct-response marketing, and the sales forces affiliated with each of its services. While the Discover card is independent and uses only direct-response marketing, it feeds Sears' other financial service efforts by keeping the Sears name in the forefront and furnishing leads.

Here's how Richard M. Jones, Sears' vice chairman and chief fi-nancial officer, once described the goal of the in-store financial service centers, which included Dean Witter, Coldwell Banker, Allstate Insur-ance, and Sears Savings Bank (since sold to Citibank): "We intend to establish long-term relationships with the 36 million American house-holds who shop at Sears, as early as possible in their development, and to serve these families' changing needs as they move from one stage in their consumption/accumulation/investment life-cycle to the next." Sounds logical, but it has not been a bed of roses for Sears. Only its very deep pockets and several years will decide whether it is correct.

Another important delivery method is the use of *incentives* or commissions. Incentives are an integral part of the securities, mutual fund, and insurance industries, but not banking.

Banks have built their businesses by "taking orders." They are accustomed to customers walking in, "hat in hand," and asking for a loan or a mortgage. To switch from this to an incentive (even a partial incentive) system is practically impossible to accomplish in less than a few years, and during that time, employee turnover increases and morale is often not good. But it can reap great rewards.

The culture is slowly changing in banking and those other areas of financial services that have not traditionally used incentive compensation. Managements are testing variable compensation programs both to reward all levels—from top management down to the production level—and to attract and keep key personnel. By adopting performance-oriented bonus plans and similar types of incentive programs, individuals and departments can be compensated for superior performance and meeting or exceeding defined goals.

Below middle management, the banking industry is attempting to get greater mileage out of base salary. In the past, bonuses were automatic. Under recent innovations, however, employees might be granted a bonus or a salary increase if they meet expectations. Those who exceed them receive more. Those who fall below receive less or nothing, thus providing additional funds to reward achievers.

Currently larger banks are paying big incentives (commissions) to their investment bankers, municipal bond, arbitrage, money market, and capital markets employees that compete directly with Wall Street. It is possible for a good municipal bond salesperson at a large bank to earn between $250,000 and $500,000 a year.

Senior bank management's most stated reason for not paying incentives is that they are afraid the employees will ignore their basic jobs and just concentrate on those products or areas paying an incentive. What bank management may not realize is that the level of an incentive regulates how hard an employee will work selling a particular product. For example, paying tellers incentives that may only add $1,000 to a

$15,000 salary is not enough to make them forget their basic responsibilities.

A sales culture requires incentive compensation packages that result in many highly paid officers. Although it is not discussed publicly, some compensation consultants suspect that many bank chairmen and presidents would not tolerate having several officers in their banks earning more than they do.

A chairman of a major Wall Street investment banking firm was asked if he didn't feel slighted because he was the seventh highest paid executive in the firm. His answer was, "Those seven made that money because they generate substantial profits for my firm and increase the value of my stockholdings. I only wish I was the 20th highest paid."

Other combinations of distribution. Insurance companies are a paradox. They have been locked into the agency distribution system for so long that they are having great difficulty moving into other methods of distribution. Almost every time an insurance company with an agency form of distribution introduces direct-response marketing, the company tries it for awhile and then quietly reduces or stop its efforts. Why? Obviously, all of them didn't choose incompetent advertising agencies.

The reason is simple, if you know the insurance business. Successful insurance agents can usually move their business (customers) with them to another agency/company if they are unhappy. Thus insurance companies pay great heed to what their agents say. Because insurance agents have a distrust of any marketing system that removes them from direct contact with their customers, they feel threatened by company sponsored direct-mail efforts, even if the direct-mail solicitation asks consumers for the name of their insurance agents (so that the agent can receive credit for the sale without having done any work).

Mutual fund companies employ many methods of distribution, often simultaneously. Companies like Fidelity distribute by direct mail, through third parties such as broker/dealers, financial planners, insurance agents, and through a limited number of their own branch offices. And they offer no load, low load, regular load funds to the same markets, as well as to different ones.

Merrill Lynch and other major securities firms have been experimenting with ways to reduce their dependence on their high-cost, commissioned sales forces, which is their dominant distribution system. To date, the results have been modestly encouraging. Here again the sales

force, like the insurance agents, can take their "book" of business to another firm. Major securities firms have been able to reduce this mobility
slightly by introducing proprietary products, such as the CMA asset
management account, which tie customers more closely to the firm than
had previously been the case.

A few years ago Merrill Lynch changed its commission schedule
so that its salespeople had an incentive to open margin or non-purpose
loan accounts. Anyone looking at a Merrill Lynch annual report would
quickly discover why. Its real profits come from lending to customers.

Citibank is recognized as the most innovative distributor of financial service products in the world. Unfortunately, in spite of its mighty
marketing efforts, Citibank has found it unprofitable to induce consumers nationally to establish a relationship with it by mail, telephone, and
ATM. The reason probably goes back to why customers want their discount brokerage rep close by, or why community banks have remained
such a successful method of distribution.

One of the most effective and flexible forms of delivery, *direct-
response marketing*, is also the fastest-growing segment of advertising.
It is also the least understood. Direct-response marketing includes the
use of direct mail, print and broadcast advertising, and telemarketing.
Any marketing effort that asks the consumer to respond directly (and
hopefully immediately) is direct response.

Credit card operations, securities firms, mutual fund distributors
and insurance companies/agents have been using direct-response marketing for many years. They feel comfortable with it and use it effectively. Such has not been the case with the main areas of banking and certain areas of insurance.

Because these companies have not used direct-response marketing
to any great extent, their advertising agencies are often not experienced
in its use. The result is a subtle fear of using direct-response marketing.
There is fear of failure, and there is fear of having advertising and marketing efforts measured in great detail, because the cardinal rule of direct-response marketing is that all expenditures and customer responses
must be recorded, measured down to the last penny, then compared
with tests and other forms of marketing.

Every time potential customers call for information as a result of a
direct-response marketing effort, they must be asked, "Where did you
read (or hear) about us? Which day was that?" "What is the code number
in the upper right-hand corner of the mailing label?" Then all these re-

sponses must be recorded and analyzed. Every newspaper ad and direct-mail piece must be coded and recorded. Everything must be tested, then compared with previous results and recorded. One doesn't prepare just one ad or one version of a direct-mail effort: at least two must be tested, and the results compared.

Except for credit cards, this has not been the way most bank marketing departments have been used to operating. Sure, the number of premiums used in a promotion for deposits and the amount of deposits were recorded, but they were not measured against the account-acquisition costs of other marketing efforts. Few banks have run two different interest rates in two different markets to see what would happen and then taken the rate and the promotion with the best results into the main arena.

Once I presented a direct-response expert and the three direct response ads that had been created to introduce a new product to the chairman of a $6 billion midwest bank. The chairman looked at the rather dignified ads and made two comments: "As long as I'm around, we won't have any coupons in our ads. And by the way, if you [referring to the expert] were really so good, you wouldn't have had to waste our money trying three ads." (The chairman relented and ran the ads, but he was asked to leave the bank a year later.)

Discarding lower performing ads and mailings in favor of more productive ones is not admitting failure, it is building a stronger marketing campaign; and it demonstrates that good marketing is still an art, not an exact science.

Telemarketing is an excellent tool that can be used by just about all types of institutions, and not just by the biggest ones with the highest marketing budgets. It can be an excellent extension of marketing efforts for small and medium-sized financial institutions. Contacting present customers by telephone to introduce them to other products and services is even more cost-effective. Even if no sale is made, this technique is a good way to remind present customers of your products. Another profitable technique is to use incoming customer-service calls to introduce other products.

For those products and services that you are unable to market effectively yourself, the second-best alternative is to have an outside contractor do it for you. For example, Security Pacific used the sales force of Madison Financial Services to market its limited brokerage service to other banks around the country. It chose Madison to do the mail solicitation and follow-up because Madison had already solicited this market. While this probably wasn't the best method in the long run, because Security Pacific couldn't control the quality of the contract, it did make the most sense in terms of the need for a rapid and broad distribution at reasonable cost.

Banks have invited outside insurance and mutual funds sales forces into their lobbies with excellent results. The outside vendor controls the hiring, the supervising, and the product mix, but gives the host bank "final approval." This appears to be one of the fastest ways to bridge the culture gap and to get a banking institution into the business quickly and efficiently. The only danger is that the banking institution doesn't seem to convert to a more sales-oriented culture, which should be their objective. These banks rely on the outside vendor for their success, while bank management goes on with business as usual.

In summary, the secret of effective delivery is to combine several forms and to make them complementary to each other. For example, direct-mail campaigns can bring in the leads to the insurance agent, stockbroker, bank platform officer. Insurance agents should be rewarded for referring business to the stockbroker, and so on. The stockbroker should be rewarded for inducing a customer who just sold securities to keep the funds in the financial institution.

A profile of successful distributors of financial products shows them constantly testing new ideas and combining different methods of distribution for greater productivity.

CHAPTER ELEVEN

Marketing Financial Services: Competition Heats Up As Restrictions Cool Down

Robert Wilcox and Diane Rosen

Robert Wilcox, President and CEO of Wilcox & Associates, first demonstrated his expertise in financial services marketing as Marketing Director at Citibank for four years. Since 1980, he has been pivotal in formulating Wilcox & Associates' dynamic approach to strategic marketing and communications for competitive business.

Diane Rosen, Vice President/Creative Director, came to Wilcox & Associates after working with Equitable Life as a sales promotion manager and Prentice-Hall as a senior financial copywriter. Since 1985, she has led Wilcox & Associates' creative teams in developing effective strategic communications for their financial services clients.

Wilcox & Associates is a strategic marketing and communications firm, supporting the financial services industry throughout the United States. From planning and development to implementation of creative recommendations, Wilcox & Associates helps clients build a long-term competitive advantage in such areas as: merger communications, improving/extending distribution, and new product development/introduction.

Forget the old myths about financial services communications. A vastly broader and more complex product/consumer base demands an entirely new kind of marketing strategy.

Gone are the days when financial institutions could rely on a full-page newspaper ad or a change of logo to meet the communications challenge. Banks can no longer count on getting their "fair share" of deposits and loans simply by opening the doors of a new branch. The cross-pollination of functions in bank and nonbank institutions has blurred most of the formerly reliable distinctions. Among other hybrids, postderegulation competition and multiplication of products have spawned the "financial supermarket." Meanwhile, savvy consumers have taken to comparison shopping. Barraged by options, they search for the financial services package that gives them the greatest number of value-added features for their money.

Correspondingly, the need arises for new "super marketing" strategies. A well-thought-out and well-implemented communications program should have all the earmarks of a sound business strategy to determine content, spending level, and media mix. In the past, bank advertising managers were rarely held accountable for business results. Seldom were analytical and planning tactics brought to bear. Since the demise of regulated rates and parity products, this simply isn't good enough. A packaging-and-service approach has replaced the old status-quo attitude. The strategic development of products, distribution, and positioning will determine your organization's ability to communicate unique points of difference that will allow it to survive. The thrust of this chapter is to focus on these strategic and innovative communications issues that are critical for creating long-term competitive advantage.

PROJECTING BUSINESS STRATEGIES INTO THE MARKETPLACE—WHY ADVERTISING ALONE ISN'T ENOUGH

Communications should be understood as a phenomenon that is larger than the sum of its parts. More specifically, advertising is just one component among many and, by itself, does not suffice for today's financial services institutions. To stand above competitors who are clamoring after the same customer base, you need an edge. That edge is created and honed by planning for the combined effect of what you say and do. The power of this synergy to influence your market is tremendous.

Nutritionist Adele Davis once said, "You are what you eat." For financial institutions, "You are what you do." Of course, all the usual advertising tools must be understood and considered: print, broadcast, direct mail, etc. But the bottom line is that the quality and consistency of your products and services say more about where you stand than any amount of advertising.

How do you get this across? What are the essentials in this customer-driven communications process? To begin with, the market-oriented, customer-sensitive issues that once applied primarily to retailing are now crucial to the financial-services industry. Positioning, research, and marketplace sensitivity are no longer exotic terms that are relevant only to the promotion of Coca-Cola or Maxwell House coffee.

Because it is a retail service business, consumer banking has a highly transactional aspect that must be accommodated. Point-of-sale communications via collateral and personal contact not only produce sales but create a definite image. Some of the following characteristics of retailing should be incorporated into marketing tactics that are the key to positioning your organization as different:

- *Consumer initiates the transfer of services.* Know your market segments and the direction in which they are moving even before *they* know it. The more financial advertisers know about the target consumers, the more success they will have in attracting them to their company or bank.

- *Sense of urgency.* People generally want services soon after they become aware of their own needs. Product and promotional offers must be countered quickly because of the close proximity of the competition.

- *Small quantities.* Consumers have a variety of financial needs and generally will purchase each service individually. Periodic servicing of particular products will bring the customer back time after time to execute relatively insignificant transactions. (Depending on your perspective, this can be a risk or an opportunity.)

- *Service: created at the moment of contact; cannot be inventoried.* With products that are also services, consumer banking breeds certain marketing anomalies that deserve special attention. Quality control, capacity planning, and perceptual factors must be managed closely.

All too often, advertising people (agencies and financial marketers) view the creative side as the beginning and the end of their responsibility. That misses the point. We want to place advertising in a *total business context.* In doing so, the emphasis is on *how* we do it (the process) not *what* we do (the creative).

The key is in developing and managing communications strategies that can put you in control to help influence your target segments. You need an integrated communications program that achieves business results for you, not just a lot of intra-industry back patting. It seems that every move taken by the regulators to help our volatile industry simply accelerates the progress toward Mr. Wriston's "level playing field." Now, basically, it's every bank—or nonbank—for itself!

MARKETING YOUR INSTITUTION— NOT JUST YOUR PRODUCTS

As we see it, the dynamic nature of the current economic/ regulatory environment must be viewed in context with the consumer and the competitor. When developing strategy, the following are some of the key issues to consider in evaluating the financial services marketplace:

- Stagnant or shrinking markets.
- Product-line expansion.
- Rapid (seemingly ad hoc) deregulation.
- Changing consumer expectations and needs.
- Creative (thematic/image) churn.
- Changing distribution systems, e.g., home banking and shared ATM networks.
- Accelerating concentration of traditional financial service institutions through acquisition and merger.
- Proliferation of nonbank competitors.

These are only some of the various marketplace, organizational, and business-income factors that combine to become the driving reality behind your marketing, planning, and decision making. Consumer needs and consumers' perceptions of their needs must be addressed.

Our research and experience with financial mass marketing has been extensive. Drawing on that background, we believe that the consumer perceives his or her needs as threefold: transactional, coping/

planning, and interpersonal. In each category, consumers seek to re-solve their needs in order to achieve peace of mind in managing their financial affairs, to attain a greater sense of freedom and control when dealing with money, and to give themselves heightened self-standing (reduced anxiety) in their own worlds. For example, if you asked consumers to articulate their own needs, they might say the following:

Transactional Needs

- *Time and place convenience.* I want to effect transactions when and where *I* choose.
- *Flexibility and control.* Let me manage my finances as *I* see fit, not as you tell me.
- *Freedom.* I want to be free to organize my finances as I want; I know what's good for me.
- *Ease.* Don't make it a hassle to get service—be quick; be competent; fix your mistakes; don't make me do it for you.

Coping and Planning Needs

- *Utility.* Help me save more; pay me a high rate of interest.
- *Assistance.* Provide me with tools that allow me to use money—yours and mine—more effectively/better.
- *Flexibility and control.* Help me solve my problems: buying a house, fixing up a room, educating my children, buying a car—don't simply try to make money on me.
- *Freedom.* Aid me in getting the financial standing that permits me to "deal" in the world today; *help me become resourceful.*

Interpersonal Needs

- *Recognition.* Trust me; I'm important to you.
- *Caring/sensitivity/courtesy.* Treat me well; like me (key with senior citizens).

Engineering the tactics of a successful program requires painstaking work. Substantive research must be done in special areas that impact directly on whether and to what extent any campaign can be successful—such as consumers' brand loyalty to certain financial packages, frequency of financial decisions within a target group, or the volume of business that a target group might be expected to generate. Remember: you are not only marketing your products; you're marketing your institution. It's the value-added concept: why your institution and not another? Why your package of financial services as opposed to others? To the once-sheltered banking sector, competition and meeting "consumer's needs" are relatively new and somewhat foreign concepts, but a frenzy of merchandising alone won't close the gap between customer needs and a bank's ability to provide the appropriate services.

COMPETITION-CENTERED STRATEGY
AND HOW TO USE IT

Rapid and significant changes in this newly competitive environment have made a competition-centered approach one of the major strategies used by leading companies in the financial industry. Several ground rules apply. In the area of competitive ability—back-office operations, advertising/promotion budgets, branch/ATM distributions, staff support, etc.—parity leads to continual aggression within a marketplace. The increasing variety of competitors and product/service offers also means that any one financial organization will always compete with several opponents at the same time. Furthermore, the nature of limited resources causes any redeployment of them to affect several tasks at the same time. Because more-volatile environments lead to fewer competitors, management of change is a critical factor for survival.

Within the framework of competition-centered strategy, management of change becomes the means to the end. There are five major marketing elements that can be managed to produce changes in competitive positioning. Listed in order of difficulty (from easiest to hardest) to impact, they are:

- Advertising.
- Price policies.
- New product or service development.
- Sales process management.
- Distribution development.

Because image advertising is technically easy to implement (tell the agency to create an ad!) it receives the most attention. However, it may be the least effective. One of the best ways to create a difference that can be used as a lever is to find realistic opportunities in the higher order marketing elements, that is, distribution, new products/services, and sales process.

Here are five steps that we have found to be valuable for developing a sound competition-centered communications strategy:

1. Understand the competitive situation and interaction as a complete dynamic system.
2. Predict the competition's reactions to your communications based on this understanding.
3. Allocate sufficient resources—dollars, staff, and time—to support tactics that will make a measurable impact. In the words of the well-known German general, Karl von Clausewitz, "Only great battles produce great results."
4. Forecast the risks and opportunities of what you say with enough accuracy and confidence to justify your tactics.
5. Communicate decisively and successfully through staff, controlled/owned media (statements, et al.), and public media.

One thing is certain: you should be well versed in all media *and* how they can be interfaced for greatest effectiveness. Marketing communications are much more than print and broadcast. Unfortunately, many players in the financial industry continue to ignore the many other media that are available. Do you use at least five of these media—TV, direct mail, branch merchandising, print, telemarketing, brochures, radio, sales-force support? For the medium in question, have you performed these steps:

- Articulated the medium's role in the communications mix?
- Developed a set of creative and content standards?
- Reviewed the competitive use of the medium?
- Set up a means to measure and evaluate the medium?
- Learned enough about the medium to effectively manage the staff or agency who will produce it?

People within your firm's marketing department should have a clear understanding of the pros and cons of all media. If your staff does not have sufficient knowledge, then hire an agency that does. If your agency doesn't have hands-on experience, then consider bringing in a specialist to ensure optimum use of that medium. By and large, the competition-centered environment demands a level of marketing expertise that is not always available in-house. If you do hire an agency to get your message across, be sure they take an integrated approach to financial services marketing that will result in on-time, on-budget, and—above all—on-target campaigns for you.

CREATING EFFECTIVE COMMUNICATIONS

An effective communications process is the result of leadership, teamwork, and the ability to formalize certain activities.

Leadership

The senior marketing person must set the tone for the organization. This entails the formal articulation of process as well as standards of excellence. He or she must manage the inter- and intradepartment relations proactively, promoting professionalism, mutual respect, and, most importantly, teamwork.

Teamwork

The people within the marketing department must work together. The ad manager, the research manager, and the product manager all have a common goal: meeting business objectives. This is especially critical in the development of marketing strategies for financial services where the factors that make for a difference that can be used as leverage with the target-consumer segment may be somewhat elusive.

Your marketing people must also foster a team approach with the line managers who actually deliver the products or services. The same holds true for your suppliers. In today's economic climate, profit margins are squeezed razor thin. So it pays in more ways than one to maximize the efficiency of your communications effort. A small department can accomplish the same as a much larger one if it deals with its suppliers as partners and not adversaries.

Formalizing Certain Activities

We've developed three basic guidelines for the manner in which a communications project should be developed and controlled:

1. *The Strategy Statement* is the touchstone to which both agency and client refer as you evaluate the creative and marketing efforts. By definition, the strategy statement is concise; it never goes beyond one page in length. It forms the basis of all communications projects and articulates the essential aspects of the campaign. It tells the agency *what* it should be aiming for and *how* it should get there. It launches your communications plan and serves also as a self-contained system for evaluating progress. Before reviewing any work for approval, always refer to it. Exciting copy and art work can be unacceptable because they are off strategy. The strategy statement covers the following points:

   - *Objective*, or what you want to gain from the program. State the net effect you intend to have on the behavior of your target audience, and quantify it.
   - *Strategy* establishes how you will achieve your objectives—how the promotion will work. The same objectives can be met by a number of promotion alternatives. For example, the acquisition of new relationships could be encouraged through a direct-mail premium offer or in-branch sweepstakes.
   - *Target-Audience* definition is critical. Whom are you talking to? What do you know about their demographic profile, banking behavior, account balances, etc? The look of a brochure, the selection of a premium, and the sound of your copy will be geared to the group you describe.
   - *Positioning* is the creative "nutshell." It summarizes in a few statements the net impression you wish to create in the target's mind and how that differentiates your offering. This is not the same as a headline, which actually derives from the positioning concept. Creating headlines is the agency's job.
   - *Support* provides concrete "reasons why" for your positioning, that is, proof of your benefits.

- *Competitive Stance* defines the extent to which you want to "confront" the competition. Consider the strength of your position versus competitors and the action you want the target to take.

- *Tone* is the mood, attitude, or style that overlays the ideas.

Depending on the project, the strategy statement can be accompanied by a set of milestones, a budget, and a marketing plan. In a "partnership" relationship with an agency, you can expect support in all aspects of creative development and implementation of communications projects, ranging from individual brochures and signs to multimedia campaigns. In addition, you would receive close support for your strategic marketing, planning, research, and analysis efforts.

2. *The Approval Process.* There are various milestones along the route to a successful program and specific requirements as to who should be involved. You need to develop a timetable that takes these steps into account. An approval process should be structured so that the right person sees the work at the right time. For things to run smoothly, it's essential that approval be given by the right person or department and not forwarded to the next stage of completion before it is appropriate to do so. This helps avoid such problems as (a) serious cost overruns caused by last-minute revisions, (b) disruption internally among staff and other "team players," and (c) disruption or even damage of certain external relationships, e.g., with suppliers.

3. *Measurement.* Often, the quality of a concept or campaign hinges on the marketer's ability to identify and quantify certain types of data. Seemingly simple bits of information can be the cornerstone of what you do, for whom, how, and when. Yet, many marketers may overlook this fundamental step of capturing information. Equally important as gathering the necessary start-up data are two key operating mechanisms that must also be built in at the very beginning. These are: a way to measure (track) results and a way to evaluate the results. With these elements in place, a solid program can be designed.

CONTINUING TO MEET THE CHALLENGE

The pervasive changes that we see already in financial services are only the beginning. Right now, the only predictable thing about this industry is that it will continue to be unpredictable. A bleak picture for the future of advertising and financial services? Not at all. What may sound nightmarish from one perspective is a welcome opportunity from another. With rapidly intensifying competition, we can finally begin to equate and evaluate communications excellence with the success of each financial services business.

In sum, there are two important questions financial institutions need to ask themselves apropos of communications and advertising: Who am I, and who is my target customer? These days, neither question is free of ambiguity. But that's part of the "communications challenge" we mentioned earlier, and it can be exhilarating. It's a time when you can, in a sense, *create* your marketplace and some of its needs, as well as *respond* to them. In the past, customers knew basically what financial services they were shopping for—and where to get them. Not anymore. Given today's wide-open field of choices, it could be a serious mistake to underestimate audience need for education about your image and your products.

We've tried to outline a few of the methods at your command for identifying specific market segments, deciding how to reach them, and positioning your products/services to create a leveragable difference and maximize opportunities for profit. Long-term planning and strategies can help you achieve these goals, but equally important is a commitment to action against *transitory* opportunities. Often, these disappear almost as quickly as they emerge. In such cases, executional excellence and flexibility under acute time pressure can be more significant than a fixed plan. Clearly, there are no more pat answers, and this chapter doesn't even raise or answer half the questions. But there is now lots of room to forge ahead, break new ground, and establish new standards for those who dare.

CHAPTER TWELVE

Public Relations—The Magic Wand of Marketing

Irving L. Straus

Irving Straus is Chairman of the Straus Marketing Communications Group, a Partner in the Financial Relations Board, Inc., and recipient of the Silver Anvil Award of the Public Relations Society of America. In a career that includes being a partner of a member firm of the New York Stock Exchange and an executive of a leading mutual fund, Straus has been involved for more than 30 years in top-level corporate communications and investor relations counseling, including investor and stockholder relations, media relations, communications audits and counseling, product publicity and promotion, literature and design services, institutional and product advertising, and communications for nonprofit organizations.

The Straus Marketing Communications Group, New York, is a division of the Financial Relations Board, Inc., the nation's largest consulting firm devoted to financial communications strategy and services, dedicated to serving the public relations and communications needs and interests of public and private industrial and service companies, financial institutions, investment firms, trade associations, and other organizations. For more than 25 years, Straus Marketing Communications Group has been singularly successful in assisting in the growth and development of diverse businesses and organizations, and marketing their products and services.

The successful financial service companies will, without question, be those that understand—and utilize—the magic wand of an organized and ongoing public relations program.

Historically, marketing, and the imaginative and consistent utilization of the marketing opportunities offered by the comprehensive public relations program, have not been the strong suit of the financial services industries.

Though there has been some movement toward more aggressive and imaginative development of the public relations potentials, banks, brokerage firms, insurance companies, and other players in the financial services universe have pretty much been doing things the same old way, generally emphasizing advertising and giveaways as the centerpiece of the marketing effort.

Now, however, the way financial services management think and act in regard to their marketing thrust must change. Clearly, the marketing of financial services has changed from an investment orientation to a marketing challenge. Those financial services managements who comprehend—and act upon—the changing environment will enjoy unprecedented growth in the decades ahead. Those that wait to see which way the wind is blowing will still be unfurling their sails while the competition is crossing the finish line.

There is no avoiding it—the profitability of financial services entities rests today, to a great measure, on marketing decisions.

In order to establish a credible, cost-effective public relations function, financial services managements need to address various key challenges from the point of view of their own, individual operations.

For example, recognition, on the part of financial services managements, that credibility may be the fulcrum upon which success in the financial services marketplace turns should lead, in turn, to the comprehension that credibility is not achieved solely through the advertising and gift-giving routes.

As a matter of fact, survey after survey has revealed consumer skepticism of the advertising message.

When financial services managements recognize that, while advertising does indeed have a place in the marketing mix, it cannot be relied upon to carry the major share of the marketing thrust, an important step in the direction of developing credibility will have been taken.

To the extent that the marketing mix consists of roughly equal parts of advertising, public relations, and direct marketing, the financial services manager will begin to enjoy an enhanced position vis-a-vis competitors.

In meeting the challenge of developing credibility, there is probably no better route to accomplishing this goal than the enlightened and professional utilization of public relations opportunities, with special emphasis on media relations. Simply stated, financial services companies with the highest degree of credibility with the public will be the ones that will succeed, and the media and public relations techniques such as interviews, feature stories, and public appearances by executives and professionals, are the key to an organization's establishment of this credibility.

In order to move to a level of sophistication in its public relations and media relations activities, the financial services managements will need to elevate these functions to a far higher level in the corporate hierarchy than has generally been the practice.

It will not be sufficient to relegate public relations and media responsibilities to a low echelon group. Rather, the most successful financial services organizations will be those that bring public relations activity to a first priority position in the corporate business structure.

THE MARKETING MIX

While individual financial services firms may be able to commit large amounts of money to their advertising programs, for most, advertising budgets are limited. This, coupled with the limited reach and high "noise" level of competing entries, suggest that advertising is best seen as a means of getting people to focus on the name, address, and telephone number of the sponsoring organization.

Surely advertising has its place in the marketing mix. However, rather than putting all your eggs into the advertising basket, as a rule of thumb advertising should capture no more than one third of your marketing budget. Even that one third must be examined quite closely to determine whether it is, in fact, performing the function of complementing your other marketing activities, or just being a stand-alone presentation of your story.

In this highly competitive marketing environment, the best bang-for-the-buck comes from other marketing routes.

The evidence supporting this contention is powerful. For example, a recent study by the Life Insurance Marketing Research Association shows that many consumers rely more on newspaper articles than on advertising for information regarding investments.

The Marketing Research Association concluded that financial institutions should consider beefing up their media efforts, including increasing the number of press releases, getting media coverage of new product introductions by preparing media kits and scheduling press conferences, and making personnel consistently available to reporters for comment, interviews, and the like.

The fact of the matter is that financial offerings are rather complex products and services, and because they are so vitally important to the well-being of your customers and prospects, it takes more than glamorous blandishments to get the marketing job done.

In this environment, it behooves financial services managers to devote more attention to marketing challenges than most other aspects of their operations.

It should not be assumed that simply having a viable product or service—as in the case of the better mouse trap—will cause people to beat a path to your door.

Rather, the financial services manager needs to understand the competitive marketplace as it exists today—and may exist in the years ahead—and structure the marketing effort accordingly.

In order to better understand the shape of the changing financial services marketplace and gain insight into what lies ahead, consider the findings of an exhaustive research study recently completed by the Cambridge Research Institute (CRI) of Boston.

Some of the key findings this survey developed specifically focus on the future shape of the financial services industry and suggest the challenges to the marketing manager in the years ahead.

As concluded by CRI, the financial services industry will consist essentially of four components: financial supermarkets, department stores of finance, independent firms, and personal advisors. CRI sees competition for customers' savings intensifying as deregulation continues and new firms enter the financial industry.

Financial supermarkets will be the outgrowth of commercial banks and the larger thrift institutions. They will be oriented towards serving a mass market with relatively standardized products. CRI sees banks pushed in two directions to maintain their earnings. One is towards automation and consolidation to control costs, and the other is towards expanding product lines to increase revenues.

The competitive strength of commercial banks will continue to be in distribution. In fact, it is quite likely that many banks, especially the smaller ones, will become *only* distributors of services that are produced elsewhere. CRI expects these supermarkets to be regional in character, with a few national exceptions. As a way of controlling costs, they will increasingly substitute ATMs and limited service walk-up windows for branches. Banking will become intensely competitive.

The *department stores of finance* will be oriented toward higher income individuals, that is, the few million people who represent approximately half of the assets of households in the United States. These department stores will be the outgrowth of the larger brokerage firms, such as Merrill Lynch, Bache, and others. American Express is another example, as are the so-called private banking units offered by certain banks, such as Chase Manhattan or Citibank. Some banks, such as Morgan Guaranty and Bankers Trust, will focus entirely on the higher income and business markets.

Financial department stores will carry a relatively broad line of products that can be custom packaged to a limited extent to fit the needs of each customer. These are the kinds of firms where the consumer will be able to contact a specific customer service representative who knows the client and knows his or her account.

Because they will serve high income customers, these department stores will be oriented toward very high service levels and strong brand image. They will be nationwide in scope, in order to maintain the advertising and computerized networks required to provide these services, and also because of the mobility of their customers. They are likely to produce most of their products internally, due to their strong emphasis on high quality.

The *independent specialists* will come in a wide variety of types. Group insurance plans would be an example, employer thrift plans and H&R Block would be others.

The orientation of specialists will be in two directions: either a standardized product at relatively low cost or a group term insurance plan, or greater personal and local attention such as might be provided by an independent insurance agent or one of the surviving regional brokers.

The product lines of these specialized independent firms are likely to be relatively narrow, but this in turn opens opportunities for joint ventures and network arrangements to broaden their offerings to leverage strengths they may have in distribution, transactions processing, or some other function.

Personal advisors will include tax accountants, estate planners, bank trust departments, and similar services. They will serve a high income, high net-worth clientele with relatively complicated finances. Such firms will, as they do now, place strong emphasis on professionalism and personal counseling, rather than the selling of a product.

By nature they will be mostly local and regional, many of them being one- or two-person firms. Advisors play a strong role in educating and training customers. These firms will make growing use of computer packages to enhance their own productivity and to provide a more effective service.

Clearly, stiff marketing challenges will be faced by financial services managers in the decades of the 80s and 90s. Virtually any financial services marketer will need to heed some basic tenets.

Every organization needs a strong marketing staff. Individuals charged with this responsibility need to be marketers with good training and experience.

Ideally, the marketing program must consist of a balanced mix of communications vehicles—public relations, direct marketing, and advertising activities. Every financial service organization would be wise to establish a well-thought-out, strong, comprehensive, and continuing marketing program.

This marketing program must have the interest and full support of senior management and must be adequately funded and staffed to carry out the agreed-upon programs.

To bring some sophistication into the marketing effort, goals need to be established and progress towards such goals must be continually monitored.

PUBLIC RELATIONS

A well-conceived, well-organized, and consistent public relations program can be your best investment in terms of bottom-line marketing impact. Managements that understand this and make commensurate commitments, in terms of qualified personnel, time, and budget, will receive impressive returns. PR is not a luxury. It is the best route to cost-effective marketing, especially for medium and smaller firms with modest marketing budgets.

Public relations can be defined as a planned effort to influence opinions through socially acceptable two-way communications. The scope of these communications can be very broad (a feature article in *Forbes* magazine) or very narrow (conversations with shareholders to discover their reactions to certain products).

If effectively implemented, public relations can accomplish four things that are crucial to maximizing business success. It can change or neutralize hostile opinions about your company. It can crystallize latent opinions in your favor. It can conserve opinions that are already favorable toward you, and, finally, it can generate action on the part of target audiences.

Several elements are essential for creating and maintaining a successful public relations program.

The first element is management's support of the public relations effort. The results attained from any PR program will be proportional to the amount of resources committed to it. As previously stated, when public relations is considered an important function and is allocated sufficient resources, it will contribute much to business success.

The second element for successful public relations is a well-qualified public relations staff. Your staff should be composed of professionals with knowledge of the financial services industry and experience in developing and implementing ongoing public relations activities.

The third element is centralization of the public relations program. You cannot allow each of your branch offices or regional centers to create a PR policy by themselves. Without centralized control of the program, your PR efforts will become disorganized, and mixed messages may be projected to your audiences.

The fourth element is to open channels of communication between your firm and the members of your various publics. Contact your publics on a regular basis and encourage them to contact you with comments and/or questions. Effective public relations requires a *two-way* flow of communication.

The final element for successful public relations is to set specific goals for your PR program and to measure progress toward these goals at regular short-term and long-term intervals.

Public relations works. It takes time, patience, persistence, and consistency. Ultimately, it can create relationships with the media that will enable you to project positive images to the public. Public relations can produce dramatic results for your company if you go about it in a serious and organized manner.

A successful public relations effort requires the utmost in careful planning, structuring, and implementing. It is a challenge that management should set as one of its top priorities.

Business goals, the competitive environment, organizational strengths and weaknesses, and the firm's philosophy all have to be assessed and molded into an organized public relations plan that complements the other aspects of your firm's marketing program—advertising and direct response marketing.

The PR program should consist of a statement of overall goals designating specific objectives for various aspects of your firm's operations. To develop such goals, each business segment needs to be analyzed to uncover the areas that lend themselves to public relations activities. In this manner, you match your business resources with relevant public relations activities to develop a coherent and effective public relations plan.

Some specific public relations activities that can work well for the financial services businesses include: feature articles, interviews, by-lined articles, inclusion in round-up stories, press releases on new firm developments, customer communications in the form of newsletters and mailings, and speaking dates before targeted community and national organizations that support your established PR goals.

Target audiences of course must be identified and may include individuals, institutions, and "influence keys" such as lawyers and accountants. The media that you work with can include consumer, business, and financial publications that are segmented into major magazines, daily and weekly newspapers, syndications, investment newsletters, and various professional trade publications (medical, legal, accounting, etc.). Also included are the broadcast media—radio, television, and cable television.

After completing your analysis, you are ready to specifically identify your short and long-term PR goals. While each financial services firm has its own special attributes and special market targets, certain marketing tools should be utilized on an on-going basis.

For example, an organized program of professionally produced press releases to report on internal firm developments would be one of the "musts."

Equally important would be an organized effort designed to establish relationships with all of the media—print and broadcast—which cover your area.

Then, the public relations program can move on to the development of interviews on issues affecting your business: newsletters; press conferences and briefings to discuss developments of importance; appearances by your executives on appropriate radio, television, and cable television programming; informational seminars on banking and personal finance topics; articles bylined by your economists, investment, and management people on timely investment, economic, and personal finance topics; and sponsorship of public service events, to name just a few.

These public relations activities can be developed and orchestrated in a fashion that will put your firm front-and-center in the eyes of vast audiences that can be your clients.

Literature and Direct Marketing

This latter point brings us to the matter of literature and direct marketing.

While many financial services firms have fairly comprehensive literature programs, these programs must be closely evaluated to determine exactly how they can better serve the marketing function whose bottom line is added business for your organization.

Roger Servison, Vice President of Fidelity Brokerage Services, summed it up quite well when he said recently: "We have to get more competitive in the way we market financial services to the public.

"For us at Fidelity," he said, "it's meant some new tools. We traditionally sold our mutual funds through sales force, and barely broke even on that operation. Today, it costs us less than 1% of our assets to bring new money in, and yet we bring it in at five times the rate we did with our broker-dealers.

"How do we do it? With more efficient tools. Through newspaper ads, with radio, with direct mail, and with 800 phone lines. In the future, we will be doing it with cable television, with Videotex, with telemarketing. We are experimenting today with things like voice recognition computers that take human labor out of the transaction."

In order to succeed in the present marketplace, you also must have a message that is clear and easy to understand. "We are witnessing in all areas of the marketplace a movement—a megatrend"—Joe Capo, publisher of *Crain's Chicago Business* recently wrote—"from generalization to specialization. In communications we are shifting from a society of mass communications to class communications. Network television is weakening every day because of cable television's power of specialization."

Specialization is winning out in the print media too. We used to have national publications; we now see regional publications as well as those aimed at very specific markets. We must learn to be aware of these trends and to use them for our own advantage.

IMPLEMENTING THE PROGRAM

Mounting a successful public relations effort requires careful attention to the implementation of some key aspects of the structure.

Media Relations

A key element in the development of successful media relations is to give an individual in your organization the specific responsibility of establishing and maintaining contact with the media. Depending on the size, complexity, and available budget of your organization, you can have a full-time media specialist or you can designate an individual within your firm to carry this responsibility along with additional duties. The following tasks should be included among the media specialist's major concerns:

1. *Maintain media lists.* This function requires care and attention. Your media list must be up-to-date when the time comes to send out news releases. If there is any doubt, the media specialist should verify the information on the list.
2. *Analyze carefully* story lines, identify appropriate media exposure, and time presentations.

3. *Have frequent, face-to-face, professional contact with your target media.* The ideal relationship is one that combines a fine balance between business and friendships with journalists. Such relationships are established through personal visits, lunches, occasional telephone calls, and by providing useful information. Depending on your firm's circumstances, the personal styles of editors and broadcasters in your area, and the established community public relations procedures, your media specialist will have to judge the best course of action to take when establishing your firm's media contacts.

4. *Be a primary contact to the media.* The media specialist needs to be the primary contact for press releases, feature story development, or interview and quote opportunities with local media editors and broadcasters.

5. *Cultivate out-of-town press.* In the process of developing local and national press relations, your media specialist should cultivate the bureaus of out-of-town media for possible coverage of your stories. Don't expect immediate results from this quarter. Patience and service, however, will be rewarded.

6. *Become a resource.* The first step in becoming a source of information is disarmingly simple. Let your target news media know that you exist. Inform them about your professional activities, your areas of expertise, your location. Make yourself or your media specialist available.

Once your firm becomes identified by a news department as a source of information on certain topics, you can expect to be called whenever these topics hit the news. It's good procedure for the news people and it could be good for you, too. Once your media specialist is established as a reliable source of information, the media contacts can in turn become a source of information for you.

To be a good source for the news media, your people must understand the constraints and demands of the media person's job and be aware of any current events upon which your organization may be asked to comment. Over time, as your firm provides more and more information and proves to be reliable and credible, the reporters and editors will consider your organization a primary resource for their work in covering the news.

Your firm's worth as a resource is based on the reliability and usefulness of the information you can provide. Resources are as valuable to reporters and editors as paychecks. In talking about their resources, the highest accolade reporters or editors can give is: "They have always provided solid information, have never lied to me, and can be counted on for solid information in the future."

This status doesn't develop immediately or on its own. It takes weeks, months, or even years of hard work, and includes "credibility initiatives" on your part. These initiatives may take various forms. One is to maintain good professional relationships with the media and to consistently provide usable and reliable information. Respond to the media's information requests quickly. If you or your media specialist are unable to provide the information, refer them to other sources that can. Suggest general ideas for feature stories, and provide supportive documentation and additional industry representatives to discuss the story. Initiate activities for public benefit, which may or may not have direct benefit to your organization. Finally, when providing information, try to make yours more reliable than that from other potential sources in your area of activity.

7. *Establish a public spokesperson.* Any organization seeking a presence in the news media should designate one or more public spokespersons to represent the firm. Such spokespersons should:

- Be senior executives who are familiar with all aspects of the organization.
- Have the ability and desire to develop a rapport with the media.
- Understand the techniques of speaking to target audiences.
- Have some measure of authority within the firm, since reporters like to talk to people in charge.
- Convey the image that the firm wants to project.
- Be briefed in advance for any interviews.
- Have access to information as needed.
- Have a complete understanding of the marketing process.

8. *Develop effective public working relationships.* Effective public relations requires positive working relationships with the media. The

most common pitfall is to consider media people and their inquiries as a nuisance or to treat them in a way that suggests you feel you are doing them a favor by being in touch. Successful media relations rests on mutual respect and the realization that by *helping* reporters in their work, you will be helping yourself to bigger and better press and broadcast visibility. For the most part, the media comes with a positive mindset; you can aid and abet this by being responsive; or, you can begin to build negative responses by being unavailable and unresponsive. The former course is far preferable, and from it great opportunities for free publicity will be available to your company.

9. *Use experience-proven techniques in working with the print media:*

   a. Familiarize yourself with the various sections of your local and weekly newspapers, especially the sections on finance, business, and local news. Do they handle news stories separately or capsulize them in a "What's Happening?" column? Do they run interview features? What about photos?

   b. Become familiar with each newspaper's deadline, daily or weekly. Any stories submitted should be prepared ahead of time to be delivered well in advance of those deadlines.

   c. Take the direct approach if you wish to solicit an interview. Write your contact a letter outlining your idea.

   d. Use the same approach if you wish to solicit coverage of a special event, such as the opening of a new facility or a workshop being held in the area. Phone your contacts at smaller dailies and weeklies or send a "Memo to the Editor" to those at larger papers. Give a brief outline of the event, its importance to the community, and point out the news possibilities.

   e. Unless a story is given to one newspaper on an exclusive basis, make sure it is released to all papers in the area on the same day. A newspaper that is scooped on a story of broad community interest is less apt to be cooperative the next time around.

10. *Use time-tested rules in working with radio and television:*

    a. When mailing stories of general community interest, be sure to include the news editors of local radio and TV stations. Important stories should be hand-delivered whenever possible.

    b. When soliciting radio and TV coverage of a special event, send news directors a "Memo" similar to the one for newspaper editors, emphasizing the general appeal of the event. For TV, include any special video possibilities.

c. Schedule distribution of your releases so that the print and broadcast media can run your story on the same day or as close in time as possible.

11. *Don't overlook radio and television talk shows,* which offer excellent opportunities to air fund and investment stories live or on tape.

a. Send the assignment editor a brief letter suggesting a possible interview.

b. Follow up with a personal phone call.

Many stations interview guests individually or present two or more in panel sessions. Many TV shows are videotaped for airing at a later time. Some radio stations conduct interviews by phone and tape them for later broadcast. Some radio and TV stations have "call in" shows where guests answer questions telephoned in by listeners and viewers.

12. *Be prepared for the occasions when the press calls you.* Reporters often call business executives for information or comments on financial issues. A call from a reporter presents both opportunity and risk for your organization. If you act in an uncooperative manner, your firm's reputation among the business press may suffer. On the other hand, you can build a positive image with the press, and ultimately the buying public, if you are responsive to the media's inquiries. The press can call at awkward times. You may even feel uncomfortable talking to reporters. Regardless, it's very important for you, as a representative of your firm, to answer when the press calls. Here are some tips on dealing with calls from the news media:

a. *Always answer the call*—We already noted the benefits of being responsive and the dangers of being uncooperative, but this is an important point that can't be stressed enough. Answer every time reporters call, even if you're too busy or don't want to talk about the subject in question. You can have your secretary screen the calls. Be sure to find out the reporter's deadline and specific topics of discussion or questions. The provide your response well before the deadline. It's particularly important for you to answer calls from the press during crisis situations. Remember that if reporters call about a controversial issue regarding your firm, they are giving you a chance to present your side of the story.

b. *Assume ignorance on the reporter's part*—in many cases, a reporter may be knowledgeable on several topics, but may not fully understand your profession. Many reporters know relatively little about financial services. Some could know a great deal about one facet, but nothing about your particular firm. That's why you must listen closely to reporters' questions and try to determine whether they understand the issues involved in your discussion. But in doing so, be careful not to talk down to the reporter. Never insult a journalist's intelligence.

c. *Avoid industry jargon*—Every industry has jargon and shorthand that is gobbledygook to outsiders. Talk to reporters in everyday English.

d. *Establish the ground rules*—When you agree to talk to a reporter about a certain topic, everything you say about it can be subject to quote and attribution in the next day's paper. Some reporters will accept comments off the record, but others won't. Reputable reporters will abide by any ground rules, provided they know what they are before the interview begins. Even so, try to avoid off-the-record statements, especially those that directly criticize your competition.

e. *The presses roll regardless*—A deadline is a deadline. The story will appear without you if you don't answer. Even if it's just a survey story (How will the upcoming presidential elections affect the stock market?), by not responding you've lost a chance to be identified as an industry expert.

f. *Don't try to intimidate*—Don't tell a reporter that you are a big advertiser in his publication. Don't brag that you are close buddies with the publisher. Don't accuse the reporter of writing a story only to sell newspapers. Don't comment that reporters are all biased. Don't say that the subject is too complicated for the reporter to grasp.

g. *Don't guess and don't rush*—The reporter is calling you for information that he intends to publish. If you don't know whether industry sales are up 10% or down 30% this year, don't just toss out a number. That number can pop up in tomorrow's newspaper with your name attached. If you cannot provide the requested information, give the reporter a name of an industry colleague who you think can.

h. *Don't deny the obvious*—If a reporter wants to know about a negative development, don't become defensive. Don't brush off the questions with a statement that denies the situation exists. People accept forthright responses. Stonewalling makes them nervous and suspicious.

i. *You don't have to talk*—In fact, nobody has to talk to the press. But, refusing to talk denies you an outlet for your viewpoint and an opportunity to tell the public your side of the story. If you feel that you must refuse comment, be polite but firm.

In any case, it's better to be quoted as saying you cannot presently comment on an issue than have the story appear with a notation that "firm officials refused to return phone calls regarding the matter."

13. *Be prepared for interviews.* Once you interest a news organization in a story, you will most likely be approached for interviews. Reporters and editors see your article suggestions and/or news releases as the starting points for a story. They advance the story by interviewing authorities who can provide expert information on the subject in question. Thorough preparation is essential if you are to successfully convey your messages to the interviewer and, ultimately, to the public. Here are some basic suggestions and guidelines that will assist you in preparing for interviews:

a. *Interviews are the basic tool of news gathering.* Reporters must rely on accounts of event participants and related experts to gain sufficient knowledge to write their stories.

b. *An interview is not a conversation.* It is like a formal but not unfriendly debate, during which the reporter represents the public and your responses or comments are directed to the public through the news media. You must understand this very important role structure in order to effectively convey your story.

c. *The reporter interviews you for information to develop a good story.* Reporters are not interested in flattering or favoring you, nor in damaging you personally. They just want news.

d. *Do your homework.* It is difficult enough to remember everything about your story when you aren't under pressure. It is even more difficult when you are "on stage." Take the time to brush up on current events as they affect you, recent news stories about your organization, and the latest relevant data on your industry. Good reporters will also do their homework before interviewing you.

e. *Anticipate key questions.* Your own knowledge of your story should point out areas of potential interest, hot spots, or controversies.

f. *Prepare key answers.* Have answers ready for key questions you have anticipated, including, if possible, quotable statements or phrases that present your answers in a catchy way.

g. *You have certain rights* as an interview subject, which you can either assert or negotiate for, as part of your agreement to be interviewed. This is especially true if a reporter from the news media has requested the interview.

   • You can help determine the time and location.

   • You can determine—in advance—the length of the interview.

   • You can ask in advance for a list of topics to be covered—but not specific questions—to help prepare to be a good interview subject.

   • You can set your own pace for answering questions—and give yourself time to think before speaking.

   • You can challenge questionable facts and assumptions, but be sure you are capable of refuting them before you raise any doubt.

   • You can question dubious sources of information.

   • You can use "human" language, anecdotes, illustrations.

   • You can personalize answers.

   • You can frame your answers from the public's point of view.

   • You can increase your credibility by revealing any self-interest.

h. *Have interview techniques at hand.* Once you are familiar with what an interview is, and after you have done your homework and anticipated key questions and key answers, you are ready for 17 points that can save your life during an interview.

- Make the interview worthwhile for you. Tell your story!

- Listen very carefully to each question. Questions that are "off the subject" may be a signal that the interviewer doesn't understand the topic. You might want to offer a quick overview.

- Speak only for yourself or your organization—not for your industry as a whole, unless you are an industry spokesperson.

- If you get angry, count to ten before proceeding. Never respond in anger.

- Avoid arguments with the reporter. Your argumentativeness, not the reporter's, may show up in print or on the air.

- If interrupted, wait for your turn and proceed with your answer.

- Challenge any effort to put words in your mouth. Otherwise, you may end up appearing to agree to points you disagree with, or admitting something you don't agree with.

- When presented with a laundry list of questions, identify the question you are responding to before you answer.

- Broaden your answers to make your points—don't play verbal Ping-Pong with the interviewer.

- Put your main points or conclusion first, followed by supporting points or arguments if necessary. In business particularly, many people are conditioned to give supporting points before the main point—in an interview you must do the opposite.

- Speak plain English. Industry jargon, company lingo, or abbreviations that are familiar to you as an insider may have no meaning to the general public.

- Don't be evasive. Evasiveness is a signal to the interviewer that you have something to hide.

- If you don't know the answer to a question, say so. Offer to find the answer as soon as possible and then provide the information to the interviewer. Resist any temptation to make up an answer, or to withhold information after you have promised it.

- If you absolutely cannot divulge information, state why in a matter-of-fact way.

- Be positive, not defensive. Take the trouble to present your point of view in a positive manner.

- Resist any temptation or effort to get you to attack other organizations or competitors. Your accusations or attacks may preempt the rest of your interview.

- Tell the truth. A half-truth is a half-lie. You are remiss if you allow a reporter to accept a partial truth as a truthful answer. Should the situation ever come to public attention, you will lose credibility. TELL THE TRUTH! TELL THE TRUTH! TELL THE TRUTH!

There are as many different approaches to interviews as there are people who "give" or "take" them. Your job during an interview is to convey the information you want the public to receive. Most frequently, it will be on a subject you want the journalist to write about or broadcast.

The interviewer will usually have the advantage of experience over you. Remember, interviewers may conduct as many interviews during a week or month as you may give in your lifetime. But you have the *knowledge* advantage. Very seldom will you be interviewed by a reporter who knows anywhere near as much about your subject as you do. You can plan for interviews, prepare for them and even practice. Yes, practice. In formal sessions, or informally, you can—and should—go over these suggestions and apply as many as possible to *your* story, to *your* interview. If you are thoroughly prepared beforehand, you will find your interviews very enjoyable, and highly productive.

14. *Prepare news releases*. News releases are integral facets of the successful public relations/media relations activity.

  a. First you must decide whether your news is really worthy of a press release. If the answer to that question is yes, then organize your thoughts, identify your spokesperson, and gather the pertinent facts.

  b. A printed news release form is nice, but not necessary. If you don't have one, type NEWS RELEASE in caps at the top of the first page, just under your company letterhead. To the right, type the date, the word "CONTACT:" (followed by the name and phone number of a media contact), and the date for release (either "FOR IMME-

DIATE RELEASE" or a future date you have reason to select—"FOR RE-
LEASE: June 1, 1987").

c. Leave wide margins and spaces between the release line and copy
itself so the editor will have room to write a headline.

d. ALWAYS double or triple space your releases. Type on *one side* of a
page only.

e. If your copy continues to a second page, end the first one at the
conclusion of a paragraph and type "MORE" at the bottom of page
1. Number the second and resume with the next complete paragraph. Follow the same procedure for each successive page. When
the text is completed, use # # # marks to denote the end.

f. Releases can be inexpensively duplicated by copy machine or offset printing. The principle cost will be first class mail.

g. *The meat of the story*—the *Who, What, Where,* and *Why,* and
sometimes *How*—should be in the first one or two paragraphs,
with succeeding paragraphs giving more detail. When faced with
space limitations, editors usually cut from the bottom.

h. *Keep sentences short and to the point.* Use adjectives sparingly
and enclose all of your personal observations in quotes.

i. *Names make news.* Editors prefer to have people to quote, rather
than anonymous spokespersons.

j. *Two or three page* press releases are generally an ideal maximum.
Longer releases are only applicable in special circumstances which
require added text or supporting graphics. Usually, these can be
packaged separately and used as attachments.

k. Target your press releases to specific publications, or categories of
publications. You can do this by slanting the whole release, adding
opening paragraphs, or using headlines that highlight news of interest to particular audiences.

l. After completing your release, read it over carefully for absolute
accuracy. Eliminate all typographical errors. Be as neat as
possible.

m. Photos or illustrations do increase the chances of publication.

n. Hand delivery of your news release is best. If it must be mailed, a
good attention getter is to stamp or write *News* on the outside of
the envelope.

o. Attention to your release may be heightened if you send an accompanying handwritten or typed personal note briefly pointing to some aspect of the release that may be of particular interest to the individual editor or broadcaster.

p. Observe the same release date for all newspaper and broadcast stations receiving your release.

q. A phone follow-up to the editor or broadcaster can be useful, but must be used with the greatest discretion and only when the news is important enough to the public to warrant additional input or assistance.

r. You should conclude all releases with a standard paragraph that describes your firm, etc. This may sound repetitive, but for most editors the background will be useful both in regard to your present press release and possible future contacts.

s. If you need to get tear sheets on stories that may result from your release, *don't* burden the editor with this request. Go to your newsstand, or the back issue department of the publication.

In sum, there is an arsenal of tools that can be used quite effectively to market financial services, but which are still largely untapped by most financial services businesses.

With the financial service business undergoing the revolution that it is, survival for each and every one will greatly depend on the effectiveness with which each organization markets its products and services.

No longer will it suffice to go with self-serving messages accompanied by addresses and telephone numbers.

No longer will it suffice to put most of the marketing eggs into the advertising basket.

No longer will it suffice to treat marketing as a necessary evil and relegate it to people who have other duties. And, finally, no longer will it suffice to operate without a strong marketing staff and a strong marketing plan.

Those financial service organizations that heed the call to meet the marketing challenge will be well on the road to winning an outsized market share.

INDEX

technology and
and branch as product center, 95–96
as decision-making tools, 96–97
discount brokerage and, 93–99
and increase in availability of financial
 information, 95
and independent investors, 93–99
and ways of selling investment information services, 97–98
Money market business, deregulation of,
 40–41
Money market deposit account, bank,
 40–41
Money market mutual fund
 advent of, in 1970s, 40
 tax-exempt, 27
Moody's Investors Service Inc., 16–17
Mortgage borrowing for investment, 181
Municipal bond(s)
 closed-end portfolio of, 18–25
 individual, tax-free investing and, 15–
  16
 interest-rate spread and, 8
 percent of outstanding held, by sector,
  2, 4, 5
 risk and, 12, 14
 zero coupon and stripped, 17
  in unit investment trust, 25
Municipal bond defaults, 14
Municipal bond insurance, 17
Municipal bond mutual funds, 25–27
 open-end, 25–26, 27
 sponsors of, and market-movement
  risk, 28
 versus unit investment trust, 27
Mutual fund companies, methods of distribution and, 203
Mutual fund factor in brokerage business,
 64
Mutual fund industry and bank in joint
 venture, 107–108
Mutual fund industry wholesaling to
 banks, 39–49
 banks' "make or buy" decision in, 45–
 46

discount brokerage and, 41–42
enormous market for, 43–44
fund families and banks involved in
 Dreyfus, 47–48
 Federated Investors, Inc., of
  Pittsburgh, 48
 Fidelity Investments, 41–43, 45–49
 Kemper Financial Services of Chicago, 48
 Massachusetts Financial Service
  Company, 48
 Security Pacific Bank (Florida), 41–
  42, 48–49
 Southeast Bank (Florida), 48–49
 market segmentation in, 44–45
 study of, by Market Facts, Inc., 43–44
 tax-free investing and, 48
Mutual fund sales charge (or "load"), unit
 trusts versus, 28
Mutual funds
 available through banks, 42–45
 bank distribution of, 107–109
 and banks as competitors or partners,
  40–41
 and entry-level barrier, 126
 money market, 40
  tax exempt, 27
 municipal bond, 25–27
 open-end
  costs and fees in, 25–26
  versus closed-end, 25–27
 regulation and sale of, 107–109
 tax-free closed-end, 26–27

N

National Bank Act of 1933, see Glass-
 Steagall Act
National Credit Union Association and
 INVEST, 79, 81

O

OCC, see Comptroller of the Currency
Over-the-counter brokers, 115

and marketing of financial services, orientation of, 219
need to elevate public relations function to higher level, 220
need to understand competitive marketplace and structure marketing effort accordingly, 221
possible accomplishments of, 224
strengthening media efforts, 221
Public relations program, 223–228; *see also* Media specialist's major concerns
developing literature and direct marketing tools for, 226–227
elements essential in, 224
implementing, 227–238
specific activities in, 225–226
as statement of overall goals and objectives, 225
Put trust, 24

R

Rates of return
after-tax real, versus tax-free real, 8–9
expected, 152, 154–155
Regulations; *see also* Federal *entries*; Regulatory primer for bank brokerage
Competitive Equality Banking Act of 1987, 103
Garn-St. Germain, 40–41
Glass-Steagall, *see* Glass-Steagall Act
governing precious metals, 51
House bill H.R. 3838, tax-free investment and, 5, 6
Investment Advisers Act of 1940, 112
NASD by-laws, 111–112
1986 tax law, 6, 15–16, 181
portfolio management program and, 140
Regulation Y (12 CFR 225.25), 108
FRB amendment to, 106–107
Securities and Exchange Commission (SEC)

de novo operation, 105
INVEST, 79, 81
registration, 110–111
Rule 3b-9, 102, 110–111
Securities Industry Association (SIA) and INVEST, 81
securities liability standards, 115–116
Supreme Court doctrine
of mutual reciprocity, 15
in Security Pacific and Schwab cases, 104
on underwriting, 110
Regulatory environment
INVEST and, 79–81
prior to 1933, 79–80
Regulatory primer for bank brokerage, 100–117
alternative means for banks to enter securities business, 104–110
Competitive Equality Banking Act of 1987, 103
discount brokerage, 104–105
acquisition, 104
de novo, 104–105
joint venture, 104
early Comptroller of Currency ("OCC") regulations and interpretations re: banks as securities brokers, 102
FDIC rules affecting state nonmember banks, 108
FRB's underwriting approval, 102
Glass-Steagall Act, 101–102
investment advice, 105–107
bank department, 106
de novo, FRB 1986 NatWest approval, 105–106
limitations on advice, 106–107
routine banking activity, 105
Investment Company Act Rule 12b-1, 108
mutual funds, regulation and sale of, 107–109
bank as custodian and depository, 108–109
regulatory requirements, 110–115